BRUCE R. McCONKIE

Bruce R. McConkie

BRUCE R. McCONKIE

APOSTLE AND POLEMICIST

1915–1985

DEVERY S. ANDERSON

SIGNATURE BOOKS | 2024 | SALT LAKE CITY

To my family:
Kandy, Amanda, Tyler, Jordan,
Jason, Karla, Sophia, Mia, and Matai.

Join our mail list at www.signaturebooks.com for details on events and related titles we think you'll enjoy.

Design by Jason Francis

FIRST EDITION | 2024

Paperback ISBN: 978-1-56085-476-0
Ebook ISBN: 978-1-56085-494-4

CONTENTS

CHAPTER ONE

BIRTH TO MANHOOD

1915-1934

"I was born with a testimony, and from my earliest days have known with absolute certainty of the truth and divinity of his great latter-day work," wrote Bruce R. McConkie in 1978 as he introduced the first of his six-volume *Messiah* series, which, with its completion four years later became his crowning publishing achievement. "Doubt and uncertainty have been as foreign to me as the gibberish of alien tongues."[1]

Even a cursory examination of McConkie's life reveals that this statement is not entirely hyperbole. His deep, unwavering commitment to his religion, and a lifelong mission to expound its theology and teach its doctrines, both over the pulpit and through his writings, is abundantly clear. Yet that passion and his dogmatic approach often invited controversy, and throughout his years as a public figure, he was no stranger to it.

It is nearly impossible to imagine McConkie's life without Mormonism at its very center. But his grandfather would have set his own life in an entirely different direction, and that of his posterity, had he not discovered the Church of Jesus Christ of Latter-day Saints, which happened quite by accident four decades before Bruce's birth. Twenty-seven-year-old George Wilson McConkie, an Ohioan of Scottish descent, and his Alabama-born wife Susan Smith McConkie, were passing through Salt Lake City in April 1874 while headed to California. They learned about the relatively new American born religion, became converted, and were baptized. With this

---

1. Bruce R. McConkie, *The Promised Messiah: The First Coming of Christ* (Salt Lake City: Deseret Book, 1978), xvii.

new life came the acceptance of the church's practice of plural marriage, and George eventually married two additional wives. The three
women in his life bore a total of fifteen children.[2]

George's second wife, whom he married in the Salt Lake City
Endowment House in 1881, was twenty-four-year-old Emma
Somerville. Her father, William, had joined with the Mormons
in Scotland in 1840 and emigrated to America the following year,
settling at church headquarters at Nauvoo, Illinois. He served as a
bodyguard to Joseph Smith, the church's founding prophet. William
married Eliza Smith, whose family came to Nauvoo shortly before
the Mormon exodus from the city in 1846.[3]

Emma Somerville McConkie gave birth to five children over the
course of her marriage to George, one of whom was stillborn. Later,
in 1886, fifteen-year-old Elizabeth Slade became George's third and
final wife. The 1880s were a difficult time for Mormon polygamists as
US marshals hunted and arrested them. During that decade George,
his wives, and his children, moved 230 miles southeast to Moab,
Utah, hoping to elude federal agents. While there, Emma's third
child, a boy named Oscar Walter, was born on May 9, 1887, in one of
two cabins that housed the family in an area known as Poverty Flat.[4]

Oscar became quite ill in his infancy and over the years several
family members relayed a story that convinced them—and him—
that God had intervened to spare his life. "A light gathered over my
bed as I lay in the dark corner of the room, and they saw it, took it
to be a sign that I would recover."[5] Moments like this reinforced in
their minds the notion that God had a plan for him.

2. Joseph Fielding McConkie, "Biography of Oscar W. McConkie," unpublished
paper, Graduate Religion #544, Brigham Young University, Provo, Utah, 1966, Church
History Library, Salt Lake City, 1–2; S. Dilworth Young, "Elder Bruce R. McConkie of
the Council of the Twelve," *Ensign*, Jan. 1973, 5; Joseph Fielding McConkie, *The Bruce
R. McConkie Story: Reflections of a Son* (Salt Lake City: Deseret Book, 2003), 26; Dennis
B. Horne, *Bruce R. McConkie: Highlights from His Life and Teachings*, second enlarged
edition with epilogue (Salt Lake City: Eborn Books, 2010), 23.
    3. McConkie, "Biography," 2; McConkie, *Reflections*, 15, 26.
    4. McConkie, "Biography," 1; McConkie, *Reflections*, 26; familysearch.org. In *Re-
flections*, the author says Elizabeth Slade was sixteen, but the LDS Church's online
genealogical database indicates she was fifteen. She died in 1973 at age 102, making
her one of the last surviving plural spouses whom the church would have considered
"authorized" to have taken part in the practice.
    5. McConkie, "Biography," 4.

It did not take long for George and his plural families to discover that Moab was not far enough away for them to elude the marshals. They made their way to Mexico, ultimately settling at Pacheco, Chihuahua. They were not there long, however, before George died on December 9, 1890. Susan, Emma, Lizzie, and their fourteen living children, moved back to Utah, with Emma settling near family members in Mona, seventy-five miles south of Salt Lake City.[6]

Young Oscar learned hard work early through his many chores, which included hauling milk—sometimes rather clumsily, trying his mother's patience. Starting at age seven he began earning money by digging potatoes and herding rams for twenty-five cents a day. But soon the family moved back to Moab, where forty-year-old Emma began caring for the two children of her recently widowed brother. Over the next eight years Oscar attended school, was ordained to the Aaronic Priesthood, and continued working a variety of jobs, including pitching hay for two dollars per day and working as a janitor at both Moab's Central School and the ward building where he attended church. As part of his duties as a young deacon, he also cut and hauled wood for those in need.[7]

Oscar believed he possessed several spiritual gifts, which he saw as the fulfilment of promises made in his patriarchal blessing, where he was told that he would see things through dreams and visions. He claimed that in many cases he learned of the upcoming deaths of individuals just days before the events occurred. He felt God in his life, but also saw much in Moab that he attributed to Satan. "I saw the spirit of the devil there," he later wrote. "A girl, Luster, about my age, committed suicide. I saw drunken men on the streets, staggering in the gutter, heard their oaths, saw them fight, saw the flash of knives and the crack of pistol fire, saw hell boiling over upon many." Among the atrocities, he saw men killed by law officers and a sheriff murdered by outlaws.[8]

In 1906 Oscar graduated from Grand County High School, left Moab, and began attending Brigham Young University in Provo. He was back in Moab by the summer of 1907 and kept busy working

---

6. McConkie, *Reflections*, 26–27.
7. McConkie, "Biography," 5; McConkie, *Reflections*, 35.
8. McConkie, "Biography," 6–7; McConkie, *Reflections*, 36–37.

and enjoying life out in the community, which his hometown newspaper occasionally reported on. In August 1907 he was laboring in road construction just across the Colorado River. Over the next few years, he sometimes worked out of town shearing sheep. But Oscar, known for his social skills and outgoing personality, also developed a love for acting and found time to perform in local theater. In February 1908, he and other young adults put on a play to raise money for a local reading room. The following winter he was away teaching a school term at Manning, Utah County, but returned to Moab in March 1909. He was apparently taken care of and fed well during his time away. "Mr. McConkie is well groomed, fat and saucy," reported the Moab *Grand Valley Times* upon his return home, where he "shows every evidence of having received kind treatment during his sojourn with the Manningites."[9]

A few months later, as Oscar prepared to receive ordination to the Melchizedek Priesthood, he contracted typhoid fever, as did his brother George. In early June his fever "reached a dangerous point," noted the local newspaper, "but is again under control and no serious complications are expected." Two weeks later he was "getting along very well," his doctor reported.[10]

A grandson who later wrote about this episode said that Oscar's temperature remained at 106 degrees for over two months as he lay unconscious, and during that time he lost over 110 pounds, weighing in at less than ninety. The sickness was said to have taken such a toll that he did not fully regain his strength for around a year. However, the *Grand Valley Times* reported that only four months after his fever had reached its peak in June, he and his sister Emma were performing in the play *The Steel King*, in which Oscar had the lead role, a conman who defrauded his sister-in-law. A review lauded him for his performance. "Mr. McConkie brought out his 'cussedness' very nicely and succeeded in gaining the cordial hatred of the

9. "Cutting Affray at Monticello," *Grand Valley Times* (Moab, UT), Aug. 9, 1907, 1; "Shearing at Dewey," *Grand Valley Times*, Mar. 27, 1908, 8; "Local and Personal," *Grand Valley Times*, Apr. 30, 1909, 4; "Show Coming Up," *Grand Valley Times*, Feb. 7, 1908, 4; "Local and Personal," *Grand Valley Times*, Mar. 5, 1909, 8; "Local and Personal," *Grand Valley Times*, Mar. 12, 1909, 8.

10. McConkie, *Reflections*, 40; "Local and Personal," *Grand Valley Times*, June 4, 1909, 4; "Local and Personal," *Grand Valley Times*, June 18, 1909, 4.

audience." During the daytime he filled in for his brother Russell as county school superintendent while Russell was out of town, and again in December, after Russell became ill.[11] None of this could have occurred had Oscar remained as ill as his grandson maintained.

Oscar's priesthood ordination finally came that same fall while he was still active in the theater. Performances of *The Steel King* continued through the end of the year. In December he appeared at the Star Opera House in a play called *Brookdale Farm*, put on by the Home Dramatic Club. The newspaper noted that "much work has been put into the preparation of this excellent drama and it will undoubtedly be better than the average entertainment. You can't afford to miss the show." Oscar played the role of a tramp named Richard Willard.[12]

Russell and Emma also had roles in this play, and four months later the three siblings performed in *East Lynne* at the same theater. "If there were any 'Doubting Thomases' who thought the Moab bunch couldn't put on a heavy play, they took it all back and denied ever saying it," noted the *Grand Valley Times*.[13]

At some point, Oscar briefly attended Agricultural College of Utah in Logan and during the summer of 1910 he began taking summer classes in Salt Lake City at the University of Utah. He also was hired that fall to both teach and serve as principal of Centerfield public schools, in San Pete County, something he did for the next two years. In between academic years he spent another summer at the University of Utah.[14]

After the 1911–12 school year, Oscar appears to have returned to Moab and on at least one occasion helped record stats at a basketball game between his former high school and the Monticello high school. This game ultimately changed his life. Also sitting at the officials table, but for the opposing team, was a young woman named Margaret Vivian Redd. Vivian, as she was called, was born in

11. McConkie, *Reflections*, 40–41; ad for *The Steel King*, *Grand Valley Times*, Oct. 29, 1909, 4; "The 'Steel King,'" *Grand Valley Times*, Nov. 12, 1909, 8; "Local and Personal," *Grand Valley Times*, Dec. 3, 1909, 5.

12. "Brookdale Farm Star Opera House Thursday Evening December Thirtieth," *Grand Valley Times*, Dec. 24, 1909, 1; "Show Was Good," *Grand Valley Times*, Dec. 31, 1909, 8.

13. "East Lynne was Splendid," *Grand Valley Times*, Apr. 29, 1910, 5.

14. "Comings and Goings," *Grand Valley Times*, July 29, 1910, 1; "More Locals," *Grand Valley Times*, June 9, 1911, 8; "Local and Personal," *Grand Valley Times*, July 28, 1911, 5.

Bluff, San Juan County, Utah, to James Monroe Redd and Lucinda Pace Redd. Vivian's LDS roots ran deeper than Oscar's. All her grandparents and even six of her great-grandparents had embraced Mormonism in the 1830s and '40s.[15]

Two of those great-grandparents, John Hardison Redd and his wife, Elizabeth Hancock, converted to Mormonism in Tennessee in 1843 and moved to Nauvoo the following year. After crossing the plains to Utah, the couple settled in Spanish Fork. After John's death in 1858, his son Lemuel Hardison Redd, his wife Keziah Butler Redd, along with Lemuel's plural families, settled at New Harmony, a community about forty miles northeast of St. George. But in 1879 he and around 230 others, under the direction of Silas Smith, were called to settle in San Juan County, where they established the towns of Bluff and Blanding.[16]

James Monroe Redd was sixteen when, in October 1889, he accompanied his father, Lemuel, and his brother Lemuel Jr., and Lemuel Jr.'s family, on this six-month expedition into territory occupied by warring Navajo and Paiute indigenous tribes. The journey was difficult due to a variety of obstacles caused by rocky and otherwise rough terrain, but when the group decided to take a previously untraveled route by crossing the Colorado River through Escalante, the trek proved to be fortuitous. A cleft separating the cliffs above the river was too narrow to allow wagons to pass through. But after three months of intense labor by several men to widen the cleft and build a road descending 1,200 feet down, they created what is called the Hole-in-the-Rock. The first wagon made its way through on January 26, 1880, and eighty-two others, along with 1,000 head of livestock, successfully followed. After a six-month journey, most of the settlers arrived at Bluff on April 6.[17]

Not much is known about Vivian's youth and upbringing, but Bluff, which sits along the banks of the San Juan River, had been settled for less than a decade when she was born on October 13, 1889. Bluff was considered one of the United States' last remaining

15. McConkie, *Reflections*, 15–20, 41.

16. Young, "Elder Bruce R. McConkie," 5, 7; Robert S. McPherson, *A History of San Juan County: In the Palm of Time* (Salt Lake City: Utah State Historical Society, 1995), 98.

17. McPherson, *History of San Juan County*, 98–99; Young, "Elder Bruce R. McConkie," 5, 7; McConkie, *Reflections*, 24.

frontiers when settlers arrived. Those early inhabitants were forced to build homes, fences, and everything else out of the cottonwood trees that grew plentifully in their midst, but cutting and shaping the lumber proved difficult. Living in this isolated part of the territory meant that Vivian and most everyone else had to learn all the skills needed for pioneer living, such as spinning and weaving wool and cooking over a wood fire.[18]

When Vivian and Oscar began courting, Oscar quite willingly rode the sixty-mile distance to Monticello on horseback to see her. Things became easier after Vivian received a basketball scholarship to the University of Utah and Oscar resumed his studies there. Both were busy and dedicated to their course work, but they could now see each other frequently and would often meet on campus for walks or to just sit and talk.[19]

The couple married in the Salt Lake Temple on September 10, 1913, and one year later moved to Ann Arbor, Michigan, where Oscar began attending the University of Michigan Law School. Vivian's sister Hortense, who was also set to study in Ann Arbor, left with them. Oscar finished his course work after only a year and the McConkies moved back to Utah, this time to Monticello, where Oscar began practicing law and took on the editorship of a new weekly newspaper, *The San Juan Record*. An influx of new citizens to San Juan County created considerable demand for the paper and Oscar had some journalistic background that put him in a position to lead the new enterprise. "The first edition of the new paper will be issued next Wednesday," noted the Moab *Grand Valley Times* on September 24, 1915. "Mr. McConkie was accompanied to Monticello by his wife and son."[20] That son was two-month-old Bruce.

The birth of the McConkie's first child was traumatic for both mother and son. Bruce Redd McConkie was born on Thursday, July

---

18. McPherson, *History of San Juan County*, 23, 95, 99, 220; Young, "Elder Bruce R. McConkie," 7.

19. "Oscar W. McConkie, 78, Judge, Churchman Dies," *Salt Lake Tribune*, Apr. 10, 1966, C5; McConkie, "Biography," 7.

20. Untitled note, *Grand Valley Times*, Sep. 3, 1915, 5; "Local and Personal," *Grand Valley Times*, Sep. 10, 1915, 5; "Newspaper for San Juan County," *Grand Valley Times*, Sep. 17, 1915, 1; "First Issue Next Week," *Grand Valley Times*, Sep. 24, 1915, 1. As of this writing, the *San Juan Record* continues to be published at Monticello, Utah.

29, 1915, in a hospital in Ann Arbor, weighing in at ten pounds. Vivian lay on the operating table for nine hours. Although a specialist oversaw the delivery, the baby suffered head injuries caused by the extreme measures taken during the birth. Bruce, who had briefly been given up for dead while doctors gathered to assist his mother, retained marks from forceps on his forehead for the rest of his life.[21]

The newspaper did business for a year out of the *Times-Independent* building in Moab, but construction was soon completed in Monticello for the *San Juan Record*'s own office. Monticello, located sixty miles south of Moab, was a small town of just under 350 people when the McConkies arrived. At the time the town provided no running water or electricity. Vivian's parents lived there, and Oscar and Vivian built a home on the Redds' property. Young Bruce eventually created a path between the two houses so that he could more easily visit his grandparents. Over the next decade during the family's Monticello sojourn, Vivian bore four more children, but did so at the hospital in Moab. She also found ways to supplement the family income by raising turkeys, which Bruce learned to herd to fields where they feasted on grasshoppers. Monticello was a tightknit community where people helped each other.[22]

Oscar became heavily involved in both church and civic affairs at Monticello. Six months after arriving in town, he was elected secretary-treasurer of the San Juan Commercial Club. Serving as county attorney, he prosecuted the murder case against Ramon Archuleta and Ignacio Martinez. On August 23, 1918, forest ranger Rudolph E. Mellenthin was killed when he tried to arrest Archuleta, who had deserted from the army and, with the help of Martinez, his father-in-law, hid out on the Navajo Reservation. Both men were convicted in June 1919—Archuleta to life in prison, and Martinez to fifteen years hard labor. Mellenthin's murder was perhaps the most notorious crime committed in San Juan County up to this point, as criminal behavior typically only involved the theft of livestock or various forms of assault.[23]

21. Young, "Bruce R. McConkie," 7; McConkie, *Reflections*, 56–57.

22. "Notice to Contractors," *Grand Valley Times*, Aug. 18, 1916, 4; McConkie, *Reflections*, 58–62, 64.

23. Untitled note, *Grand Valley Times*, Mar. 17, 1916, 7; "Murderers of Ranger Get Heavy Sentences," *Grand Valley Times*, June 13, 1919, 1; McPherson, *History of San Juan*

The following year Oscar was called as bishop of the Monticello Ward and ordained to that position by Richard R. Lyman of the Council of the Twelve Apostles. Only months later Oscar was elected Monticello's member of the San Juan Board of Education, eventually serving two terms in that capacity. In addition, he held the position of juvenile judge for several terms. In 1922 he became the Democratic nominee for the twelfth senatorial district and won that seat. He was a leader in organizing the Monticello State Bank, serving the institution as both attorney director and vice president.[24]

As a student, young Bruce earned grades ranging from average to a little above, and teachers described him during these years in Monticello as "ordinary." On the spiritual side of things, Oscar and Vivian taught their children the Latter-day Saint gospel, and the experiences they had as a family reinforced their faith. When Bruce was around five years old Oscar became ill with the flu. After Bruce prayed for his father, Oscar, who spoke about this incident, said he recovered instantly. Bruce was on the receiving end of what the family believed to be divine intervention as well. When a doctor diagnosed his stomach pains as appendicitis, he and Vivian traveled to Salt Lake City to see a specialist, but further examination failed to show any sign of the condition.[25]

The family routinely discussed the scriptures and Mormon principles during dinner and at other times. On Sundays, Oscar always wanted to know what the kids had been taught in Sunday School, corrected it when he felt necessary, and supplemented those lessons with additional insights. "I had a very spiritual home life," Bruce said. "I would be surprised if there were anyone that I'd ever run across who spent as much time just deliberately discussing and thereby teaching gospel principles to his children as my father did. He was a great conversationalist and he just kept me everlastingly

County, 326–27. Martinez was released after two years due to uncertainties about his role in the slaying. Archuleta served only six years before he was released on parole.

24. "Oscar W. McConkie is New Monticello Bishop," *Times-Independent* (Moab, UT), May 20, 1920, 1; "Local and Personal," *Times-Independent*, Dec. 16, 1920, 5; "Southeast Utah Man for State Senator," *Times-Independent*, Aug. 17, 1922, 1; "Each Party Elects Four Officers," *Times-Independent*, Nov. 9, 1922, 1; "McConkie Opens Law Offices in Salt Lake City," *Utah Statesman* (Salt Lake City), Sep. 3, 1927, 1.

25. McConkie, *Reflections*, 61

thinking and evaluating on principles of the gospel." Moments like these helped Bruce's readiness for baptism when the time came. Oscar performed the ordinance on Bruce's eighth birthday in a little building next to the ward meetinghouse.[26]

A near-fatal episode happened at some point during McConkie's Monticello childhood. Neither he nor his father said how old he was, but both shared the story separately. Bruce was riding a horse at the apple orchard at their farm. "The horse bolted," McConkie remembered, "and I slipped from the saddle with one leg going down through the stirrup, and I was forced to hang onto the little leather thong on the side of the saddle with my head hanging down." Oscar was inside reading the newspaper but felt prompted to rush outside to the orchard. Not knowing why, or what he was even looking for, he suddenly saw the horse running through the trees. "I had been scraped off the saddle and was hanging on the other side and he couldn't see me so he didn't know why he was there. He stopped the horse, and when he did, he found me on the other side of the horse, just ready to fall off."[27]

In November 1923, after three and a half years as bishop, Oscar received a call to the San Juan stake presidency as second counselor to President Wayne H. Redd, an uncle of Vivian. The following year the family experienced a difficult loss with the death of Oscar's mother, sixty-six-year-old Emma Sommerville McConkie, who had spent her past few decades in Moab. Bruce would have spent time with his grandmother during visits there, but these moments may have been rare. "I remember visiting my grandmother Emma Sommerville McConkie a time or two in Moab," he said. "She seemed to be a very old lady. She was a very good woman and had been the ward Relief Society president for many years in the Moab Ward." A photo exists of Emma holding the infant Bruce that would have been taken only months after his birth.[28]

---

26. McConkie, *Reflections*, 66; Young, "Elder Bruce R. McConkie," 8; Dell Van Orden, "Elder Bruce R. McConkie: 'A Challenging Future,'" *Church News*, Oct. 21, 1972, 3; Sheri L. Dew, "Bruce R. McConkie: A Family Portrait," *This People*, Dec. 1985/Jan. 1986, 52.

27. Van Orden, "Elder Bruce R. McConkie," 3; McConkie, *Reflections*, 69.

28. McConkie, *Reflections*, 58, 63, 69; "Wayne H. Redd is Named President," *Times-Independent*, Nov. 29, 1923, 1. In *Reflections*, Joseph Fielding McConkie says the stake president was Lemuel H. Redd, as does his father; "Revered Pioneer Woman Called Home," *Times-Independent*, Jan. 10, 1924, 1.

Even though Oscar was a practicing attorney and had passed the bar exam back in 1917, he and his family left Monticello in 1925 and returned to Ann Arbor, where Oscar resumed his law school studies for one year. At the time five children had been born into the family. Besides Bruce there was France Briton "Brit" (1918); James Wilson (1921); Margaret (1923); and Oscar Walter Jr. (1926). The McConkies were the only Latter-day Saints in the community. Occasionally they traveled the forty miles or so to attend the LDS branch in Detroit, but usually they held church at home, with Bruce using his knowledge of the Book of Mormon, which he was then reading for the first time, to teach the family Sunday School. To avoid total isolation spiritually and perhaps socially, and to maintain the routine of going to meetings, they sometimes attended a local Presbyterian church. Bruce and Brit both enrolled in summer school and Bruce later took part in a music program and began playing the saxophone.[29]

After Oscar finished his final term at Ann Arbor, the McConkies returned to Utah, but Oscar decided not to run for reelection to the Utah Senate. This may have been because after eleven years in Monticello he had decided to sell their land and move the family to Salt Lake City and practice law there, where his additional legal training would provide him greater professional opportunities. By September his children were enrolled in school in Salt Lake, but Oscar took another year to permanently move as he wrapped up unfinished business in Monticello.[30]

Bruce, now eleven years old, began attending Lowell Elementary School as a seventh grader, and several months into the school year he was ordained a deacon in the Aaronic Priesthood. This occurred on February 27, 1927, five months before his twelfth birthday, during one of Oscar's visits to town. After a year of traveling back and forth between Monticello and Salt Lake City, Oscar finally settled in at the family's new home on C Street in the Salt Lake City Avenues and opened his law office on the seventh floor of the Continental

29. McConkie, *Reflections*, 14, 71, 74; "Servants in the Lord's Kingdom," *Improvement Era*, Nov. 1967, 57.

30. "Election Time Again Draws Near; Few Candidates Out," *Times-Independent*, July 22, 1926, 1; "Politics in Grand County Shows Life; Candidates Discussed," *Times-Independent*, Aug. 19, 1926, 1; untitled note, *Times-Independent*, Sep. 23, 1926, 8; "Price and Nearby," *The Sun* (Price, UT), Sep. 2, 1927, 5; McConkie, *Reflections*, 72.

Bank building. He also began lecturing part-time at the University of Utah law school. The family returned to Monticello each summer to work at Vivian's father's farm. Oscar managed to do this by trading cases with a local judge who took Oscar's docket during that judge's visits to Salt Lake City. During one of those summers as Bruce got a little older, he helped install a water pipeline for the Blue Mountain Irrigation Company.[31]

For eighth and ninth grade, Bruce attended Bryant Junior High School, where he participated in a variety of activities. As a Boy Scout, he earned his Star award in a Court of Honor held on Friday, May 25, 1928, at West High School. He also played for the Tigers in Bobby Richardson's Junior Basketball league at the Deseret Gymnasium. On June 6, 1929, Bryant held an assembly to honor graduating ninth-grade students and the program featured music by the Bryant orchestra in which McConkie was the lone C-melody saxophone player. There was also a harp solo and a performance by a girl's chorus. McConkie described himself as being a "very poor" saxophonist but remained in the orchestra due to the school's lenient policy of allowing anyone in who wanted to play. McConkie, then thirteen, was among the speakers at the ceremony, his subject being "Education and Training."[32]

At the time, junior high school lasted only two years, followed by two years of high school. This timeframe was an experimental program that McConkie happened to fit into because of his age. He began LDS High School in the fall of 1929 and was on track to graduate at fifteen years old in the spring of 1931. The school was located where the LDS Relief Society building and Church Office Building stand today, near the corner of North Temple and Main Street in Salt Lake City. In September 1929 the last of the McConkie children was born. Oscar and Vivian named their sixth child and fifth son William Robert.[33]

---

31. McConkie, *Reflections*, 61, 73, 75–76; Young, "Elder Bruce. R. McConkie," 8; "McConkie Opens Law Offices," 1.

32. "Coyotes, Wildcats, Bears Lead Play," *Salt Lake Tribune*, Jan. 21, 1929, 10; "Scouts Make Award Record," *Salt Lake Tribune*, May 26, 1928, 19; Gertrude Ingbar, "Junior Students Plan Hard Work as Seniors," *Salt Lake Tribune*, June 5, 1929, 23; McConkie, *Reflections*, 74.

33. McConkie, *Reflections*, 14, 73; Young, "Elder Bruce R. McConkie," 8.

During high school, Bruce became involved in a variety of activities. He played football, even though he was not athletically inclined nor apparently all that coordinated. But, based on how he described them, neither were the others on the team. He was also part of the debate team, which probably suited him much better, and he also put his editorial skills to work as manager of the school yearbook. Shortly before graduation, McConkie was one of sixteen students to receive "Gold and Blue" and "S" book awards for publications at a school assembly. Afterward all the students were excused for an outing at Lagoon, the amusement park located eighteen miles north of Salt Lake City. After the class of 1931 graduated, LDS High School closed and the remaining students began attending other area schools the following year.[34]

While growing into his teens in Salt Lake City, McConkie frequented the public library and became captivated by the animal stories of Canadian-American author Ernest Thompson Seton, whose book, *Wild Animals I Have Known*, was his most popular.[35] By the time he graduated from high school McConkie was well rounded, happy socially, and satisfied academically as he took part in a variety of extracurricular programs. He had tried sports, had attempted a musical instrument, was a Boy Scout, and had done some public speaking. By next enrolling at the University of Utah, he followed in the footsteps of his father.

McConkie became immediately involved at the university. He joined the Sigma Pi fraternity his freshman year, one of 215 students to pledge with the various fraternities and sororities. Like his father, who enjoyed performing in community theater when young, Bruce thought he would give acting a try, but he did not get a part he auditioned for. He believed this was because dramatics advisor Marion Redd, a relative, "did not want me around so that I could make any comments or reports to my parents of what a jackrabbit she was." He lost interest in acting after that, a turn he felt grateful for. "If I had gotten involved with the clique of people whose lives centered in dramatics and the applause that comes to those behind the footlights, there is no telling what bad companions I would have

---

34. "L.D.S. Pupils Win Awards for Activity," *Salt Lake Tribune*, May 23, 1931, 6.
35. Young, "Elder Bruce R. McConkie," 8.

picked up with." He tried football again, but because he was so young compared to others on the team, he was given few opportunities to play. He became involved in ROTC, however, and stayed with that program throughout the course of his college career.[36]

On Friday, February 5, 1932, sixteen-year-old McConkie was driving near South Temple and 700 East in Salt Lake City when his car collided with another driven by E. V. Theriot, who received cuts and bruises to his head, face, and chest. McConkie was not injured in the accident. Apparently, another car turned in front of him when he tried to pass it, forcing him to hit Theriot's car.[37] If McConkie was shaken by this encounter, a positive, lifechanging moment was around the corner.

That moment occurred when McConkie attended a party at the home of Joseph Fielding and Ethel Reynolds Smith. Fifty-five-year-old Joseph was then a member of the Council of the Twelve Apostles in the LDS Church and had been serving in that capacity for twenty-two years. His first wife, Louie Emily Shurtliff, died in March 1908 and he and Ethel married seven months later. A son of the late church president Joseph F. Smith, and a grandson of Hyrum Smith, brother of LDS founder Joseph Smith, Joseph Fielding was one of the most recognized leaders in one of the most prominent families in the church. Ethel became impressed with McConkie for a number of reasons that evening and encouraged her fifteen-year-old daughter, Amelia, to ask him out, which she obediently—and nervously—did. That date, a formal dance at Salt Lake City's Memory Grove, occurred on May 21, 1932. Amelia, the Smith's seventh child, later reflected on the occasion and remembered that "the dance could not have been a greater success." As to McConkie, "he was fun to talk to, pleasant to be with, and friendly with everyone."[38]

Afterward they went out for ice cream at the Coon Chicken Inn,

---

36. "Greek Letter Units Pledge New Members," *Salt Lake Tribune*, Apr. 24, 1932, 6A; "Utah Greeks Make Freshman Pledges," *Daily Utah Chronicle*, Apr. 27, 1932, 3; McConkie, *Reflections*, 74–75. Although McConkie did not reveal the first name of the relative, the faculty advisor for drama at the University of Utah with the correct last name was Marion Redd. See *The 1937 Utonian* (Salt Lake City: Sherman R. Slade and Robert C. Flandro, 1936), 228.

37. "Auto Accident Victims Recover from Injuries," *Salt Lake Telegram*, Feb. 6, 1932, 2.

38. McConkie, *Reflections*, 76–77; Young, "Elder Bruce R. McConkie," 9; Horne, *Bruce R. McConkie*, 105.

a popular restaurant in Salt Lake City's Sugar House area, whose entrance featured a twelve-foot face of a bald Black man wearing a porter cap on his head, all done in an exaggerated, minstrel-show fashion. This was reflective of the era in which its patrons lived and indicates the level of racial prejudice then present in the North as well as the Jim Crow South, which most whites seemingly ignored, found amusing, or simply tolerated, but which few objected to. Mormon teachings and practice at the time had relegated Blacks to a second-class status and they were barred from the church's highest ordinances and to any level of priesthood office. Raised with a theology that cemented discrimination against Blacks in religion in addition to its prevalence in social settings throughout the country, Bruce and Amelia likely thought nothing of the racism behind the restaurant's name and entrance. The only uncomfortable moment at the Coon Chicken Inn was when Amelia spilled her malt on her formal dress.[39]

The pair did not see each other again until the fall. The McConkies spent the summer at the San Juan County farm as they always did. In July Bruce spoke at an event there sponsored by the Monticello Camp Daughters of the Pioneers.[40]

After the new school year began, McConkie was featured as one of several speakers, accompanied by musical numbers, that performed at a special "Era" program sponsored by the church's Mutual Improvement Association, held at the family's ward on Sunday, October 2, 1932. Several days later he saw Amelia for the first time since their date five months earlier, but it was under less-than-preferred circumstances. It turned out that they were both part of a double date and attended a post-football game dance, but with different companions. Neither was interested in the person they were with and managed to dance with each other during one song. That was the only time they were together. But that reunion motivated McConkie to call Amelia a few weeks later for a second date. "From then on," Amelia said, "we only dated each other," and they had a fun

39. McConkie, *Reflections*, 78. Coon Chicken Inn in Salt Lake City stayed open until 1957. Its Washington and Oregon locations closed earlier. See Sheena McFarland, "Whatever Happened to ... the Chicken Restaurant with the Racially Charged Name?" *Salt Lake Tribune*, Jan. 13, 2015; Dew, "Family Portrait," 52.

40. "Monticello's Fourth of July Program Arranged," *San Juan Record*, June 30, 1932, 1; McConkie, *Reflections*, 78.

time doing it. "When we were dating Bruce would carry a notebook full of jokes in his shirt pocket. He had a fantastic sense of humor." Amelia graduated from East High in the spring of 1933.[41]

That fall McConkie began his junior year at the University of Utah, and Amelia entered as a freshman. McConkie was on the committee for the Harvest Ball, held at the Memory House at Memory Grove on November 3. If he also attended this dance, he surely had Amelia by his side.[42]

McConkie remained active in the ROTC and served as a third lieutenant under Captain David H. Rees in Battery C. He attended a camp at Fort Francis E. Warren at Cheyenne, Wyoming, beginning June 3, 1934, for cadets from the University of Utah and Colorado Agricultural College.[43] But further training, his senior year, and even his relationship with Amelia would soon be put on hold as he turned his attention to serving an LDS mission.

---

41. "Church Notices," *Deseret News*, Sep. 29, 1932, 6E; Amelia Smith McConkie obituary, *Deseret News*, Sep. 23, 2005, B7; McConkie, *Reflections*, 79; Dew, "Family Portrait," 50.

42. "Harvest Ball, *Deseret News*, Nov. 1, 1933, 8.

43. *The 1935 Utonian* (Salt Lake City: William C. Winder and Richard A. Van Winkle, 1934), 255; "Cadet Camp Chief Named," *Salt Lake Tribune*, May 31, 1934, 6.

CHAPTER TWO

A MISSION AND EARLY MARRIED LIFE

1934-1940

In late August 1934, Bruce R. McConkie began talking with his local church leaders about his desire to serve a fulltime mission. He even told them he'd like to serve in England, if possible. On Sunday, August 27, he spoke in his ward sacrament meeting and shared the program with his stake president and a man in town from New York named Don B. Colton, president of the Eastern States Mission. McConkie must have made an impression, because after listening to him speak, Colton noted that if he had his choice, the soon-to-be-missionary would be assigned to him. When McConkie received his mission call in the mail on September 8, to his dismay, he saw that Colton's wish had been granted. Before long, however, McConkie felt good about serving in his assigned mission and believed he was headed where he was meant to be.[1]

McConkie, who now stood six feet five inches, was spiritually ready to begin his time in the mission field. He had read the Book of Mormon three times and the Bible, Doctrine and Covenants, and Pearl of Great Price at least once. Things moved quickly over the next forty days. Oscar ordained Bruce an elder and he received his endowments in the Salt Lake Temple in preparation to enter the mission home. The night prior to his departure, Oscar gave his son a blessing, one Vivian preserved for him by writing it out in longhand as Oscar spoke.

"The day will come, while you are yet tabernacle in the flesh, that all men who know you will look to you for counsel and for the

---

1. Joseph Fielding McConkie, *The Bruce R. McConkie Story: Reflections of a Son* (Salt Lake City: Deseret Book, 2003), 80–81.

witness of the truth, for through your faithfulness you shall become a chosen vessel, exalted among your brethren in the holy order of the priesthood of our God," Oscar said. "The Lord will bless you and your heart will be filled with understanding. Your wisdom shall be great, extending beyond the bounds of the earth, and you shall comprehend the mysteries of the kingdom of God, and many revelations will be given unto you, and many things will be understood and taught you which are and shall ever be mysterious unto those who are not willing to pay the full price of obedience to God's exalted law." This blessing became a lasting source of strength to Bruce.[2]

McConkie entered the mission home located in Salt Lake City on State Street, not far from the Beehive House, on Thursday, October 18. But by the following evening he became so ill with infectious hepatitis that he returned home. While there he also developed jaundice. The illness was severe, but the timing made it worse because his missionary farewell sacrament meeting was scheduled for Sunday, October 21 at the Twentieth Ward chapel.[3]

The meeting, which drew a crowd of 600 and featured Oscar McConkie and Joseph Fielding Smith as speakers, went on without Bruce present. But the ailing missionary got to read the talks thanks to two women who attended and recorded them in both long and shorthand. That evening he received a priesthood blessing that promised him he would leave for his mission assignment with the others in his group, who were set to leave on Wednesday. When the day came, he was well enough to receive his patriarchal blessing from the church's presiding patriarch, Nicholas G. Smith. After Joseph Fielding Smith laid his hands on McConkie's head and set him apart as a missionary, McConkie boarded the train bound for New York. Amelia Smith was among the family and friends there to see him off. "I said goodbye to my family and Amelia," noted

2. S. Dilworth Young, "Elder Bruce R. McConkie of the Council of the Twelve," *Ensign*, Jan. 1973, 9; McConkie, *Reflections*, 82–84; Joseph Fielding McConkie, "Bruce R. McConkie: A Special Witness," *Mormon Historical Studies* 14, no. 2 (Fall 2013): 191–92.
3. Dell Van Orden, "Elder Bruce R. McConkie: 'A Challenging Future,'" *Church News*, Oct. 21, 1972, 3; McConkie, *Reflections*, 84; "Wards Honor Missionaries on Departure," *Salt Lake Tribune*, Oct. 14, 1934, 8B. Although the missionary farewell program states the date of the service as October 14, this was either a misprint or the date had changed. The *Tribune* article and McConkie's journal are clear that the farewell was held on October 21. Matthew B. Christensen to Devery S. Anderson, email, May 9, 2022.

McConkie in his journal. His "last image of Amelia [was] an image which will stay with me forever. I was in [the] train door and she on the platform. No words were spoken. We just looked. She was so pathetically sad and beautiful. I shall never forget it. She's so wonderful to me and I love her so much."[4]

The Eastern States Mission had originally been established in 1839 with John P. Greene presiding. After three suspensions between 1850 and 1869, it was reorganized in 1893 with Brooklyn, New York, serving as its headquarters. Boundaries changed a few times, but by 1934 it included Connecticut, Delaware, New York, Maryland, Massachusetts, Rhode Island, southern West Virginia, and West Pennsylvania. President Colton had led the mission since July 1933, which followed his twelve years' service as a member of the US House of Representatives from Utah. At the time McConkie came to the mission, Colton was actively running for the US Senate as a progressive, New Deal Republican. In fact, his campaign ads against incumbent Sen. William H. King were running in the church's monthly *Improvement Era* magazine.[5]

McConkie spent the first six months of his mission in Pittsburgh, where he found the work less than productive and the missionaries unmotivated. Sometimes he went canvasing alone when his companion refused to accompany him. But in April 1935 Colton transferred him as one of forty missionaries assigned to the area of Mormonism's beginnings in Palmyra, New York, for a three-month assignment that culminated in the dedication of a new forty-foot-tall shaft made of Vermont granite, topped with a nine-foot bronze statue of the Angel Moroni, erected on the Hill Cumorah. The church hired Sculptor Torleif S. Knaphus of Salt Lake City to create the monument. In LDS teachings, Moroni was the ancient custodian of the Book of Mormon plates who, as an angel, delivered them on that hill to seventeen-year-old Joseph Smith in September 1827. The church had big public relations and proselytizing plans centered around the monument, which had been in planning stages for over three years. Twelve companies anxious to construct it submitted bids

4. McConkie, *Reflections*, 85–86.
5. "L.D.S. Church Names Two Mission Heads," *Salt Lake Tribune*, July 19, 1933, 20; see *Improvement Era*, Oct. 1934, inside front cover, for one of Colton's political ads.

from around the country. Construction began shortly before Mc-Conkie arrived.[6]

It was an exciting time for the church in the region where Smith published the Book of Mormon in March 1830 and officially founded his church the following month. President Colton wanted a twenty-mile radius of Palmyra to be the focus of intense proselytizing by missionaries. McConkie and his companion hitchhiked most of the 300 miles from Pittsburgh to Palmyra. After McConkie received a new companion upon his arrival, the pair rented a room in Canandaigua. Over the next few months, they held street meetings and knocked on every door they could in their assigned areas. The street meetings included singing by the missionaries. McConkie, who could not carry a tune, sang so poorly that on one occasion the sister missionary standing next to him demanded that he "either stop singing or go down to the other end of the line." He obliged. The missionaries experienced success in teaching as well as opposition by a local evangelist who held public meetings lecturing against the church.[7]

The culmination of all the intense missionary labors was, of course, the dedication of the Angel Moroni monument during a four-day Pioneer Day celebration planned and carried out by the mission in late July 1935. The monument's progress over the months made news in papers around the country and the Canandaigua *Daily Messenger* announced on May 29 that the statue on top of the $35,000 structure was in place. Soon after workers installed four floodlights for $3,000 to illuminate it all. Church leaders left Salt Lake City by train on July 16 to take part in the dedication.[8]

President Colton made sure all the missionaries in the area were utilized for the celebratory events. "Prior to the dedication," noted

6. McConkie, *Reflections*, 87–88; "L.D.S. Monument Will Depict Discovery of Golden Plates," *Salt Lake Telegram*, Feb. 2, 1935, 8; "Cumorah Monument Nears Completion," Church Section, *Deseret News*, Feb. 23, 1935, 1; "Cumorah Shaft Bids Considered," *Salt Lake Tribune*, Dec. 15, 1934, 29; "Monument Set on Tablet Spot," *Birmingham News*, Feb. 3, 1935, 10.

7. "Mormon Workers Leaving Elmira for Palmyra, N.Y.," *Star-Gazette* (Elmira, NY), Apr. 26, 1935, 13; Max Smith, "New Church Monument on Hill Cumorah," *Lehi Sun* (Lehi, UT), June 13, 1935, 4; McConkie, *Reflections*, 88–91, 271.

8. "New Statue Is Put in Place," *Daily Messenger* (Canandaigua, NY), May 29, 1935, 8; "Officials of L.D.S. Plan Cumorah Trip," *Salt Lake Telegram*, May 22, 1935, 6; "Place Lights at Monument Hill Top," *Democrat and Chronicle* (Rochester, NY), July 4, 1935, 13.

the *Deseret News*, the missionaries laboring within the twenty-mile radius of the hill "plan to take the message of Mormonism to every home in that section. It is thought to be the most thorough preaching of the gospel to be made in the Church's home state since the early labors of Oliver Cowdery, Samuel H. Smith and Parley and Orson Pratt." McConkie was a dedicated presence in those labors.[9]

The campaign did not involve just going door-to-door. The missionaries led a public relations endeavor under Colton's direction, and they formed a special publicity committee that created newspaper and radio station ads promoting the ceremonies and the church itself. In the days and weeks prior to the dedication, around one thousand visitors came to the hill each week to see the statue, and missionaries remained onsite to meet people and answer questions. Workers constructed a grandstand seating 2,500. Missionaries preparing for the dedication worked well into the night Friday filling in trenches near the lights and beautifying the grounds for Sunday's event.[10]

On Sunday, July 21, LDS president Heber J. Grant offered a dedicatory prayer at the monument as forty-foot drapes covering the entire shaft and statue fell to the ground and revealed the structure. First Presidency counselor David O. McKay spoke. McConkie got to see very little of the ceremony because he had been assigned to park cars. That afternoon, however, McConkie baptized three people at a service that saw a total of twelve join the church. Another ceremony included talks by S. Nelson Sawyer and Robert F. Thompson, former and current members of the New York State Supreme Court. Sawyer was then the mayor of Palmyra and grew up in the area. He spoke of his own experience hearing and believing lurid stories about Joseph Smith before he later had a change of heart.[11]

The next few days included ceremonies at the Sacred Grove, where Joseph Smith was said to have received his "First Vision" in

---

9. "Missionaries Promote Wide Interest in Hill Cumorah Monument Dedication," Church Section, *Deseret News*, June 15, 1935, 2.

10. "Missionaries Promote Wide Interest," 2; "Church Prepares for Cumorah Fete," Church Section, *Deseret News*, July 13, 1935, 1; "Mormon Officials Arriving for Dedication Ceremonies," *Democrat and Chronicle*, July 18, 1935, 6; "Labor after Sunset to Finish Work on Mormon Monument," *Ithaca Journal* (Ithaca, NY), July 20, 1935, 1.

11. "Monument Dedicated Sunday at Palmyra in Mormon Ritual," *Daily Messenger*, July 22, 1935, 5; "Church President Dedicates Shaft at Hill Cumorah, *Deseret News*, July 22, 1935, 1; Van Orden, "Elder Bruce R. McConkie," 3; McConkie, *Reflections*, 91–92.

which God the Father and Jesus Christ appeared to him when he was only fourteen years old. When the festivities ended, McConkie became junior companion to the district leader of the newly formed Seneca District. This meant McConkie remained in the Palmyra area and occasionally came to Cumorah and answered questions posed by tourists. Sometimes he went to the monument alone with just his "thoughts and the spirit of the Lord." He and his companion paid $100 for a six-year-old Ford, which allowed them to save valuable time getting to and from the hill or any of their work areas. They eventually crashed the car, however, and sold it for less than a quarter of their original purchase price.[12]

In September McConkie took over as Seneca district leader after his companion transferred to Hudson. His new companion, Elder Dennis Flake, later recalled an evening that the pair needed a place to stay and had counted on lodging the night with a church member. When that failed to work out, they went to a car lot and tried to open doors until they found one that was unlocked. They crawled inside and spent the night.[13]

McConkie soon took the opportunity to play matchmaker when he became friends with a new sister missionary from Idaho, Carol Read. Back then it was not against the rules for an elder and sister to work together and knock on doors, which McConkie and Read sometimes did. One day at Read's apartment McConkie spotted a photo of a young man Read identified as her fiancé. "You'll never marry him," McConkie told her. "You're going to marry Elder Dennis Flake." Although Read was surprised and mildly offended by this declaration, when she shortly met Flake, she fell immediately in love, as did he. Flake asked to be transferred so that he could continue his mission labors undistracted. The pair eventually married.[14]

While McConkie continued to work in the area, President Colton developed big plans at the Hill Cumorah for the summer of 1936. Coinciding with a conference of the Eastern States Mission, he held another Pioneer Day celebration from July 24–26. Friday, the opening day, began with a morning meeting at the Sacred Grove. That night

12. McConkie, *Reflections*, 95–97.
13. McConkie, *Reflections*, 97–98.
14. McConkie, *Reflections*, 98–99.

there was a campfire meeting at Cumorah, complete with covered wagons. Saturday began in the grove once again, but then attendees traveled to several historic LDS sites. That night speakers from Salt Lake City closed the day out. Sunday, the final day, began with a sunrise meeting at the hill and another gathering at the Sacred Grove. A baptismal service followed in the afternoon, after which they held another meeting at the grove. That evening the entire three-day celebration culminated in a large pageant, "Truth from Earth," depicting the events surrounding the coming forth of the Book of Mormon. The large cast included missionaries and church members who lived in the area and a crowd of 5,000 came to watch on the slopes of the hill. Just like the year before, McConkie spent his time parking cars and was unable to see the pageant. The evening concluded with talks by Colton and others. Colton announced that the pageant would become an annual event. The following day all 118 missionaries in the Eastern States Mission met together to take stock of all their efforts and to plan strategies for the future.[15]

When the Cumorah celebration ended, McConkie had three months left on his mission. One of the highlights was on September 18 when he spent time with Joseph Fielding Smith after the apostle came to tour the mission and speak. McConkie was invited to ride with Smith and President Colton to Syracuse and then to a meeting in Canandaigua where they asked McConkie to speak impromptu. When Elder Smith wrote home a few days later, he joked to Amelia that "I met the finest missionary in the Eastern States mission," and noted that, "He spoke briefly at one of our meetings and made the most intelligent talk I have heard from any missionary. I wonder if you know what his name is? I think they call him Bruce at home. He wanted to know how you are so I think you may know him."[16]

15. "New York L.D.S. Members Plan Rites at Hill Cumorah," *Salt Lake Tribune*, July 21, 1936, 20; "Pioneer Day Being Planned at Palmyra by Mormon Followers, *Daily Messenger*, July 22, 1936, 5; "LDS Leaders Meet at Hill of Cumorah," *Honolulu Advertiser*, July 25, 1936, 1; "5,000 in Attendance at Mormon Ceremonies at Palmyra on Sunday," *Daily Messenger*, July 27, 1936, 2; "Palmyra L.D.S. Plans Annual Book Pageant," *Salt Lake Tribune*, July 27, 1936, 8; "Church Will Present Pageant at Birthplace," *Deseret News*, Feb. 17, 1937, 9; Van Orden, "Elder Bruce R. McConkie," 3; McConkie, *Reflections*, 105. The Hill Cumorah Pageant was performed annually until 2019, when LDS leaders ceased future productions.

16. Francis M. Gibbons, *Joseph Fielding Smith: Gospel Scholar, Prophet of God* (Salt Lake City: Deseret Book, 1992), 270; McConkie, *Reflections*, 107.

Bruce and Amelia had, of course, corresponded throughout Bruce's mission and fully expected to resume their relationship once he was home. He would often enclose copies of his talks in his letters to her. "I'd show those to dad," Amelia recalled in 1985, "and he'd say they were very fine. In fact, I had a date with somebody else one night and dad lectured me about it. He was in Bruce's corner from the beginning."[17]

McConkie's two-year mission was scheduled to end in October 1936, but President Colton asked him to stay an additional six weeks with an assignment to travel the mission and speak. McConkie happily accepted. After his extended mission officially ended, he traveled back to Salt Lake City and arrived there on Monday, December 7.[18]

After making his way to the family home and cleaning up, he went to visit Amelia, who was thrilled to see him after nearly twenty-six months apart. Later that month McConkie bought her a ring and visited her father to seek his approval of their marriage. "When I asked Joseph Fielding Smith if I could marry his daughter, he said yes and then abruptly scooted me out of his office." That was it. Christmas Day found Bruce and Amelia engaged and planning a wedding. They had no doubts about their decision, and on more than one occasion McConkie spoke about how he never prayed about whether he should marry Amelia; he simply knew she was the one for him. "Now, if I'd done things perfectly," he later said, "I'd have done some counseling with the Lord, which I didn't do."[19]

In early January 1937 McConkie returned to the University of Utah, where Amelia also attended and was working toward her degree in bacteriology and pathology. The following month McConkie joined the Delta Phi fraternity for returned missionaries and on February 28 was ordained a seventy in his ward. Typically, after classes ended for the day, McConkie walked Amelia to her family's home on Douglas Street and then walked all the way back to his own home alone. While doing so he liked to think about a particular scripture

17. Sheri L. Dew, "Bruce R. McConkie: A Family Portrait," *This People*, Dec. 1985/ Jan. 1986, 52.

18. McConkie, *Reflections*, 108, 276.

19. McConkie, *Reflections*, 109–10; Dennis B. Horne, *Bruce R. McConkie: Highlights from His Life and Teachings*, second enlarged edition with epilogue (Salt Lake City: Eborn Books, 2010), 43.

and then outline a talk in his head. He lived about a forty-five-minute walk from the university, and he also used this time going to and from the campus to imagine he'd been assigned to speak on a particular topic. "I would then say the first word on the subject and the last word, and then in the 40 minutes or whatever time I allotted myself, I would attempt to cover the subject in some intelligent way, just for the purpose of training myself to think in outlines."[20]

His desire to become an exceptional speaker went back to his mission, at least, when on his twentieth birthday he created a list he called "Resolutions of Obvious Necessity." One of those was a determination to "Acquire 'speaking genius.'" Throughout his mission he rated his talks in his journal, often calling them "poor" or "very poor," an indication he was hard on himself and would not be satisfied until he mastered, in his own mind at least, the art of speaking.[21]

The twenty-one-year-old recently returned missionary soon had the opportunity to test his skills by addressing a large audience during a meeting in the tabernacle on Temple Square on Sunday, March 28, one week before the church's general conference. How this talk came about is unknown, but it is possible that Joseph Fielding Smith had a hand in arranging it. The text of McConkie's speech, titled "From Eden to Cumorah," was published in the Church Section of the *Deseret News*. Many of the themes recurred in his speeches later in life, and it's not difficult to picture a young McConkie standing at the tabernacle pulpit, delivering his address.

"I thank God I am a Mormon," he declared. "The Latter-day Saints conceive of the Gospel as coming in a mighty chain of eras or dispensations. Through them the purposes of God are culminated by bringing to pass the immortality and eternal life of man.... The Gospel is all truth; all truth is the Gospel. The truths in the philosophies and sciences of men are parts, portions, and ramifications of the Gospel in its broadest signification," he taught. "There are no principles of eternal truth anywhere in the universe that are not embraced in the Gospel of Jesus Christ. It is the true order of heaven;

---

20. Dew, "Family Portrait," 52; Dorothy O. Rea, "Amelia Smith McConkie," *Church News*, Oct. 31, 1964, 6; Van Orden, "Elder Bruce R. McConkie," 3; McConkie, *Reflections*, 110.

21. McConkie, *Reflections*, 95, 100–01.

the pathway to perfection for man; and the system of laws by which Gods and angels are governed. Because of it men are; and through it we live and move and have a being."

Spiritual knowledge, McConkie asserted, is far more valuable than secular, because coming from God, it can be trusted. "Contrary to common worldly concepts, people in Adamic days were supremely intelligent. Father Adam had more of the knowledge that saves than all the so-called divines and scientists combined who believe contrary-wide. It was Mormonism that saved Adam; Adam was the original earthly founder and first member of this church. He holds the keys of salvation under Christ for all the dispensations, and he will preside over the whole human family forever. He is our Prince."

Yet, he believed, there are many falsehoods taught to humankind, both in science and religion. "For long centuries of apostasy 'darkness covered the earth, and gross darkness the minds of the people.' The Gospel was not had among men. One of the many sure ways of knowing this is to remember that the Gospel is the God-Story. People have no knowledge of God, have not the Gospel; the knowledge of God is the Gospel; it is eternal life to know God, and Jesus Christ whom He hath sent."

False concepts about God were a theme he continued to expound upon throughout his life, and this is one of his earliest examples. "A belief that God is an uncreated, unknowable, incomprehensible trinity, is to a true knowledge of God as dark night is to noon day.... To assert that God is without 'body, parts, or passions' when He walked and talked with the prophets, and made man in His own image, and proclaimed from Sinai: 'I, the Lord, Thy God, am a Jealous God,' is to be utterly blind concerning the scriptures and is an announcement to all the world that you know not God, and hence, have not the Gospel."[22]

McConkie's knowledge of and passion for Latter-day Saint doctrine came from years of discussion and study, beginning in his youth at church, at home at the dinner table, and on his mission. He also had a new mentor, Apostle Smith, who he spent time with one-on-one and who had already written several books and numerous

22. Bruce R. McConkie, "From Eden to Cumorah," Church Section, *Deseret News*, Apr. 10, 1937, 4, 8.

articles in church publications and was recognized then as perhaps the church's most respected living theologian. McConkie seemed sure of his own words and the doctrines he was now beginning to teach in public. This, together with his quest to become an effective speaker, put him on a path toward quickly fulfilling that goal. He did not know it at the time, but it all would prove valuable once he was in the public eye.

On Tuesday, June 8, 1937, Bruce and Amelia, having each earned Bachelor of Arts degrees, received their diplomas at the baccalaureate ceremonies at the University of Utah. That same month McConkie became one of forty-nine Utah men appointed by the war department as members of the reserve officer's corps, each receiving commissions as second lieutenants. He spent that summer at a military camp in Wyoming and, while he was gone, Amelia took a train to Chicago to visit her sister.[23]

Sadly, as Bruce and Amelia planned for their October wedding, Amelia's mother, Ethel Reynolds Smith, died on August 26. She had been sick for months, but she took a sudden turn for the worse. Amelia now had to face her wedding without her mother. There were other concerns as well, most immediate being a job for Bruce, which would enable him to support the two of them once they were husband and wife. He began driving an unreliable truck delivering ice to homes without electric refrigerators. Although the couple had been engaged since the previous December, they announced it officially at a luncheon at the Smith home on Saturday, September 26, and again the following day in the local newspaper. The *Salt Lake Tribune* referred to them in its headline as a "popular couple." It gave a wedding date of October 13.[24]

Indeed, Bruce and Amelia were popular locally largely due to the families they came from. Amelia was a daughter of an LDS apostle, himself a descendant of Mormon royalty. McConkie's father, Oscar, had been a judge in the Third District Court since 1928. Amelia was

23. "University Registrar Lists Graduates to Get Diplomas," *Salt Lake Tribune*, June 7, 1937, 5; *The Nineteen Hundred Thirty-Eight Utopian* (Salt Lake City: University of Utah, 1937), 38, 44; "Utahns Added to Reserves," *Salt Lake Tribune*, June 29, 1937, 7; McConkie, *Reflections*, 111.

24. McConkie, *Reflections*, 110–13; Gibbons, *Joseph Fielding Smith*, 271, 273; "Engagement of Popular Couple Told," *Salt Lake Tribune*, Sep. 26, 1937, 4C.

honored at two parties hosted by friends shortly after the announcement, and another hosted a bridal shower for her. All three of these
were held between October 1 and 6.[25]

Finally, the day came for the couple to be married, which turned
out to be a beautiful Wednesday morning. McConkie went to the
Smith home, picked up Amelia, and they met her father at the
Salt Lake Temple. Apostle Smith performed the ceremony for his
daughter and now son-in-law, with Oscar and Amelia's brother
Lewis serving as witnesses. Forgoing the expense of a reception,
members of both the Smith and McConkie families hosted a dinner
that evening for the couple at the Smith home, with forty guests
seated around a large table. The following morning the newlyweds
left in a borrowed car and spent three days honeymooning at Bryce
Canyon and Zion national parks.[26]

Following their return, the McConkies created an apartment for
themselves in the Smith basement at 998 Douglas Street in Salt
Lake City. They began a daily routine of studying the scriptures
together and over the next few years read each of the four standard works several times. McConkie also attended law school at the
University of Utah, where his experience was made harder because
he was forced to endure some discrimination from a professor who
failed to hide his anti-Mormon bias. Despite the long hours his
studies required, McConkie found time to occasionally travel with
his father-in-law to stake conference assignments. On January 8,
1938, the pair spoke in Alpine, Utah, where Smith urged attendees
to obey the Word of Wisdom and McConkie told those assembled
that whatever spirit possesses their bodies now will continue to do so
after the resurrection. During another visit to a stake in Springville,
McConkie did not learn he was to talk until Smith asked him to do
so on the way to the meeting. There were also social activities for the

---

25. Joseph Fielding McConkie, "Biography of Oscar W. McConkie," 9, unpub-
lished paper, Graduate Religion #544, Brigham Young University, Provo, Utah, 1966,
in Church History Library, Salt Lake City; "Number of Fetes Being Arranged for
Bride-Elect," *Salt Lake Tribune*, Oct. 1, 1937, 26; "Dinner Party on Friday Compliments
Bride-Elect," *Salt Lake Tribune*, Oct. 2, 1937, 20; "Amelia Smith Complimented," *Salt
Lake Telegram*, Oct. 5, 1937, 17.

26. McConkie, *Reflections*, 114, 116–17; "Popular S.L. Couple Wedded," *Salt Lake
Tribune*, Oct. 14, 1937, 18.

young couple. In February Bruce and Amelia attended a reunion at Brigham Young University in Provo for missionaries from the Eastern States Mission.[27]

Bruce and Amelia had only been married a few months when Amelia became pregnant with their first child. That was not the only good news within the family. On April 11 the twice-widowed sixty-one-year-old Joseph Fielding Smith married thirty-five-year-old Jessie Ella Evans, who worked as the Salt Lake County recorder, was a former singer in the Metropolitan Opera, and was then a member of the Mormon Tabernacle Choir. At the time she moved into the Smith home, Bruce and Amelia were still living there, as was Amelia's sister Lois and her family, while Lois's husband, a medical student, completed his studies.[28]

The following fall McConkie became ill with pneumonia, and his condition became so serious that he had to be hospitalized. After his release he moved in with his parents to complete his recovery. This gave Amelia, who was soon to give birth, some relief. But on the evening of September 8, she knew the baby was coming and went to the hospital. The child, a son, was born at 12:42 the following morning. The McConkies named him Bruce Redd McConkie Jr., but the father, still ill, had to wait a few days to meet the baby. After ten days in the hospital Amelia was released, but at Vivian's insistence, Amelia and Bruce came to stay with her and Oscar so that she could care for all three of them. On top of everything else, Amelia began suffering from a breast abscess, which laid her up for several days. Around the middle of October, the McConkies returned to their apartment in the Smith basement.[29]

All the joy the young couple felt over becoming parents was unexpectedly short lived and soon turned to grief. Just under eight weeks after Bruce Jr.'s birth, Joseph Fielding Smith noticed that his grandson looked sick. He called his brother Silas, a doctor, who came over and examined him. He agreed the baby was ill but thought home remedies would help. The next day, after examining him a second

27. McConkie, *Reflections*, 118–19; Van Orden, "Elder Bruce R. McConkie, 3; "Quarterly Conference Well Attended by Membership," *Pleasant Grove Review*, Jan. 14, 1938, 5; "Missionaries at Social," *Daily Herald* (Provo, UT), Feb. 21, 1938, 5.

28. Gibbons, *Joseph Fielding Smith*, 274–78; McConkie, *Reflections*, 119–20.

29. McConkie, *Reflections*, 120–22.

time, Dr. Smith felt that the baby's condition had worsened enough that he should be hospitalized. McConkie skipped his law classes and with Amelia took Bruce Jr. to LDS Hospital. Despite the care Dr. Smith and the nurses administered, little Bruce died Wednesday evening, November 2. The diagnosis was an intestinal infection. The family held a small service at the Smith home and buried the baby at the Salt Lake City Cemetery. Amelia described her son as "a beautiful baby," and took comfort in LDS teachings about the resurrection as expounded by her father later that day after the burial. These doctrines now held new meaning for Amelia and her husband. Unbeknown to them, Apostle Smith had begun fasting as soon as he saw the baby was sick and did not stop until after the child's death.[30]

Despite this loss, life went on for the McConkies. Amelia began working at the Utah Genealogical Society to help the family financially but did so for only six months. Around June 1939 she became pregnant for a second time. Bruce graduated from law school and then passed the bar in October, ranking number three out of the seventy-five who took the test. Then, on January 8, 1940, he was one of thirty-three new attorneys who took the oath and were admitted to the Utah State Bar at the Utah Supreme Court at the state capitol. After the ceremony, McConkie was elected chairman of the Utah State Bar Class.[31]

This began a new era for Bruce and Amelia as Bruce opened an office in downtown Salt Lake City with three other attorneys from his class.[32] The couple looked forward to expanding their family and anticipated a bright future on their own in a home of their own, which was just around the corner.

---

30. McConkie, *Reflections*, 122–25; Bruce Redd McConkie Jr. obituaries, *Salt Lake Telegram*, Nov. 3, 1938, 22, and *Salt Lake Tribune*, Nov. 3, 1938, 22.

31. McConkie, *Reflections*, 118, 125–26; "33 Young Attorneys Take Oaths," *Deseret News*, Jan. 8, 1940, 9.

32. McConkie, *Reflections*, 126.

CHAPTER THREE

LEGAL CAREER AND MILITARY
1940-1946

McConkie tried his first case the month following his admittance to the bar, and did so before his father, Oscar, who was still judge of the Third District Court. Before that trial even got underway, however, there was talk that Bruce was one of two "likely candidates" to fill the open position of first assistant city attorney. He shortly applied for the post, but the job went to future LDS apostle Marion G. Romney in late February 1940. Romney resigned only five months later, however, so that he could dedicate more time to his private practice. The city commission appointed McConkie to the position effective August 1, thus ending the law practice he had opened with his friends only months earlier. He started at a salary of $200 per month, but it went up to $210 in November, making it consistent with the starting wage of his predecessor.[1]

Meanwhile, Amelia's second pregnancy resulted in the birth of a daughter on March 2, 1940. Bruce and Amelia named her Vivian, after Bruce's mother. A local paper reported the news and highlighted that the baby was a granddaughter and fifteenth grandchild of Joseph Fielding Smith, who learned about the birth while attending an LDS conference in New York City.[2] The McConkies could now begin anew their life as parents.

---

1. Joseph Fielding McConkie, *The Bruce R. McConkie Story: Reflections of a Son* (Salt Lake City: Deseret Book, 2003), 126; "Fisher Harris May Resign as City Attorney," *Salt Lake Telegram*, Feb. 2, 1940, 17; "Fisher Harris' Resignation Is Put in Record," *Salt Lake Telegram*, Feb. 6, 1940, 13; "City Announces Job Changes in Legal Staff," *Salt Lake Tribune*, July 31, 1940, 13; "City Increases Salary Rate of Prosecutor," *Salt Lake Tribune*, Nov. 15, 1940, 15.

2. "Elder Smith Informed He Has New Grandchild," *Deseret News*, Mar. 2, 1940, 7; McConkie, *Reflections*, 125.

As assistant city attorney, McConkie's job was to try any criminal cases on the city's docket. For example, in October 1940 he motioned that a case against a local attorney who resisted arrest be dismissed due to a lack of evidence. The man and the police officer involved resolved the issue by apologizing to each other over the incident. A year later a young woman attending the University of Utah, who the *Salt Lake Tribune* described as an "attractive sociology student," argued her own case when charged with a traffic violation. She put forth a defense, which impressed Judge Frank Moss, but McConkie held firm and won the case. The driver of the other car involved offered to pay half of the defendant's $10 fine.[3]

On Monday, November 4, the night before the 1940 presidential election, Utah Democrats held fifteen large rallies throughout the state in a final effort to urge voters to elect President Franklin D. Roosevelt to an unprecedented third term. McConkie did his part for the party by speaking at a rally in Scipio. Utah Democratic Party chairman Parnell Black predicted a record turnout for the incumbent president, and in the end, he won the state with 154,277 votes, or 62 percent of the total votes cast.[4]

The McConkie family kept growing when, in April 1941, Amelia bore a son, Joseph Fielding, named after his grandfather. After nearly four years living in the Smith family basement, and now with two children, Bruce and Amelia bought a home that June at 1980 Michigan St.[5]

A holiday tradition in the city allowed that those charged with minor infractions be released from jail each Christmas Eve, and this occurred as usual on December 24, 1941. After attorney J. Arthur Bailey made the motion, Judge Moss granted it and suspended the

---

3. "Resisting Officer Charge Dismissed," *Salt Lake Telegram*, Oct. 22, 1940, 22; "Coed's Oratory Wins Cut in Traffic Fine," *Salt Lake Tribune*, Nov. 4, 1941, 8.

4. "Democratic Leader Predicts Record Vote Tuesday in Utah for Roosevelt," *Salt Lake Tribune*, Nov. 4, 1940, 8. Although McConkie's son Joseph characterized his father as a Republican in *Reflections*, 30, it is clear that in 1940 he was not. A nephew who knew the apostle well maintains that even later Bruce was, like most McConkie family members, a Democrat. James W. McConkie, author interview, July 20, 2023. As shown later in this chapter, however, Bruce R. McConkie appears to have later soured on the New Deal and became opposed to a president staying in office without term limits.

5. "Babies Are Born to These Couples in S. L.," *Deseret News*, Apr. 4, 1941, 18; McConkie, *Reflections*, 126.

sentences for either thirty-six or forty-two inmates—newspaper reporting varies—then held at the jail. This was done "in reverence for
one who was merciful." McConkie, however, "contrary to tradition,"
entered an objection to the release on behalf of the city, which means
he either felt the leave was unjustified or he simply wanted to make
an official statement on behalf of his office. The *Deseret News* noted
that Moss "urged the men being released to find their places as useful
citizens and to cease being a burden and start being a help to society."[6]

During his time in the city attorney's office, McConkie remained
a lieutenant in the Army Reserves and, along with Lieutenant Frank
E. Moss, was nominated to the post as judge advocate in May 1941.
Besides home and church life, other activities kept McConkie busy
outside of the office. In October he addressed members of the Ante-
lope Island chapter of the International Footprint Association in Salt
Lake City on the principles of freedom as found in the US Constitution. He warned his audience that unless Americans remain aware
of those freedoms, they risked losing them. Two months later he and
many of his attorney colleagues set aside the stress of their work and
entertained members of the state bar association convention at the
Hotel Utah by performing their own production of Arthur Sullivan's
Trial by Jury. McConkie played the role of one of the jurors.[7]

Following the bombing of Pearl Harbor in December 1941, Mc-
Conkie's military duties took precedence over his work in the city
attorney's office. In February 1942, when Judge Moss took a leave of
absence to begin active duty, it was widely rumored that McConkie
would fill in during Moss's leave. He was indeed offered the position,
but because he too expected to be called to duty, he turned the job
down rather than accept it and put the city in a position of having to seek another replacement. However, he was willing to accept
the judgeship should he be guaranteed a return to his position as
assistant city attorney once Moss returned to the bench. Oscar Mc-
Conkie, who had just made an unsuccessful run for Utah governor
on the Democratic ticket, left his own judgeship in November 1940

---

6. "Court Releases 36 From City Jail for Christmas," *Deseret News*, Dec. 24, 1941,
16; "S.L. Jail Prisoners Get Freedom as Yule Gift," *Salt Lake Tribune*, Dec. 25, 1941, 25.

7. "Attorney Warns Footprinters of Citizens Duties," *Deseret News*, Oct. 9, 1941, 7;
"Lawyers Turn Talents to Light Opera," *Salt Lake Tribune*, Sep. 28, 1941, 2C.

to become city commissioner, and any appointments to cover these leaves would come through his office.[8]

As expected, McConkie was called to active duty, and reported to Fort Douglas on March 5, 1942, where he received an assignment in military intelligence. Located at the University of Utah, Fort Douglas was only a thirty-minute walk from his home. During the required physical he underwent at the time of his induction he learned that he had contracted polio during his childhood, something no previous doctor had ever known. Although he failed his eye test, he managed to convince personnel to allow him to serve anyway. McConkie's replacement in the city attorney's office, Arthur H. Nielsen, started out at $15 more per month than McConkie had earned, but would serve only until McConkie returned from duty, or "until further action of the commission." In all, records showed that 118 members of the Utah State Bar were in fulltime military service by the time of the bar's annual convention the following December.[9]

During the next four years McConkie traveled regularly around the west and met with governors and city mayors about issues surrounding security. On September 21, 1942, he was the first speaker for the six biweekly lectures sponsored by the Citizens' Defense Corps. The talk, delivered at West High School, was titled, "The Functions of the Military and How to Cooperate with Military Authorities in an Emergency."[10]

On October 29, 1943, McConkie, who had already been promoted to captain, was one of three Utah officers to receive a temporary promotion to major. The following month he spoke about army facility security requirements to representatives of Utah industrial and

8. "Utah Officer Unit Will Pick Leaders," *Salt Lake Tribune*, May 1, 1941, 10; "City Studies Filling of Judicial Post," *Salt Lake Tribune*, Feb. 7, 1942, 21; "Jurist's Post Waits Filling," *Salt Lake Tribune*, Feb. 8, 1942, B1; "City Bench Vacancy May Go Unfilled," *Deseret News*, Mar. 4, 1942, 9; "McConkie to Assume New Post Tomorrow," *Deseret News*, Nov. 14, 1940, 16; "Judge McConkie Takes Oath as Commissioner," *Salt Lake Tribune*, Nov. 15, 1940, 15; Dennis B. Horne, *Bruce R. McConkie: Highlights from His Life and Teachings*, second enlarged edition with epilogue (Salt Lake City: Eborn Books, 2010), 25.

9. "City Bench Vacancy," 9; Bruce R. McConkie, military card, familysearch.org; McConkie *Reflections*, 130; "City Names Prosecutor for Vacancy," *Deseret News*, Apr. 22, 1942, 9; "City Puts Okeh [*sic*] on Prosecutor," *Salt Lake Tribune*, Apr. 23, 1942, 15; "118 members of Utah Bar Join Service," *Deseret News*, Dec. 4, 1942, 12.

10. "Citizen Defense Corps Maps Lecture Series," *Salt Lake Tribune*, Sep. 11, 1942, 17; "Officer Slates Speech on Civil Defense," *Salt Lake Tribune*, Sep. 21, 1942, 16.

manufacturing plants at a conference sponsored by the Utah Council of Defense.[11]

Bruce and Amelia welcomed another child on February 8, 1944, a boy they named Stanford Smith McConkie. Later that month Bruce found himself on the receiving end of some criticism, and his response reveals the firm and unflinching views that the twenty-nine-year-old had already developed and would champion later in life when he was in a position of authority to advocate them more publicly. Apparently during a meeting of Sunday School teachers held during a conference at the Bonneville, Utah, Stake, conducted by Dr. William M. McKay, McConkie made some critical remarks about the current churchwide Sunday School manual, *The Synoptic Gospels*, written by BYU religion professor Russel B. Swensen, one of several LDS scholars who had been trained in biblical studies at the Divinity School of the University of Chicago.[12]

Milton Bennion, the general superintendent of the Sunday School since 1943, learned of this and wrote McConkie a letter on February 24 in which he accused him of having made untrue accusations against the manual's author. "We are informed that you charged that the manual contains false doctrines," Bennion said. "You were asked, we are informed, to furnish specific evidence and you refused to do so. We think it entirely unfair and misleading for you to make these statements before a group of Sunday School teachers. We think you should point out specifically what these false doctrines are." Bennion sent the letter to several general authorities, including Joseph Fielding Smith, who then served as chairman of the publications committee.[13]

McConkie responded in a lengthy letter on March 1. "The report that was made to you was in error. I did not say any of the charges or

---

11. "Officers Promoted, Called to Duty," *Ogden Standard Examiner*, Oct. 29, 1943, 8A; "Utah Industrialists Set Meet on Safety Measures," *Salt Lake Telegram*, Nov. 22, 1943, 7; "Parley Sets Study Topics," *Deseret News*, Nov. 22, 1943, 10.

12. "The Youngest Generation," *Deseret News*, Feb. 9, 1944, 6; McConkie, *Reflections*, 132. For the manual under discussion, see *Gospel Doctrine Sunday School Lessons, The Synoptic Gospels, for the Church of Jesus Christ of Latter-day Saints* (Salt Lake City: Deseret Sunday School Board, 1944); Russel B. Swensen, "Mormons at the University of Chicago Divinity School: A Personal Reminiscence," *Dialogue: A Journal of Mormon Thought*, 7, no. 2 (Summer 1972): 37.

13. McConkie, *Reflections*, 132–33.

statements contained in your letter either as you have written them or in substance, nor did I say anything that could be construed or interpreted to mean what I am quoted to have said." He denied that he or anyone in the room disparaged Swensen or the Sunday School superintendency, yet he did acknowledge pointing out two instances in the manual where he felt it taught false doctrine. In the first, the manual states that Jesus used "exorcism" to cast out demons, a description McConkie found troubling. "Exorcism connotes to me magical formulas and incantations associated with an evil power," he wrote. "I do not believe that Christ cast out devils by any such means, but rather by the authority of his priesthood and the power of faith."[14]

In the second case, the manual referred to John the Baptist's vision of the Holy Ghost during his baptism of Jesus and called it a turning point where Jesus came to understand his role as the Son of God, choosing this divine path over a simple life as a carpenter. For McConkie, this was too much. "I do not believe it to be the doctrine of the Church that Jesus faced a grave crisis at the time of his baptism at which time he had to choose between a humble profession and the Messiahship. Rather, I believe that at least from the time he was 12 years old he knew who he was and had begun to understand his mission, and that prior to the day of his baptism he knew with a perfect knowledge, and therefore was not subjected to the crisis of any great choice."[15]

McConkie had other problems with the eighty-four-page lesson book and noted that "in my opinion the manual as a whole was written from the perspective of worldly knowledge and the wisdom and philosophies of men, rather than from the viewpoint of latter-day revelation and the gospel." He found it unfortunate that all twenty-one scholars listed under the acknowledgements, and whose works were cited, were non-LDS, and that Mormon sources were hardly used at all. He said it contained naturalistic explanations for miracles and taught that the canonization of the books of the New Testament was a "survival of the fittest in the fierce competition for popular approval," which in his view was an entirely human process.

14. *Synoptic Gospels*, 26–27; Bruce R. McConkie to Milton Bennion, Mar. 1, 1945, in John A. Widtsoe papers, CR 712/2, box 127, fd. 10.

15. *Synoptic Gospels*, 18; McConkie to Bennion.

McConkie was clear that a view other than the direct hand of God or inspiration through the Holy Ghost in the canonization process essentially invalidated those books as the word of God.[16]

The manual did use a scholarly approach to the New Testament, and one that has held up well in the years since. McConkie believed that the writers of the various books understood that they were creating scripture as they wrote, but history shows the gathering and compilation of the books came much later and that the status of the texts evolved. Swensen clearly wanted to provide a credible way for Latter-day Saints to both believe in the texts yet have a deeper and more solid understanding of the history behind them. McConkie believed that anything other than the most conservative approach to the New Testament (or any scripture in the LDS canon) was unacceptable.

"I regret that you sent copies of your letter to your Sunday School Advisors and others of the General Authorities without first having referred the matter to me," McConkie concluded in his letter. "If you had been fully and correctly advised, I do not think you would have attributed the hearsay report to me." He told Bennion that he was therefore going to send his response to the same nine individuals Bennion had sent his own letter.

Neither Bennion nor his counselors responded to McConkie, but two of the general authorities who received copies of both letters did. First Presidency counselor J. Reuben Clark was vague when telling McConkie that "a cursory examination of it [the manual] does not give me basis for disagreeing with what you say." Joseph Fielding Smith told his son-in-law privately that he fully agreed with him. Over the years Smith also had voiced his share of criticism toward trained LDS biblical scholars, most recently Mormon educator Heber C. Snell. McConkie's written defense of his views was his first exposure to some of the church leaders who received both Bennion's rebuke and McConkie's response.[17]

---

16. McConkie to Bennion. The young attorney's response to the criticism he received and his views on the manual are also dealt with in McConkie, *Reflections*, 131–37.

17. McConkie, *Reflections*, 136–37. For Smith's views see Richard Sherlock, "Faith and History: The Snell Controversy," *Dialogue: A Journal of Mormon Thought*, 12, no. 1 (Spring 1979): 27–41.

Smith may well have helped cement McConkie's views on biblical studies. After Smith's son Lewis was killed in World War II in December 1944, Smith and McConkie became much closer, and Smith more proactively mentored him in LDS gospel principles. Even so, many of McConkie's thoughts on such things had become ingrained at a young age. Lowell L. Bennion, Milton Bennion's son and seven years McConkie's senior, was a young teacher at the LDS Institute at the University of Utah in the 1930s and had a more liberal take on the Bible. McConkie had been one of his students while an undergraduate. "I will say that while I appreciated Bruce McConkie, I don't think I taught him anything," Bennion said nearly fifty years later. "I think he already had his mind made up on a lot of things and was not very amenable to my ideas." Bennion also taught Bruce's siblings Brit, Oscar Jr., and Margaret, who were more open to Bennion's approach. "I don't mean to be critical of Bruce. I just think he's done his own thinking right along and is not as open to other points of view."[18]

If the exchange between Milton Bennion and McConkie put him on the radar of at least a few church leaders, he got more of their attention and that of the general church membership through the pages of the church's monthly magazine, *The Improvement Era*. He had already become an experienced public speaker throughout the city, and now his public writings were about to give him more exposure. An article by McConkie, in which his bio line referred to him as a "Major, U.S. armed forces," appeared in the March 1945 issue of the magazine. Whether he was asked to write it or submitted it on his own initiative is unknown. Titled "Can Man Govern His Thoughts?" the essay addressed the path one must take to achieve exaltation in the Kingdom of God. "What is the relationship between salvation and the thoughts which men think?" he asked. "Reflection suggests that there is no more fundamental measure of the true inner man than the thoughts resident in his heart." Evil thoughts lead to evil deeds, McConkie warned. But righteous thoughts can be nurtured and win in the end by having a transforming effect. "I believe there are those now living who are almost complete masters of the thoughts

---

18. McConkie, *Reflections*, 128–29; Lowell L. Bennion, oral history interview with Maureen Ursenbach Beecher, Mar. 9, 1985, James H. Moyle Oral History Program, Church History Library.

that they think and the desires that are formed in their hearts." Controlling one's thoughts allows for controlling one's words, and from there, one's actions. "Salvation is for those who endure to the end. The mechanics of enduring to the end consist of so governing spirits that we think only righteous thoughts, develop only true beliefs, speak only discreet and wise words, and then finally perform only those acts which are in harmony with the mind and will of the Lord."[19]

Following this article's appearance, McConkie began publishing a twenty-part series in the *Deseret News* beginning March 15, 1945, focusing on the United States Constitution. Because this series provides rare insight into McConkie's thinking outside of religion (although it does carry religious overtones), it is important to detail the articles here. His knowledge is impressive, and his unwavering opinions on even secular subjects are clear. In other words, the style is what would one day become classic McConkie.

"The Constitution of the United States of America is the document nobody knows. Like the Bible, all Americans make reference to it, and some profess to revere it, but few read it," he noted in the opening lines of his first installment. "Few still understand the written words and appreciate the effect of its provisions upon their daily lives and interests." The Constitution was under attack by many who feel it is obsolete, he insisted, but in this, he said unequivocally, they erred. "The Constitution is the very foundation and substance of the freedom of all men of this nation, and it is as needful, or more needful that its precepts be kept alive today than at any other time in the history of man's struggle for freedom." At this time the Second World War was nearing an end. A month earlier President Roosevelt, Winston Churchill, and Joseph Stalin met at Yalta to discuss their plans for rebuilding Germany and Europe after the war and asked that an international peace organization be created, which became the United Nations. Germany would surrender two months later, in May, and Japan would follow formally in September, marking the end of the global conflict.[20]

---

19. Bruce R. McConkie, "Can Man Govern His Thoughts?" *Improvement Era*, Mar. 1945, 124–25, 165–67.

20. Bruce R. McConkie, "Know Your Constitution," part one, "The Unknown Constitution," *Deseret News*, Mar. 19, 1945, 4; *David M. Kennedy, Freedom from Fear: The American People in Depression and War, 1929–1945* (New York: Oxford University Press, 1999), 799–806, 851–52.

Much of the series provided straight facts about the Constitutional convention—the rules and process of creating the document in Philadelphia from May 14 through September 17, 1787—and in that sense it was informative to a general reader. Yet McConkie was quick to add his own beliefs, based on well-established LDS teachings. "There are those who believe, and the author is one, that the document signed in the convention on the 17th of September in 1787 did not emanate from the wisdom of the Founding Fathers alone, wise and experienced as they were. Rather the inspiration of the Almighty was with that little body."[21]

McConkie spent a good deal of time talking about the essential freedoms found in the Bill of Rights. "Rights are being infringed today even as they were in the days of George III," he insisted. Yet being in the midst of war, as the United States then was, meant that, justifiably, "certain rights are suspended or restricted." However, "Americans must preserve their rights after this war. If they know what they are and the value they have, they will preserve them."[22]

For him and the LDS Church, God was particularly behind religious freedom. "The denial of religious freedom in other nations is a crime for which their rulers will be held accountable before the judgment bar." This seemed obvious to him during the present time of war. "Germany and Russia have formally and as an official act of state denied Christ and forbidden or limited His worship." Nazi Germany initially suppressed Christianity, promoting pagan beliefs and undermining religious influence. While some Christian leaders collaborated, dissenting groups, such as Jehovah's Witnesses, faced persecution. Later, as war strained resources, the regime co-opted Christianity for propaganda, allowing limited practice to maintain control but targeting those who opposed Nazi ideology. Hence McConkie's firm belief that any attempt to scrap or revise the Constitution should be met with fierce resistance. But the challenges to religious freedom did not exist only outside of the United States. "The Missouri persecutions of the Latter-day Saints in the 1830s

---

21. McConkie, "Know Your Constitution," part three, "The Men Who Made It," *Deseret News*, Mar. 21, 1945, 4.

22. McConkie, "Know Your Constitution," part eight, "Americans Have Their Rights," *Deseret News*, Mar. 27, 1945, 4.

were as reprehensible and iniquitous as any in the history of the world.... Religious liberty is not yet secure in actual practice even in the United States. We have yet to arrive at the day spoken of by the legislature of colonial Rhode Island in 1647 when all men may walk as their consciences persuade them, and that without molestation."[23]

One installment focused on the Electoral College and McConkie provided a glimpse into its history and purpose. "The people of the United States have never elected a president or a vice-president," he wrote, noting, however, his belief that this system of electors had outgrown its purpose. "In the absence of political parties and under the conditions existing in the 13 original states the Electoral College undoubtedly was an ingenious success. Today it is completely outmoded." By that time in history, two presidential candidates— Rutherford B. Hayes (1876) and Benjamin Harrison (1888) had lost the popular vote but won the election because of the Electoral College. For McConkie this result from an outdated system was a travesty, but he recognized that there was only one way to remedy it. "There is no method for changing the Electoral College setup except by an amendment to the Constitution. This ought to be done."[24]

McConkie had other suggestions for change. He believed the powers of the chief executive "are almost too great to be entrusted to one man. Even by staying strictly within them, and it is said that none of our dynamic presidents actually have, a power and influence is built up that makes it easy for the presidency to perpetuate himself in office." This article came shortly after President Franklin D. Roosevelt's reelection five months earlier to a fourth term. No president had ever been elected to more than two prior to Roosevelt, nor had they ever run for a third. McConkie, who had previously campaigned for Roosevelt, had a proposal for addressing this issue. "I suggest a constitutional amendment limiting the president to one term of 4, 5, or 6 years." He recommended that abolition of the electoral college

---

23. McConkie, "Know Your Constitution," part ten, "Shall it Be Jehovah or Baal?" *Deseret News*, Mar. 29, 1945, 4; Jane Caplan, *Nazi Germany: A Very Short History* (New York: Oxford University Press, 2019), 76–77.

24. McConkie, "Know Your Constitution," part thirteen, "America Chooses a Successor to George III," *Deseret News*, Apr. 2, 1845, 4. Since this article was written, two other candidates who lost the popular vote have been elected president: George W. Bush (2000) and Donald Trump (2016).

be part of that amendment. "The limitation of his tenure to one term is the only feasible way to place the executive department back in its true perspective with the legislative and judicial departments." McConkie was not a lone Democrat in his view. Alfred E. Smith, former governor of New York, was a vocal, conservative member of the party opposed to Roosevelt serving beyond his first two terms.[25]

The power granted to the US Supreme Court was less of a worry to him. That body, he recognized, decides what legislation is "unconstitutional and void. Thus the will of the people is defeated—or is it." He maintained that it is not, even if a slim 5–4 majority of the court rules against a law. "Congress may enact a law which is in conflict with the permanent will of the people," meaning, the US Constitution. "If this occurs and a proper case comes before the court, a choice must be made between a higher law and the lesser. The effect of this choice is to declare the act of Congress void, or, as is commonly said, unconstitutional.... This is the natural function of courts. If this country is to have a written Constitution, then the courts cannot be denied this power." If it were not this way "there would be nothing to uphold the supreme law of the land as against any lesser law, and the Congress would become supreme and have all sovereignty."[26]

McConkie clearly saw Congress at war with the Constitution when it passed the New Deal, a not uncommon criticism among conservatives who believed it gave too much power to the federal government and that it's related spending would lead to the total downfall of the country. Democrats typically thought differently, so McConkie's criticisms are unusual. But there were exceptions, such as former governor Smith, a critic of the New Deal. "When the Congress steps outside of its delegation of authority and attempts social and economic reforms and experiments and these same courts determine that such laws conflict with the Constitution, then the courts are condemned and maligned and people say that they are a hindrance to economic progress and industrial development....

---

25. McConkie, "Know Your Constitution," part fourteen, "When the Wicked Rule the People Mourn," *Deseret News*, Apr. 3, 1945, 4.

26. McConkie, "Know Your Constitution," part fifteen, "Thus Saith the Supreme Court: It Shall Not Stand," *Deseret News*, Apr. 4, 1945, 4.

The multitudes seek the loaves and the fishes at the expense of their rights as free men," McConkie continued. He also worried about an amendment proposed by Democratic Sen. Henry F. Ashurst, from Arizona, delegating all authority to Congress to "make laws to regulate agriculture, commerce, industry and labor." If this had passed, then all measures of the New Deal would have remained intact. "This amendment would put the federal government in the position of being capable of regulating every detail of the economic life of every person in the nation. State and local governments would be reduced to mere nothingness. Centralization and its offspring bureaucracy would reign supreme."[27]

Too much power within the federal government, McConkie believed, was becoming more and more prevalent and came at the expense of local freedom and governance. "Recent trends have been toward centralization. But the remedy is simple. It consists in sending to Congress men who will strictly construe the powers of the federal government; men who will desert the pork barrel and champion state rights." If American citizens understood how dangerous the loss of local self-government was to their own liberties, "they would require their Congress to preserve the integrity of the states and diminish the influences of the federal government." Because Congress represents the people, McConkie argued, it should be the strongest of any of the three branches of government and the one that champions the people's rights. [28]

Congress has many powers, he noted, and those can be abused too. The Supreme Court, for example, has consistently broadened the meaning of interstate commerce to where it controls every aspect of the nation's economy. This can't be blamed on the court or the president. "The fault lies with the Congress, or perhaps ultimately with the people, for sending to Congress men who will vote for social and economic measures which usurp the powers of states over their internal and domestic matters." Unless Americans prefer "a strong central government controlled from Washington and that

---

27. McConkie, "Know Your Constitution," part sixteen, "The Congress Shall Have Power," *Deseret News*, Apr. 5, 1945, 4.

28. McConkie, "Know Your Constitution," part seventeen, "Bureaucracy Comes of Age," *Deseret News*, Apr. 6, 1945, 4.

necessarily by bureaus," then "Congress must be required to confine regulations governing commerce to goods in transit, and return the control of manufacturing back to the states." Again, this all boils down to whether the people want a local self-government or would prefer to be controlled by a "centralized bureaucracy. They can have either. The Congress can give them either. It is their Congress."[29]

In the nineteenth installment, McConkie talked about the method—and rarity—of passing amendments to the Constitution. It takes two-thirds of Congress and three-fourths of the states to do so. "It is in the interest of the people to make it difficult to override these rights and freedoms. The easier it is to amend a constitution, the easier it will be for the rights of the people to be lost in times of war or of other emergencies." The three Civil War amendments proved that during times of crisis amendments can be passed quickly. Yet by design, McConkie concluded, "The Constitution is neither too hard nor too easy to amend. It is just right."[30]

In concluding this series, McConkie stressed that "the principles established and the freedoms guaranteed in the Constitution were the outgrowth of over 700 years of struggle by English free men. Every phrase, word and letter was sanctified by the shedding of the blood of those who loved freedom and right more than life. The Constitution was the crowning capstone of all the common law." Yet the people of the United States must not ignore the problems they face and the fact that freedom is tenuous should they fail to fight to preserve the rights guaranteed by their governing document. "The constitutional sun is rising, and it has not reached its zenith, nor will it, so long as the love of freedom is sufficiently dear that men will sacrifice their all for it." Indeed, it all boils down to the people, who "must love freedom more than they love money. The cause is just. The God of fre[e]dom has approved. The event is in the hands of the people."[31]

In May 1945 McConkie, having been ordained a seventy around eight years earlier, was called as one of the seven presidents of the

---

29. McConkie, "Know Your Constitution," part eighteen, "Has Congress Failed Us?" *Deseret News*, Apr. 7, 1945, 4.

30. McConkie, "Know Your Constitution," part nineteen, "The People Change Their Government," *Deseret News*, Apr. 9, 1945, 4.

31. McConkie, "Know Your Constitution," part twenty, "It is a Rising Sun," *Deseret News*, Apr. 10, 1945, 4.

340th Quorum of Seventy in the Yalecrest Ward in Salt Lake City. He was still in the army, as was evident in a newspaper photo of the quorum where he was the only one of the seven men wearing military attire. But as he approached his discharge date, the local press began speculating about whether he and others about to return to civilian life would run for a local judgeship. With a bump in salary from $3,000 to $5,000 per year, the job was highly attractive and competitive.[32]

While any future job decisions were still to be decided, Bruce and Amelia took a vacation in August. This was Bruce's first furlough during his military career. While Bruce's sister Margaret Pope and her husband, Bill, took care of the children, the McConkie's took a road trip to Yellowstone National Park. When they arrived on September 2, they noticed that people were carrying out a celebration outside of the lodge. They shortly learned that Japan had formally surrendered, which meant that World War II was over. The surrender was announced earlier on August 15 but was now made official with a signing aboard the USS Missouri in Tokyo Bay. During this trip Bruce and Amelia also traveled to Idaho Falls, Idaho, to attend the open house for the new LDS temple while it was open to the public between September 15 and 20.[33]

Any talk of a judgeship for McConkie ended when he wrote Salt Lake City mayor Earl J. Glade in December 1945 and asked to be reappointed to his previous job as city prosecutor. McConkie explained that he was no longer on active duty and would remain on terminal leave until February 27, 1946, when he would be officially discharged. A few months later, before any decision was made to reinstate him, he was appointed a chaplain in the new Mervyn S. Bennion Post No. 83 of the American Legion. At the time of his discharge from the military he held the rank of lieutenant colonel

---

32. Photo caption in "Melchizedek Priesthood Section," *Church News*, June 2, 1945, 2; "Corporal Seeks Judge Bench," *Daily Herald*, July 27, 1945, 9; "City Elections Candidates Still Wanted," *Deseret News*, Aug. 25, 1945, 9.

33. In McConkie, *Reflections*, 137, Amelia says that they went to the Idaho Falls Temple first, but the open house came after Japan's surrender, not before. Although she does not identify which of the two dates announcing the surrender that they arrived at Yellowstone, it makes more sense that it was the latter. Otherwise, their trip away from their children would have lasted much longer, which was unlikely; "48,000 Persons Visit Idaho Falls Temple," *Salt Lake Tribune*, Sep. 20, 1945, 7; Kennedy, *Freedom from Fear*, 851–52.

and had been awarded both the American Campaign Medal and the World War II Medal.[34]

On the day before his formal discharge, McConkie resumed his job as city prosecutor, but immediately resigned from that position, the *Salt Lake Tribune* reported, so that he could "devote himself to other work." That work, surprisingly, was a new career as a reporter for the *Deseret News*. Thus, McConkie permanently left behind both the legal profession and his work in city government. Amelia recalled later that her husband soured on the law because "he had to prosecute petty criminals," and reign in prostitution, neither of which he enjoyed doing. "He much preferred to write."[35]

This was shocking to his father because Oscar had long anticipated his son taking over his law practice. That plan was especially relevant now because in March Oscar and Vivian accepted a call from President David O. McKay of the First Presidency to preside over the California Mission. The presidency announced the appointment the following month. With Bruce adamant about ending his legal career, Oscar may have closed his office during his time in California, but at some point after his assignment ended Oscar reopened his Salt Lake City office and his sons Brit and Oscar Jr. joined him there.[36]

Articles McConkie wrote for the *Deseret News* report stories on the LDS Church, as well as local, secular news. He worked under the direction of Apostle Mark E. Petersen, who served as managing director of the paper. As a reporter McConkie followed and wrote on a scandal involving Salt Lake City commissioner Fred Tedesco, who had used city funds and personnel for his own private use, including painting projects at his home.[37]

34. "Army Officer Seeks Old City Post," *Ogden Standard-Examiner*, Dec. 8, 1945, 2; Kenneth Miller, "Veterans' Affairs," *Salt Lake Tribune*, Feb. 15, 1946, 8; "New Legion Post Names First Slate of Officers," *Deseret News*, Feb. 15, 1946, 20; McConkie, *Reflections*, 131.

35. "Irvine Keeps City Post," *Salt Lake Tribune*, Feb. 27, 1946, 13; Horne, *Bruce R. McConkie*, 45.

36. McConkie, "Biography," 10; France Briton McConkie obituary at findagrave. com; McConkie, *Reflections*, 52, 140.

37. See, for example, Bruce R. McConkie, "Seventies of Church Called to Stand Forty as Special Witnesses of Christ," *Church News*, Apr. 13, 1946, 5; Bruce R. McConkie, "Mission Head Report at General Conference," *Church News*, Oct. 5, 1946, 6, 8; Bruce R. McConkie, "Tedesco Admits City Property Use," *Deseret News*, July 30, 1946, 1, 3; Bruce R. McConkie, "Tedesco Scandal Mere Start, Pres. McKay Says," *Deseret News*, Aug. 6, 1946, 1, 6.

As McConkie focused on his new job, he and Amelia celebrated the birth of their fifth child and fourth to survive, a daughter they named Mary Ethel. The following month Salt Lake City mayor Earl J. Glade wrote LDS Church President George Albert Smith to let him know how pleased he was with McConkie's job at the paper and as one "guided only by the utmost discretion.... Bruce's fine legal mind makes us want to counsel with him. We highly value his judgment."[38]

Life could hardly have been better for this young family of six as Bruce settled into a new job that seemed to satisfy him. But things were about to change dramatically for the McConkies, and as a result, their lives would be forever altered.

---

38. "Sidelights," *Deseret News*, June 17, 1946, 11; McConkie, *Reflections*, 140–41.

CHAPTER FOUR

NEW GENERAL AUTHORITY

1946-1955

When the LDS Church's 1946 semi-annual general conference commenced in the fall, McConkie was on the staff of the *Deseret News* and took notes on the various sessions from behind the press table in the tabernacle on Temple Square. The conference opened on Friday, October 4, but the church's seventeen North American mission presidents gathered two days earlier for a special meeting in the Salt Lake Temple. McConkie attended that event and reported on it for the paper in an article that took up all five columns of one page and part of two others.[1] Writing this piece, which appeared in the Saturday edition, must have taken up much of his time, but covering the entirety of the conference surely added to the intense business of the weekend.

There was one bit of news that the press and everyone else had waited for most of the conference to hear, but by Saturday night, it was clear that they would need to wait until Sunday. There was a vacancy in the First Council of Seventy, due to the death of President John H. Taylor four months earlier on May 28. Taylor died suddenly while addressing departing missionaries at the Salt Lake City mission home. With that vacancy, thirty-one-year-old McConkie began hearing predictions from friends, family, and even strangers, that he would probably be called to fill the position. Although McConkie would usually brush off these comments with a dose of humor, he

---

1. Bruce R. McConkie, "Mission Heads Report at General Conference," *Church News*, Oct. 5, 1946, 6, 8, 12.

also began to accept the possibility that a call as a general authority might be headed his way.[2]

Shortly before the conference's final session began on Sunday afternoon, the telephone rang at the McConkie residence. Amelia answered and recognized the voice of First Presidency counselor David O. McKay, who asked for Bruce. Amelia told McKay that her husband was at the tabernacle covering the conference with other reporters. After they hung up, Amelia wondered to herself if this phone call was related to Bruce filling the vacancy. At the tabernacle, First Presidency secretary Joseph Anderson found McConkie and told him that President McKay wanted to see him. "I knew instantly what was wanted," McConkie later said. Anderson took him to a room where McKay was waiting. The two men then held an impromptu interview. McKay told him that his name would be presented to the conference as the one chosen to fill the vacancy in the Seventy. He also asked a series of questions related to McConkie's worthiness and faithfulness. McConkie answered all of them in the affirmative, and McKay then issued the official call.

"You are the unanimous selection of the First Presidency, the Council of the Twelve, and the First Council of the Seventy," McKay said. "It is the voice of the Lord. You go back to your place; we will not go out together."[3]

McConkie went back to his seat and continued taking notes as a member of the press. After President George Albert Smith's closing remarks, McKay rose and presented the general authorities of the church to the members for their sustaining vote. After listing the members of the First Presidency, the Twelve, and others, he read the seven names of the First Council of Seventy, McConkie's being the last on the list. Those present sustained the council with an uplifted hand, making it all official. After the meeting concluded Oscar and Vivian McConkie, who were in town with other mission presidents attending the conference, approached their son separately and kissed him, neither saying a word as they did so. Other church leaders

---

2. "President John H. Taylor of the First Council of Seventy," *Improvement Era*, July 1946, 429; Joseph Fielding McConkie, *The Bruce R. McConkie Story: Reflections of a Son* (Salt Lake City: Deseret Book, 2003), 143–44.

3. McConkie, *Reflections*, 145–46.

congratulated him. When his in-laws visited him later, Joseph Fielding Smith simply told him, "Just keep your feet on the ground."[4]

After calling McConkie to his new position, President Smith felt some angst about charges of nepotism immediately hurled by critics of the church. McConkie's wife was the daughter of an apostle who was also a Smith. George Albert Smith and Joseph Fielding Smith were great-grandsons of brothers John Smith and Joseph Smith Sr., two sons of Asael Smith, and were thus third cousins. This meant that Amelia Smith McConkie was a third cousin once removed to the current church president. The relationship was somewhat distant, but family ties among the general authorities were not new and were even common. For example, Joseph Fielding Smith had been called as an apostle in 1910 by his father Joseph F. Smith, who was then the president of the church and a son of a former member of the First Presidency. Church president George Albert Smith was the son and grandson of apostles also, which could have made him feel more sensitive when calling McConkie as a general authority. But the two had had little interaction prior to the appointment, and with McConkie himself not sharing a blood relationship with the Smiths, any criticisms quickly dissipated.[5]

Although his new position within church leadership would be a fulltime assignment, when McConkie met with President Smith on Thursday, October 10, Smith asked him to continue writing for the *Deseret News*. That same day, in the Salt Lake Temple, Smith set McConkie apart by the laying on of hands, with seventeen other general authorities standing in the circle.[6]

The next issue of the church's official magazine, *The Improvement Era*, contained an article about McConkie that shed light on his qualities and what his new calling meant to the church. "Despite his thirty-one years," wrote *Church News* editor Henry A. Smith,

---

4. McConkie, *Reflections*, 146–47; Dennis B. Horne, *Bruce R. McConkie: Highlights from His Life and Teachings*, second enlarged edition with epilogue (Salt Lake City: Eborn Books, 2010), 52.

5. Francis M. Gibbons, *George Albert Smith: Kind and Caring Christian, Prophet of God* (Salt Lake City: Deseret Book, 1990), 320–21.

6. McConkie, *Reflections*, 150–51; "Elder McConkie Set Apart, Oct. 10," *Church News*, Oct. 12, 1946, 5; Henry A. Smith, "Elder Bruce R. McConkie of the First Council of the Seventy," *Improvement Era*, Nov. 1946, 730.

McConkie "had earned an enviable reputation in Church service, especially in the fields of gospel study, teaching, and seventies' quorum leadership." He possessed a "sterling character," "sincerity," exhibited "loyalty to the Church" and "outstanding ability." McConkie would also "bring a viewpoint of the young people of the Church into his new duties." In fact, it had already been pointed out that he was the youngest man called as a general authority since B. H. Roberts entered the Council of Seventy at the same age in 1888. The article noted that McConkie had been a popular and highly requested speaker at sacrament meetings in the Salt Lake City area for many years.[7]

McConkie's gospel study habits involved more than just reading. Over the years he had already filled many loose-leaf notebooks with notes from his laborious analyses of the Book of Mormon, which covered over 115 different subjects, including, for example, every reference to "faith" in the text. At the time of his call, he was undertaking a similar project with the Doctrine and Covenants. Besides his public speaking, he already had vast experience teaching the Gospel Doctrine Sunday School class and had been an instructor in the seventy's quorum in his ward.[8]

McConkie's primary duties—and those that affected him and his family more than any other—were the near weekly assignments presiding at stake conferences throughout the church, which often required him to spend weekends or longer away from home. For his first few conferences he accompanied other general authorities to their own assignments. The first at which he presided on his own was a conference held in East Millcreek Stake on the weekend of October 26–27, 1946. Roscoe W. Eardley of the Church Welfare Department came along and also spoke.[9]

At the time, church leaders traveled by car or train, depending on the distance. In November McConkie left by train when he undertook a two-week tour of the Southern States Mission. When mission president Heber Meeks wrote to the First Presidency on November 28 from his Atlanta headquarters to report on McConkie's work

7. Smith, "Elder Bruce R. McConkie," 692; "Appointee, 31, Youngest LDS Leader," *Salt Lake Tribune*, Oct. 7, 1946, 1.

8. Smith, "Elder Bruce R. McConkie," 692.

9. McConkie, *Reflections*, 152–53; "Quarterly Conference Appointments," *Church News*, Oct. 19, 1946, 5.

there, he noted that, "His good counsel and warm friendship was helpful and encouraging to us. He took sufficient time to give the missionaries much helpful counsel and instruction. His fine, doctrinal sermons were an inspiration to the Saints throughout the mission. His presence in the mission was a blessing to us all."[10]

On March 27, 1947, the First Presidency published a letter in the *Deseret News* addressed to presidents of stakes and missions that rolled out a plan to meet the spiritual needs of LDS military members by seeing that they were aided sufficiently to stay in the church or enter full activity wherever they were stationed. McConkie had been in the Seventy for a little less than six months when the presidency tapped him to take on the role as coordinator for this effort and to spend a few months traveling to the church's missions to help implement the program.

McConkie's work was to be overseen by the LDS Servicemen's Committee of which he was a part, and which included Apostles Harold B. Lee and Mark E. Petersen, and Hugh B. Brown, former LDS servicemen's coordinator and current coordinator of veteran's affairs at Brigham Young University. "Our experience in the last war indicated that many of our boys yielded to temptation to some extent because they had been neglected by their brethren at home, and came to feel entirely out of touch with the Church and its program," the committee explained in a letter to Elder John A. Widtsoe of the Council of the Twelve. "We feel that in the present instance, if our priesthood organizations will do their duty, many boys may be kept in paths of virtue and activity in the Church."[11]

On Friday, April 4, church members watching or listening to the annual general conference of the church witnessed McConkie speak as a general authority for the first time. His talk opened with the words "I know that Jesus is the Son of the Living God and that he was crucified for the sins of the world. I know that he came into the

---

10. "Latter-Day Saints Official to Speak," *Birmingham News*, Nov. 13, 1947, 16; Heber Meeks to First Presidency, Nov. 28, 1947, First Presidency mission files, CR 1/49, box 56, fd. 15, Church History Library, Salt Lake City.

11. "Letter from the First Presidency," and "Presidency Takes New Steps to Provide for LDS Men in Service," *Deseret News*, Mar. 29, 1947, 1; Harold B. Lee, Mark E. Petersen, Bruce R. McConkie, and Hugh B. Brown to John A. Widtsoe, Oct. 11, 1948, John A. Widtsoe Papers, CR 712/2, box 180, fd. 10, Church History Library.

world with the definitely appointed mission to be the Redeemer and the Savior of men." This was, he said, "the great burden of the message of the restored gospel."

He testified of the mission of Joseph Smith in restoring the truth to the earth. But there was a living prophet currently among them, George Albert Smith, who all should follow at that time. "If men in this world in our day want to go back to our Father's kingdom, it is incumbent upon them to come to the Living Oracle and have exercised in their behalf the authority of the priesthood. They must accept and live in harmony with the counsels of those men whom God has chosen today."

McConkie taught that truth comes to one's soul through the Holy Ghost, and he outlined a four-part process in obtaining a testimony: 1. Desire to know; 2. Study the principles of the gospel; 3. Practice those principles; 4. Pray that God will reveal the truth to you. "There is not a person, a God-fearing and righteous person in this world," he insisted, "who cannot come to this kingdom and by obedience to that law, embracing those four steps, gain for himself a knowledge that this work is true." He concluded that "there is nothing in this world that I would rather do than have the privilege of preaching the gospel and of devoting such time and abilities as the Lord may bless me with to the building up of his kingdom."[12] For McConkie, whose focus had been strictly on preaching and teaching the message of the Restoration for the past six months, it must have seemed like a lifetime ago that he practiced law or relied on a paycheck through any secular endeavors.

On Saturday, April 12, McConkie left to begin visiting all the missions and selected stakes near army bases in the United States, and started his tour in Washington, DC. As a young, relatively recently discharged military veteran, McConkie was an obvious choice for such an assignment.[13]

In late summer, McConkie left to speak at the San Juan Stake Conference in Monticello, Utah, on September 6 and 7, 1947, and he

---

12. *One-Hundred Seventeenth Annual Conference of the Church of Jesus Christ of Latter-day Saints, Held in the Tabernacle, Salt Lake City, April 4, 5, and 6, 1947* (Salt Lake City: Church of Jesus Christ of Latter-day Saints, 1947), 38–41.

13. "2 Authorities Will Visit LDS Missions," *Deseret News*, Apr. 11, 1947, 13.

brought his family along. Because this was the home of his youth and he had not been back in over a decade, he turned the assignment into what was then a rare vacation for the McConkies. His grandmother Redd still lived there, and the family stayed with her.[14] It was not long after when Amelia became pregnant with another child, and on June 28, 1948, she bore a son, Mark Lewis. The family now consisted of three boys and two girls. Bruce was a month away from his thirty-third birthday, while Amelia had just turned thirty-two a week earlier. Daughter Vivian was eight years old, Joseph, seven, Stanford was four, and Mary was just two. With Bruce regularly away from home, Amelia understood that she would, out of necessity, take care of the children much of the time on her own. Although an absent husband and father was the norm for families of general authorities, the McConkie family was younger than most, and the burden was heavier. "She made many of our clothes, put up fruit, sewed the holes in our Levi's. She knows what it is to be left alone, to be ignored and not know what's going on, to go without—all the implications of being a Church widow," a son later said of her. Amelia herself took it all in stride, as she reflected decades later. "For me, life married to a General Authority was perfectly normal." She had been born and raised in the home of an apostle and experienced an absent father and saw what her own mother had to endure. "I know that's not the case for other women who are plunged into it suddenly. But I wasn't. I did, though, in large part have to raise the children alone."[15]

With the larger family came need for a bigger home, and the McConkies moved to a house that better met their needs at 1985 Lambourne Avenue in South Salt Lake. They made many friends in their new neighborhood and the kids had plenty of playmates. Here, Amelia served as the Relief Society president of their ward. A sixth child, Rebecca was born in 1950, and a seventh, Stephen, came along the following year, confirming further the conviction that the move

---

14. "Authorities Assigned to Stake Conferences," *Church News*, Aug. 30, 1947, 4. In McConkie, *Reflections*, 160, son Joseph Fielding McConkie says this assignment to Monticello occurred in the fall of 1946, but I could only find an assignment for Bruce in Monticello in September 1947.

15. "Elder McConkie, Wife Rejoice Over New Son," *Church News*, July 4, 1948, 20C; Sheri L. Dew, "Bruce R. McConkie: A Family Portrait," *This People*, Dec. 1985/ Jan. 1986, 61–62.

to the new house was a wise one.[16] With Stephen's birth, the family was nearing completion—but it was not there yet.

Giving what time and attention he could to his growing brood probably became more challenging when, between February and December 1950, McConkie edited a weekly Saturday column for the *Deseret News* called "History: What Happened in the World This Last Week." This column highlighted selected news stories locally, nationally, and internationally. McConkie may have been inclined on his own to stay current on such events, or perhaps the assignment made that easier for him, but pursuits like this probably help explain why his family described him as "well-rounded and well-versed in life."[17]

With American troops now serving in the Korean War, and thus more LDS men enlisted, on September 28, 1950, McConkie was reappointed to his position as coordinator for LDS servicemen. As before, he was part of a committee effort to provide activities within church units where young Mormons served. Addressing ward and stake leaders that next evening during a meeting at the Salt Lake Tabernacle, he spoke of the plight of military members trying to keep close to the church. A reporter writing about his talk noted that, "He declared the servicemen are crying for help—that they want to hear from home, get the news and be encouraged." McConkie estimated that 10,000 LDS members were then serving in the military, a number twice as high as those then away on missions. He predicted that number would likely double within the next eight months.[18]

On Sunday, October 8, McConkie was in San Diego, California, meeting Mormon military members at the naval training center, conferencing also with Willard L. Kimball, assistant coordinator for local LDS servicemen, and stake president Wallace W. Johnson, about helping to meet the needs of those serving their country. Within a year and a half, the committee sent out close to 15,500 packages containing special military editions of The Book of

---

16. McConkie, *Reflections*, 162–63.

17. See articles published Saturdays in the *Deseret News* between February 18 and December 23, 1950. The first two were given the title "The Week's News in Review." In January 1951 John R. Talmage took over the column; Dew, "Family Portrait," 50.

18. "The Church Moves On," *Improvement Era*, Dec. 1950, 944; "McConkie Chosen GI Coordinator," *Standard-Examiner* (Ogden, UT), Sep. 29, 1950, 8A; "Church Leaders Voice Need for Faith in God," *Herald Journal* (Logan, UT), Sep. 30, 1950, 1.

Mormon, *Principles of the Gospel* (a book explaining basic Mormon teachings), a directory listing the locations of Mormon chapel addresses, and a dog tag for LDS service members.[19]

McConkie turned thirty-seven on July 29, 1952. The *Deseret News*, in noting that fact, said that he spent the day outside picking apricots and that evening canning them at the church's Welfare Square. That the paper would go out of its way to note that fact may be an indication of how out of character it seemed for a man who church members typically saw as a serious-minded theologian and expounder of doctrine, one who seemed to have little time or inclination for other activities outside of reading, writing, studying, or speaking. But there was more to Bruce McConkie the man that few outside his family and circle of friends knew. "I have a keen sense of humor, actually, but it doesn't project over the pulpit and it's not generally known," he revealed years later, something which Amelia confirmed. "People didn't get to know the real him. They saw him at the pulpit, and at the pulpit he didn't believe in doing anything but preaching the gospel. I've had people ask if he quoted scriptures to me and that sort of thing when he was home. Goodness no! He was a perfectly normal man. He didn't have his nose in a book all the time, though he did study a lot. But I don't think I've ever known anyone who was more well-balanced."[20]

When he did study, however, he was usually so absorbed in what he was reading that if Amelia tried to get his attention, she sometimes waited endlessly for a reply. "Finally I'd say, 'Would you just go *ugh* or something so I'll at least know you heard me.' Then he'd start to laugh."[21]

Although the family held daily morning prayer together, surprisingly, McConkie never initiated any formal, structured gospel learning at home. The family never held scripture study together and rarely held family home evenings, as neither was heavily emphasized by the church at that time. "But we caught something, we

19. "Authorities: Pres. Smith to Leave for Denver," *Church News*, Oct. 11, 1950, 2; "LDS Group Distributes Servicemen's Packet," *Salt Lake Telegram*, Apr. 4, 1952, 6.

20. "Elder McConkie Notes His 37th Birthday," *Church News*, July 30, 1952, 15; David Croft, "Spare Time's Rare to Apostle," *Church News*, Jan. 24, 1976, 4; Dew, "Family Portrait," 50.

21. Dew, "Family Portrait," 52.

sensed something," son Joseph said in 1985. "We inherited by exposure. There was never any pretense. There was never any attempt to squeeze religion into us. But dad *lived* the gospel, he breathed it, he loved it. And he taught us more than answers. He taught us how to get answers." He also made sure he showed affection. Daughter Vivian said that, "Whenever he met us, dad would kiss us on the forehead." It didn't matter where they were. "It used to embarrass my sister Rebeca. But that changed as we got older."[22]

He was not afraid to show affection publicly toward Amelia. "There was no embarrassment about holding hands or kissing. Frankly, there were times when dad would leave in the morning and by the way he kissed mother you'd think he was off to Japan for three weeks," said son Mark. "When they were in the same room dad wanted mother sitting next to him. Obviously that physical closeness symbolized the emotional, spiritual and intellectual closeness they shared."[23]

It appears that McConkie was not all that strict with his children and was known to inject humor to prove that. Once, after Amelia had finally had enough of their son Joseph repeatedly coming home late for dinner, she told her husband, "Bruce, *you* say something to this boy!" All Bruce did was look over at his son and say, "Well, hello Joseph!"[24]

Surprisingly, this man who regularly spoke publicly, could also be very quiet in many settings, especially around extended family. An aunt once joked to him, "Bruce, I can't imagine how any of your children learned to talk. They sure didn't learn it from you." It was understandable if he kept quiet when others were singing, because his dreadful singing voice remained with him throughout his life. He learned he had better only sing when he was alone or when driving with Amelia, who apparently could tolerate it.[25]

His colleagues in the First Council of Seventy had varied experiences with him, and each perhaps saw him differently. Marion D. Hanks had been called to the Seventy in 1953 and the two became close friends. Hanks said more than once that if a better man than McConkie ever lived, he had yet to meet him. But the two could

---

22. McConkie, *Reflections*, 231; Dew, "Family Portrait," 50, 54.

23. Dew, "Family Portrait," 62.

24. Dew, "Family Portrait," 50.

25. Dew, "Family Portrait," 51, 52; McConkie, *Reflections*, 267, 271–72.

not have been farther apart in their views and attitudes, and some-times Hanks was troubled by what he observed in McConkie. In Hanks's experience McConkie could be unforgiving toward others and even seemed to delight when erring members were disciplined by the church and marginalized. Yet Hanks said in their personal in-teractions McConkie was always courteous to him. Family members insist McConkie was in fact quite forgiving and never held a grudge, even against his critics.[26]

This was all balanced by fun moments with these same col-leagues—even when he was on the receiving end of practical jokes, which were spearheaded at the office by another close friend, S. Dilworth Young. Some of these pranks, McConkie confessed, were "elaborate and extensive." The general authorities, he said, overall, were "congenial and most of them have a very rich sense of hu-mor." That fun side was evident in the neighborhood parties and get-togethers he and his family were part of. Neighbor Glen Rudd described McConkie as "the ringleader in organizing the neighbor-hood," and his informal ways were regularly observed by those who knew him best. "I remember one day my wife was out in the kitchen and he came in, went in on the front room floor and lay down—he nearly stretched from wall to wall—and kicked off his shoes and started yelling, 'I'm starving to death! I'm hungry! Marva, Marva, help a hungry man.'" After he'd consume what she brought, "He'd lie there, kick his feet, and shout" for more.[27]

Besides speaking at stake conferences, general conferences, and other meetings, or carrying on his work in helping to bolster the spiritual life of LDS servicemen, McConkie's assignments took him to various destinations to oversee other aspects of the church and its growth. In September 1952 he spent three weeks touring the Southwest Indian Mission where he reported that so far that year 400 Native Americans had been baptized, and another 200 were expected to join the church before year end. This despite tremen-dous anti-Mormon activity among them by non-Mormon clergy. He met with the Maricopa, Pima, Papago, Zuni Isleta, Navaho, and

---

26. Richard D. Hanks, interview with the author, June 13, 2023; Dew, "Family Por-trait," 61.

27. Croft, "Spare Time's Rare to Apostle," 4; McConkie, *Reflections*, 164.

Hualapai tribes. "President McConkie is a 'natural' with the Indian people," wrote Golden R. Buchanan, president of the mission. "He is able to speak in short simple sentences and to explain the gospel easily and in simple language. He felt perfectly at home with the Indian people. He was able to shake hands with them in such a manner that he won their confidence immediately. He was loved by them all." McConkie also met with the missionaries serving in the mission. "His instructions were given kindly but very much to the point. His great knowledge of the gospel was an inspiration to us all. I am sure our mission is better for his having been here with us."[28]

Two months later McConkie and Apostle Spencer W. Kimball traveled to Mexico where they dedicated two chapels. On November 1, 1952, Kimball dedicated the Tlalpan branch chapel, and two days after that McConkie dedicated the new building for the Monte Corona branch. While there they held conferences and met with government officials and the twelve missionaries who then served within the local branches. Two years later he toured the Central States Mission with its president, Alvin R. Dyer, on a two-week assignment. They held conferences in Kansas, Oklahoma, Arkansas, Missouri, and in western Illinois. They met with missionaries and military members and held another conference with an LDS branch made up almost entirely of Native Americans. In reporting back to Joseph Fielding Smith, McConkie wrote on November 4, 1954, "In the course of the tour we held 17 public meetings, four with servicemen, 10 with missionaries, dedicated five buildings, and met with approximately 30% of the entire membership of the mission. A goodly number of investigators and friends attended most of the public meetings."[29]

McConkie's passion for spreading the LDS gospel message extended beyond his own talks, writings, and travels. Around 1953 he began compiling many of the teachings of his father-in-law into a three-volume work he titled *Doctrines of Salvation: Sermons*

28. "Elder Bruce McConkie Reports Big Gains," *Church News*, Sep. 27, 1952, 12; Golden R. Buchanan to the First Presidency, Sep. 19, 1952, Joseph Fielding Smith Papers, MS 4250, box 76, fd. 15, Church History Library.

29. "Elders Kimball and McConkie Dedicate Chapels, Select Sites," *Church News*, Nov. 15, 1952, 14; "Elder McConkie Dedicates Five Chapels During Tour," *Church News*, Oct. 30, 1954, 7; Bruce R. McConkie to Joseph Fielding Smith, Nov. 4, 1954, Smith Papers, box 74, fd. 13.

and Writings of Joseph Fielding Smith. "Joseph Fielding Smith is the leading gospel scholar and the greatest doctrinal teacher of this generation," McConkie wrote on November 10, 1954, in the preface to volume one, released soon after. "Few men in this dispensation have approached him in gospel knowledge or surpassed him in spiritual insight." The material came mostly from sermons published in church periodicals and from instruction extracted from letters written to church members who had questions for which they could find no answers. McConkie even supplemented the volume with letters written directly from Smith to him. Volume two was published the following year. McConkie may have gained his interest in publishing partly from Smith, who was indeed a prolific writer, but also from his father Oscar, who had penned two books of his own, *A Dialogue at Golgotha* in 1945 and *The Holy Ghost* in 1952.[30]

It is not surprising that McConkie found Elder Smith's writings important and deserving of wider circulation. At the time Smith was perhaps the most prolific and respected theologian in the church. McConkie, who had long possessed his own interest in gospel study and in analyzing gospel topics, certainly found his father-in-law's insights to be of great value, not to mention how their one-on-one discussions over the past decade and a half must have inspired him. Their views were similar in their conservative leanings. Smith explained that this project was one McConkie did on his own without even consulting him, yet he approved of the compilation and believed it to be of importance. "Elder McConkie has devoted a great deal of time in collecting and arranging the material for these 3 volumes, all of which was done unbeknown to me," Smith noted in a letter to an inquirer. "I hope that these books will find a ready response, for in my judgment, they answer many questions that are constantly arising."[31]

---

30. Joseph Fielding Smith, *Doctrines of Salvation: Sermons and Writings of Joseph Fielding Smith*, 3 vols., Bruce R. McConkie, comp. (Salt Lake City: Bookcraft, 1954–56), 1:v. Full citation for books by Oscar W. McConkie are *Dialogue at Golgotha: An Analysis of Judaism and Christianity, and of the Laws, Government and Institutions of the Jews, and of the Jewish and Roman Trials of Jesus* (Salt Lake City: Oscar W. McConkie, 1945) and *The Holy Ghost: A Study of the Holy Ghost According to the Standard Works of the Church* (Salt Lake City: Deseret Book, 1952).

31. Joseph Fielding Smith to J. K. Orton, July 30, 1956, Smith Papers, box 31, fd. 14.

Some of McConkie's own writings were done as official church publications. As a member of the Missionary Committee, he authored four twenty- to forty-page pamphlets for use by missionaries while proselyting. Released in July 1955, the four tracts formed a series on the Godhead and were titled, *The Truth about God*, *What the Mormons Think of Christ*, *Second Coming of Our Lord*, and *The Holy Ghost Speaks Again*.[32] All footnotes were linked to the church's four accepted books of scripture, which added to the authoritative status of the tracts.

For the now forty-year-old McConkie, that some of his own works were officially sanctioned and distributed certainly elevated his reputation as a gospel scholar to a new level. After he compiled the works of his father-in-law and published them, the reception for that work was favorable. The trust the First Presidency placed in him nearly a decade earlier with a call to the presiding quorums of the church possibly led him to feel that his voice and the ideas he espoused were entirely on safe ground. He soon discovered, however, that despite the best of intentions on his part, this was not always the case.

---

32. "New Mission Tracts: Bruce R. McConkie Authors New Series," *Church News*, July 9, 1955, 3.

CHAPTER FIVE

CONTROVERSIAL AUTHOR

1955-1960

As Bruce R. McConkie wrapped up volume two of the *Doctrines of Salvation* compilation in September 1955, he also planned the release of another book, the first of several volumes he envisioned as part of a series.

Between 1854 and 1886, a semi-monthly publication called *Journal of Discourses* published 1,438 speeches by fifty-five different church leaders and others. Brigham Young provided 390 of these, while John Taylor, Orson Pratt, Heber C. Kimball, and George Q. Cannon gave well over one hundred each. The sermons had been recorded by George Watt, David W. Evans, and George F. Gibbs, and once transcribed, they were compiled and eventually bound into twenty-six volumes. Although many of the talks contained valuable and instructive information, they were never officially sanctioned by the church.[1] Indeed, some of them contained doctrines the church never adopted, while others taught ideas the church once believed but no longer embraced.

McConkie believed that these sermons were significant enough that church members would benefit from the best among them. He contracted to produce the series with a local publisher, Bookcraft, his publisher for *Doctrines of Salvation*. It called for a ten-volume set of around 350 pages each that would reproduce about a fifth of the original work. He believed his project was important because one day someone would undertake something similar, and their

---

1. Ronald G. Watt, "Journal of Discourses," in Daniel H. Ludlow, ed., *Encyclopedia of Mormonism*, 4 vols. (New York: Macmillan, 1992), 2:769–70.

qualifications might be lacking or their motive questionable. He talked it all over with Joseph Fielding Smith.[2]

He called this project *Sound Doctrine: The Journal of Discourses Series*, and a photo of the completed and soon-to-be-released first volume appeared in the December 1955 issue of the *Improvement Era* as part of an ad for Christmas titles. "At long last a great wealth of authoritative information comes to light from a series of books unknown and unavailable to this generation," the accompanying text noted. "This vital doctrinal source contains important sermons of the Presidency and the Council of the Twelve during the all important 40-year period in which most of the doctrines of the church were being revealed and recorded. These sermons, delivered by men who knew the Prophet Joseph and were taught by him in public and private, are published in full." The advertised price was $3.00.[3]

When First Presidency second counselor J. Reuben Clark learned of the upcoming release of volume one, he became concerned about the wisdom in publishing these sermons. He then called McConkie in to meet with the presidency on November 9 to explain his reasons for undertaking this project. McConkie left proofs of the first 150 pages for them to review. At this time the presidency consisted of church president David O. McKay, Stephen L Richards, and Clark. McConkie followed up this conversation with a December 1 letter to the presidency. At this point, apparently they wanted to delay publication until they could read the manuscript and decide. "As the Brethren know," McConkie wrote in his letter, "my purpose and aim in this matter is to further and protect the interests of the Church, and I am amenable to such changes as may be desired, both as to the name of the book and as to its contents." He lamented the fact that although all publicity for the book had been pulled since their meeting, one bookstore had kept advertising it. "I am sorry these ads have appeared and wish to assure you that every effort was made to stop the appearance of those published since my interview with the First Presidency, and that they are not intended in any way to embarrass or pressure you Brethren."[4]

2. Bruce R. McConkie to the First Presidency, Dec. 1, 1955, copy courtesy of Smith-Pettit Foundation, Salt Lake City.

3. "This Christmas, give LDS Books…," *Improvement Era*, Dec. 1955, 882.

4. McConkie to First Presidency, Dec. 1, 1955. An ad announcing *Sound Doctrine* appeared in the *Salt Lake Tribune* on Nov. 30, 1955, 16.

Two months later on February 9, 1956, the presidency drafted a letter to McConkie apologizing for the "considerable delay in reaching conclusions embodying our feelings concerning your proposal to print an abbreviated edition of the Journal of Discourses." They had read the pages he left them and "tried to look at the problem as wisely as we can," but decided, in the end, to suspend publication. The omitted sermons, they feared, would serve as an invitation by people to seek them out, causing them to get more attention than they would have otherwise. "Sometimes the Brethren in earlier days advanced ideas for which there is little or no direct support in the scriptures (they are largely speculative) and which have not received the support of the Brethren since then who have felt that the views expressed contained matters that might be called 'mysteries,' concerning which the Lord has not yet revealed the Truth." Thus, "Under this situation we feel constrained to request that you give up the idea of an abridged edition of the Journal of Discourses."[5]

For whatever reason, the presidency did not send this letter. Instead, McConkie met with President Clark in Clark's office five weeks later, on March 15, to learn of their decision. Clark had read the manuscript pages and talked with McKay and Richards. One concern for Clark was that leaving out the Adam-God teachings of Brigham Young and others "would give the cultists an opportunity of attack which might increase our present difficulties instead of mollifying them." Clark also frowned upon McConkie's intent to publish a talk that one apostle gave on electricity, because it failed to hold up against current scientific developments. McConkie understood and agreed.

Clark also questioned the book's title of *Sound Doctrine*, which "implied that there was other doctrine that was unsound." McConkie agreed with that also. He proposed another title, but Clark thought it too "was open to somewhat of the same objection." Clark was upset that there were many books being published by church authorities that did not always align with everyone within the hierarchy. He emphasized to McConkie that "it would have been better if he had conferred with the Brethren before he began the printing of his book,

---

5. First Presidency to Bruce R. McConkie, Feb. 9, 1956, draft copy, copy courtesy of Smith-Pettit Foundation.

instead of afterward, and he [McConkie] admitted that that was a mistake which he had made." Clark said he would talk further with McKay and Richards about the matter, but because he was sure the views he just expressed to McConkie would mirror theirs, "it would not be wise to issue the publication as he had planned it."[6]

The book was already advertised and marketed for Christmas when the First Presidency took notice of it, so it may have already been printed or was in the process of being so. No copies are known to exist, which means they may have halted it in time or what copies did come off the press were disposed of. Although this decision of the presidency ended McConkie's quest to publish his series, twenty years later his son Joseph issued it through Bookcraft under his own name as compiler. He called it *Journal of Discourses Digest*, volume one. No additional volumes ever came to fruition.[7]

On July 19, 1956, the *Deseret News* advertised that all three volumes of *Doctrines of Salvation* were now complete and for sale. If McConkie was stinging from the *Sound Doctrine* controversy, this certainly gave him reason to feel proud of his publishing record. Seven months later, on February 19, 1957, Amelia gave birth to their last child, a daughter who became Joseph Fielding Smith's fiftieth grandchild. With Sara Jill, the eight children in the family now ranged in age from newborn to seventeen years old. With a larger family came more responsibility at home, but McConkie's assignments kept him away just as much as they had before. He continued to travel to stake

---

6. *The Diaries of J. Reuben Clark, 1933–1961, Abridged, with Appendix 1. The Diaries of Stephen L Richards 1951–1954, and Appendix 2. The Diaries of Marion G. Romney, 1941–1961, Abridged* (Salt Lake City: privately published, 2010), 224–25. See also D. Michael Quinn, *Elder Statesman: A Biography of J. Reuben Clark* (Salt Lake City: Signature Books, 2002), 222–23.

7. Joseph Fielding McConkie, comp., *Journal of Discourses Digest*, vol. 1 (Salt Lake City: Bookcraft, 1975). Joseph Fielding McConkie, in *The Bruce R. McConkie Story: Reflections of a Son* (Salt Lake City: Deseret Book, 2003), makes no mention of the *Sound Doctrine* episode. Another biographer of McConkie is also silent on the controversy and says only that *Sound Doctrine* "never got off the ground and was discontinued." He also said that Joseph Fielding McConkie told him that future volumes of the *Digest* never came about because Bookcraft manager Marvin Wallin thought the company would be better off selling a reprint of the full twenty-six volume *Journal of Discourses* instead of an abbreviated version. Dennis B. Horne, *Bruce R. McConkie: Highlights from His Life and Teachings*, second enlarged edition with epilogue (Salt Lake City: Eborn Books, 2010), 88, 101n3. The full run of the *Journal of Discourses* has been reprinted numerous times by various publishers.

conferences on weekends and remained in his role as coordinator of the general servicemen's committee. In July 1957 he announced that a new directory for LDS military members listing meetinghouses adjacent to all military installations would soon be ready and sent to bases for distribution. New recruits would be given theirs upon entry. Bishops would provide the committee an address, and they in turn would send the pocket-sized military editions of the Book of Mormon and *Principles of the Gospel*, and the LDS dog tag to those serving. That same month it was the McConkies' turn to host the annual family dinner honoring Joseph Fielding Smith on his birthday.[8]

When not busy with his church assignments, McConkie was hard at work on another book, and it would be released the following year. In fact, he began it years earlier when he was in the military.[9] He would not be a compiler or an editor, but the book's author. It would prove to be his most popular among the several volumes still to come from his hand, and it would make him a household name among most active Latter-day Saints. Yet it would also prove to be his most controversial. He titled this book *Mormon Doctrine*.

The 776-page volume went on sale in July 1958. In his preface, dated June 1, McConkie explained that it was "unique" and "the first book of its kind ever published." Indeed, *Mormon Doctrine* was a first. Written in encyclopedic form, "It is the first extensive compendium of the whole gospel." It contained over 2,000 entries, arranged alphabetically, beginning with "Aaron" from the Old Testament, and concluding with "Zoramites" from the Book of Mormon. There were many "apostate, sectarian" Bible commentaries and other works, he explained, but "never before has a comprehensive attempt been made to define and outline, in a brief manner, all of the basic principles of salvation—and to do it from the perspective of all revelation, both ancient and modern."

Mormon Doctrine was not an official publication of the church, McConkie pointed out, and "for the work itself, I assume sole and

---

8. "Now! The Complete Series," ad posted in *Salt Lake Tribune*, July 19, 1956, 8; "Welcome New Arrival," *Church News*, Feb. 23, 1957, 2; "LDS Prepare Guide to Servicemen," *Salt Lake Tribune*, July 6, 1957, 6; Joseph Lundstrom, "Pres. Smith Notes 81st Anniversary," *Church News*, July 20, 1957, 4.

9. Stirling Adams, "Oh, Say, What Was Mormon Doctrine," 14, unpublished paper courtesy of author.

full responsibility." Yet, "Observant students, however, will note that the standard works of the Church are the chief sources of authority quoted and that literally tens of thousands of scriptural quotations and citations are woven into the text material." In addition, McConkie referenced Joseph Smith 215 times, Joseph Fielding Smith 178 times, and various others a few dozen times or less, for a total of 607 such author citations outside of the scriptures.[10]

Bringing this book about was no easy task, but it was one McConkie was inclined to undertake. "One of the things that I enjoy doing more than anything else," he later said, "is just the simple matter of studying the doctrines of the gospel and organizing them by subject and solving and analyzing doctrinal problems." That method of study and organization is what culminated in *Mormon Doctrine*. He used holidays and days off to write much of it.[11]

Mormon Doctrine sold well from the beginning, but that soon became a concern to President McKay, thanks to his second counselor Clark, who briefed him on it. Clark had learned of the book's title and then began reading it upon its release. Perhaps with the *Sound Doctrine* controversy still on his mind, Clark wasted no time in consulting the church president. "I was urgent in saying I did it only because I felt he must know. I was sure we had to do something because this book would raise more trouble than anything we had had in the Church for a long while."[12] Being caught off guard as they were meant that McConkie, despite acknowledging in 1956 that it had been a mistake not to clear *Sound Doctrine* with the presidency, kept this book quiet also until it hit the shelves.

Although McConkie was likely thrilled with the release of the book, he was also occupied with the upcoming wedding the following month of daughter Vivian to Don Carlos Adams. The couple married in the Salt Lake Temple in August and Bruce and Amelia hosted an open house at their home.[13]

That October McConkie was away late in the month for two

---

10. Bruce R. McConkie, *Mormon Doctrine* (Salt Lake City: Bookcraft, 1958), 5; David John Buerger, "Speaking with Authority: The Theological Influence of Elder Bruce R. McConkie," *Sunstone*, Mar. 1985, 9–10.

11. David Croft, "Spare Time's Rare to Apostle," *Church News*, Jan. 24, 1976, 4.

12. J. Reuben Clark memorandum, July 9, 1958, in Quinn, *Elder Statesman*, 224.

13. 'McConkie-Adams," *Salt Lake Tribune*, Aug. 27, 1958, 13.

weeks as he toured the Southern States Mission, unaware thus far of any concerns about his new book. He was pleased to report in early November that the mission had enjoyed a 300 percent increase in baptisms over the past three years. The tour was a busy one; he personally interviewed 173 missionaries and even flew to Puerto Rico to visit two branches there.[14] After he returned, however, he soon learned that *Mormon Doctrine* was creating a buzz he had not expected nor wanted. It had been three months since McKay and Clark had discussed it and, so far, they had done nothing about the matter. But some of their feared backlash was about to begin, which undoubtedly played a role that finally forced them to act.

In an entry titled "Church of the Devil," a phrase from the Book of Mormon, McConkie said that it could be defined in two ways. "All churches or organizations of whatever name or nature—whether political, philosophical, educational, economic, social, fraternal, civic, or religious—which are designed to take men on a course that leads away from God and his laws and thus from salvation in the kingdom of God." The second was not vague at all: "The *Roman Catholic Church* specifically—singled out, set apart, described, and designated as being 'most abominable above all other churches.'" The scripture McConkie referenced was 1 Nephi 13:5. Other articles in *Mormon Doctrine* critical of Catholicism were found under the headings "Indulgences," "Mariolatry," "Penance," "Supererogation," and "Transubstantiation."[15]

McConkie was not the first church leader to criticize Catholicism or even to apply this Book of Mormon verse to them. That had already been done by J. Reuben Clark and B. H. Roberts in the 1930s and '40s. McConkie, however, took it to a new level.[16]

Duane G. Hunt (1884–1960), then bishop of the Catholic Diocese of Salt Lake City, had been raised Methodist but converted to Catholicism in 1913 before he moved to Utah to teach at the University of Utah. He was ordained to the priesthood in 1920 in Salt Lake City and, in 1937, was appointed the fifth bishop of the

14. "Elder McConkie Reports Tour of Southern States Mission," *Church News*, Nov. 8, 1958, 4.
15. McConkie, *Mormon Doctrine*, 1958 ed., 129. For the various other headings referred to, see pages 346, 425–26, 697, and 730–31; Buerger, "Speaking with Authority," 9.
16. Adams, "Oh, Say, What Was Mormon Doctrine?" 4–6.

Salt Lake City diocese. With that, he became the first convert from Methodism to enter the American Catholic hierarchy. During his tenure he developed a good relationship with the Mormons, even broadcasting the weekly "Catholic Hour" over the LDS Church-owned KSL radio station for twenty-two years. But Hunt was hurt by McConkie's characterization of his church, and after the general election of 1958, Hunt visited David S. King who had just been elected to the US House of Representatives. A tearful Hunt, holding a copy of *Mormon Doctrine*, said, "We are your friends. We don't deserve this kind of treatment!"[17]

Hunt also went to President McKay to complain. McKay's son Lawrence remembered Hunt asking, "Is this the attitude of the Church, that the Catholic Church is the 'Great and Abominable Church,' as expressed in this latest book of Bruce McConkie's?" McKay was embarrassed and perhaps even outraged.[18]

McConkie not only failed to tell the presiding brethren about *Mormon Doctrine* in advance of publishing it, but his father-in-law claimed he was never told about it either. Yet for as often as McConkie and Joseph Fielding Smith interacted, it seems improbable that Smith had remained completely in the dark about it.

On January 5, 1959, McKay asked Apostle Marion G. Romney to review the book, and he submitted his report three weeks later on January 28. On a positive note, Romney describes McConkie as "an able and thorough student of the gospel. In many respects he has produced a remarkable book. Properly used, it quickly introduces the student to the authorities on most any gospel subject." However, Romney went on, "its nature and scope and the authoritative tone of the style in which it is written pose the question as to the propriety of the author's attempting such a project without assignment and

---

17. Bernice M. Mooney, "Duane Garrison Hunt," in Allan Kent Powell, ed., *Utah History Encyclopedia* (Salt Lake City: University of Utah Press, 1994), 264; Gregory L. Prince and William Robert Wright, *David O. McKay and the Rise of Modern Mormonism* (Salt Lake City: University of Utah Press, 2005), 122.

18. Prince and Wright, *David O. McKay*, 122; McConkie, *Reflections*, 184–85; Rev. Joseph T. Fitzgerald to David John Buerger, Mar. 24, 1981, David J. Buerger Papers, 1842–1988, MS 0622, box 3, J. Willard Marriott Library, Special Collections, University of Utah. Hunt responded to McConkie in his own book published soon after this. See Duane G. Hunt, *The Unbroken Chain: The Continuity of the Catholic Church* (St. Louis: Queen's Work, 1959); Adams, "Oh, Say, What Was Mormon Doctrine?" 7.

supervision from him whose right and responsibility it is to speak for the Church on 'Mormon Doctrine.'" That supervision could have spared McConkie all the controversy surrounding the work.

Romney then listed dozens of problematic teachings from the book that he grouped into four different categories: McConkie's unflattering characterizations of other churches; his certitude around various controversial doctrines, or teachings; "miscellaneous interpretations"; and finally, McConkie's use of words such as "apostate" to characterize others in a negative way. Romney concluded this letter: "I have promised to contact Marvin Wallin, manager of Bookcraft Company, by the 9th of February about the 4,000 volume edition of Mormon Doctrine which he is holding."[19]

McKay's diary notes on February 6, 1959, that during a meeting of the First Presidency, "I stated that the General Authorities of the Church should be informed that the First Presidency expect no book to be published unless it be first submitted. The Authority will still be the author, but the First Presidency wants to know what is in the book before it is published. In the minds of the people the General Authorities in their individual capacities cannot be separated from them in their official capacities." Two days later McKay came to his office, called up First Presidency secretary Joseph Anderson, and asked him to get a copy of *Mormon Doctrine* and put it on his desk. McKay took the book home and began studying it that night. He "made an outline of questions that I shall take up with Brother McConkie when he meets with the First Presidency next Wednesday morning." That February 11 meeting lasted from 8:30 to 9:45 a.m.[20]

Although McKay's diary says nothing about the discussion that took place during the meeting, six days later McConkie wrote letters addressed to the editors of both the church's monthly magazine, *The Improvement Era*, and its weekly *Church News*, which he obviously did at the First Presidency's insistence. "As you may know, I am the

19. Marion G. Romney to David O. McKay, Jan. 28, 1959, in David O. McKay diary, transcript, David O. McKay Papers, 1897–1983, MS 0668, box 43, J. Willard Marriott Library, Special Collections, University of Utah. The typescript is cited for references not included in Harvard S. Heath's condensed publication of the McKay diaries cited below.

20. David O. McKay, diary, Feb. 6 and 8, 1959, in Harvard S. Heath, ed., *Confidence amid Change: The Presidential Diaries of David O. McKay, 1951–1970* (Salt Lake City: Signature Books, 2019), 262–64; McKay diary, Feb. 11, 1959, McKay Papers, box 43.

author of a book entitled 'Mormon Doctrine,' an encyclopedia-type publication which attempts to digest and explain many of the basic doctrines of the Church." Addressing the issue as to whether the book had official church approval "or whether it contains only my personal views," he stressed that it was not endorsed by the church and "contains my personal views only, and I am solely responsible for all statements or opinions expressed in it." He wrote also that although he intended to present accurately the doctrines of the church, he was not trying to speak on behalf of the church. Mc-Conkie added a memo to President McKay that said, "If I caught the vision of what should be done perhaps these letters will help. If you think they should be changed, modified, or expanded in any way I will be happy to revise them."[21]

McKay, Richards, and Clark wrote McConkie the following day to inform him that his letters "were considered this morning by the First Presidency, and we feel that they do not cover the situation as it was discussed by us, and particularly that they do not conform to the ideas that we have that you cannot be disassociated from your official position in the publication of such a manuscript. The letters do not indicate that there will be corrections of items which you yourself indicated were over or not well stated." It appears that McConkie's letters were never sent into the *Improvement Era* or *Deseret News* for this reason. The presidency suggested "that pending the final disposition of this problem no further edition of the book be printed."[22]

The matter would not be resolved anytime soon. Two weeks later on March 5, McKay asked to see Apostles Mark E. Peterson and Marion G. Romney. Although Romney had already submitted a preliminary report in January, McKay directed the two men to read *Mormon Doctrine* and "make a list of the corrections that should be made preparatory to his sending out an addendum to all members of the Church who have purchased his book."[23]

In the meantime, McConkie continued his usual assignments, and that summer he toured the Western Canadian Mission and held

21. Bruce R. McConkie to editors of *The Improvement Era* and *Church News*, Feb. 17, 1959, transcribed copy courtesy of Smith-Pettit Foundation.
22. David O. McKay, Steven L Richards, J. Reuben Clark to Bruce R. McConkie, Feb. 18, 1959, transcribed copy courtesy of Smith-Petitt Foundation.
23. McKay diary, Mar. 5, 1959, in Heath, *Confidence amid Change*, 270.

conferences in British Columbia, Alberta, and Saskatchewan, interviewing 145 missionaries in the process. The branches there had seen tremendous growth. They had totaled only 125 members nine years earlier, but now there were 1,800. "All of the branches seem to have grown substantially since I was last there," McConkie reported upon returning. That same month the General LDS Servicemen's Committee released a report that there were now 12,000 church members serving in the military. It broke down their activity rate within the church and showed which ones were receiving church publications in the mail, letters from their bishops, and letters from quorum leaders.[24]

It took ten months for Petersen and Romney to review *Mormon Doctrine*, but on January 7, 1960, the two apostles had finished their report. They confirmed that the manuscript had never been given to the reading committee prior to publication and that "President Joseph Fielding Smith did not know anything about it until it was published." Petersen said that he had marked up his own copy of the book which listed 1,067 errors in it, and that some could be found on almost every page. Petersen urged that "no book should be published without a specific approval of the First Presidency." McKay's diary then notes with emphasis that, "I stated that the decision of the First Presidency and the Committee should be announced to the Twelve."

They still had to deal with the fact that the book was already in the hands of thousands of church members. The number of corrections needed was such that a revised version "would be such an extensive repudiation of the original as to destroy the credit of the author." Thus, they decided it should not be republished and that "the book should be repudiated in such a way as to save the career of the author as one of the General Authorities of the Church." All agreed that McKay should convey this to the Twelve Apostles before talking with McConkie. They directed Petersen to prepare an editorial for the *Improvement Era* addressing the situation, but he would first submit a draft to them for approval.[25]

The presidency met again the next day and discussed reports that

24. "Elder McConkie Tours W. Canadian Mission," *Church News*, July 11, 1959, 6; "12,000 LDS Servicemen Listed as Members of Armed Forces," *Church News*, July 18, 1959, 6.

25. McKay diary, Jan. 7, 1960, in Heath, *Confidence amid Change*, 300–1.

had come to them indicating that McConkie had made corrections to the book and was planning to publish a revised edition. They were adamant, however, that *Mormon Doctrine* "must not be re-published, as it is full of errors and misstatements, and it is most unfortunate that it has received such wide circulation." They further reiterated the new policy that general authorities were not to publish any books without receiving prior First Presidency approval.[26]

Peterson turned in the draft of his editorial six days later, which he titled, "Seek Ye Out of the Best Books." He noted that, "Speculation becomes rife at times. Private interpretations of doctrine and extremes of dogma are thrust upon an unsuspecting public, some of whom seem to accept any unusual idea that is promulgated if they see it in print." Some of these are geared toward Latter-day Saints, and even come from the church's general authorities. "When the Brethren have done this they have acted upon their own responsibility, doing so without the knowledge or consent of the presiding authorities of the Church." These works should never be accepted as the official voice of the church. "One such book," Petersen said, "was the recently published 'Mormon Doctrine' by Elder Bruce R. McConkie of the First Council of the Seventy. This volume presumes to give the final word on many doctrines of the Church, some of which have never been completely explained even in revelations." He also mentioned another speculative title, Milton R. Hunter and Thomas Stuart Ferguson's *Ancient America and the Book of Mormon*. In the end, the presidency decided Petersen should pull direct references to the two books and that the editorial should simply focus "on the subject of selecting good books." But any final decision on publishing the editorial at all would be postponed until after a meeting between McKay and Joseph Fielding Smith.[27]

McKay called Smith on Wednesday, January 27, and told him that "we are a unit in disapproving of Brother Bruce R. McConkie's book, 'Mormon Doctrine,' as an authoritative exposition of the principles of the gospel." Yet this posed a problem that was obvious to both of them.

---

26. McKay diary, Jan. 8, 1960, in Heath, *Confidence amid Change*, 303–4.

27. McKay diary, Jan. 14, 1960, in Heath, *Confidence amid Change*, 305–6, and 306n11. Mark E. Petersen, "Seek Ye Out of the Best Books," J. Reuben Clark Papers, Ms 303, box 289, fd. labeled McConkie, L. Tom Perry Special Collections, Harold B. Lee Library, Brigham Young University, Provo, UT.

"Now, Brother Smith, he is a General Authority, and we do not want to give him a public rebuke that would be embarrassing to him and lessen his influence with the members of the Church." McKay planned to announce at the meeting with the Twelve the following day in the Salt Lake Temple that *Mormon Doctrine* "is not approved as an authoritative book, and that it should not be republished, even if the errors (some 1,067 of them) are corrected."

"That is the best thing to do," Smith agreed.

McKay next said that he had learned that McConkie "is advocating by letter some of the principles as printed in his book in answer to letters he receives."

"I will speak to him about that," Smith responded.

"He is also speaking on these subjects," McKay then told him.

"I will speak to him about that also." Smith also believed as "wise" the proposed policy that books by general authorities must first be submitted for approval.[28]

That next day McKay reported to his counselors his conversation with Smith. "It was decided that the First Presidency should inform Brother McConkie before he learns of our decision from some other source, so Brother McConkie was asked to come into our meeting this morning." When McKay told him that the First Presidency did not want the book republished, McConkie agreed. They then recommended McConkie "answer inquiries on the subject with care."

"I am amenable to whatever you Brethren want," McConkie responded. "I will do exactly what you want. I will be as discreet and as wise as I can." He promised he would not express any views that went counter to those the presidency had stated and would conform to their wishes completely.[29]

Later that afternoon the First Presidency and Council of the Twelve met in the temple and discussed the McConkie meeting from

---

28. McKay diary, Jan. 27, 1960, in Heath, *Confidence amid Change*, 307. Both Horne, *Bruce R. McConkie*, 63–64, and Joseph Fielding McConkie, "Bruce R. McConkie: A Special Witness." *Mormon Historical Studies* 14, no 2 (Fall 2013): 198, insist that many of the items deemed errors in *Mormon Doctrine* were references to the Joseph Smith Translation of the Bible, which the Reorganized Church of Jesus Christ of Latter-day Saints owned and was a document the LDS Church did not fully trust. Even if this were true, Horne points out, this would only account for around 170 of the errors Petersen and Romney found. Joseph McConkie numbers those references at around 300.

29. McKay diary, Jan. 28, 1960, in Heath, *Confidence amid Change*, 307–8.

that morning. McKay emphasized once again that *Mormon Doctrine* "had caused considerable comment throughout the Church, and that it has been a source of concern to the Brethren ever since it was published." The recommendation was "that the book be not republished; that it be not republished even in corrected form, even though Brother McConkie mentions in the book that he takes all responsibility for it; and that it be not recognized as an authoritative book." There would be no public rebuke because that could seriously damage McConkie's influence within the church. As a result, Petersen's editorial, even with its revisions, never appeared in *The Improvement Era*. "The First Presidency recommend that the situation be left as it is, and whenever a question about it arises, we can answer that it is unauthoritative; that it was issued by Brother McConkie on his own responsibility, and he must answer for it." The assembled brethren then adopted the policy that all books by general authorities receive approval prior to publishing. "It may seem all right for the writer of the book to say 'I only am responsible for it,'" McKay told them, "but I said 'you cannot separate your position from your individuality.'"[30]

Between his attempt to publish *Sound Doctrine* in 1955 and his experience with *Mormon Doctrine* between 1958 and 1960, McConkie learned some painful, yet important lessons.[31] Or did he? The *Mormon Doctrine* story, it turns out, was not over, although the next chapter would need to wait a few years. But McConkie eventually discovered that time was indeed his friend in this matter.

---

30. McKay diary, Jan. 28, 1960, in Heath, *Confidence amid Change*, 308–09. Although Petersen's editorial never appeared, McKay shortly published an article which borrowed some of the ideas found in Petersen's draft, although it did not reference McConkie at all. See David O. McKay, "The Printed Companions We Choose," *Improvement Era*, Mar. 1960, 142–43. I was made aware of this essay by Adams, "Oh Say, What Was 'Mormon Doctrine'?" 15.

31. In *Reflections*, Joseph Fielding McConkie spends a chapter on "The *Mormon Doctrine* Saga" (182–93) but writes it in the form of a question-and-answer exercise. Although he admits that McKay was embarrassed about the book's portrayal of the Catholic Church after being confronted by Hunt, he says nothing about the committee formed to read and report on the book, and nothing about the many errors they found. He says that, "In January 1960 President McKay asked Elder McConkie not to have the book reprinted," as though the decision were being left to McConkie. McKay's diary clearly indicates that McConkie did not have a choice in the matter.

CHAPTER SIX

MISSION PRESIDENT

1960-1964

In the fall of 1960, ten months after the *Mormon Doctrine* controversy had been quietly dealt with, S. Dilworth Young planned and
elaborately carried out a practical joke on his good friend McConkie,
one that took some creative skill to pull off. Young sent McConkie
a letter under the fictitious name of Balwant Singh, who said he
lived in India but wanted to come to the United States, live with
McConkie, and learn about the LDS Church. To make this believ-
able, Young enlisted the help of an East Indian professor at BYU
who secured people in India to allow the use of their address and
whose authentic postmark guaranteed McConkie would not suspect
a thing. McConkie responded and after he and "Singh" exchanged a
few letters, Singh said he was coming to the United States with his
wife and some friends named Ghlema Rhoodh, Vulmh Arveh, and
Seehkmoor Dhl Jung, a play on the names of McConkie's friend
and neighbor Glen Rudd, his secretary, Velma Harvey, and Young,
the mastermind of the entire prank. The unsuspecting McConkie
offered to have the group over for dinner, but in the end, Young and
the others backed down, fearing a backlash from church members
who might not think this joke was funny should they hear about it.[1]

For over fourteen years McConkie had enjoyed Young's friendship as a fellow member of the Seventy. Lighthearted moments with
him and others assured that McConkie maintained the healthy balance in his life he enjoyed. But a new phase was about to start that

---

1. Benson Young Parkinson, "S. Dilworth Young of the First Quorum of Seventy,"
Journal of Mormon History, 27, no. 1 (Spring 2000): 232–33; Sheri L. Dew, "Bruce R.
McConkie: A Family Portrait," *This People*, Dec. 1985/Jan. 1986, 50.

would take him away from his friendships for a time. McConkie was at his office on February 9, 1961, when President Henry D. Moyle of the First Presidency called and asked him to come to his office. There Moyle gave McConkie a letter signed by David O. McKay, J. Reuben Clark, and Moyle calling him as president of the Southern Australia Mission. When Amelia came with the car to pick her husband up after work, he got behind the wheel and drove them up to Ensign Peak, which overlooks the city. Once there he let her read the letter herself.[2]

At this point the family had six children still at home. Vivian had been married for two years and Joseph was in Scotland on his mission. Amelia immediately thought of the challenges such an assignment would bring, but she accepted it and, along with Bruce, kept the calling quiet until church leaders made a public announcement a week later. The McConkies had a little over five months to make all preparations before leaving the country for this three-year assignment.[3]

Was there any correlation between this calling and the hullabaloo surrounding *Mormon Doctrine*? If so, it would not be the only time a general authority was assigned to preside over a mission to temporarily remove them from church headquarters and lessen their influence among members. Two years after McConkie began serving in Australia, Apostle Ezra Taft Benson received a call as president of the European Mission after years of polarizing behavior in his public support for the right-wing John Birch Society. This calling was believed by some within the church hierarchy to have been a way to exile him. "I think it is time that Brother Benson forgot all about politics and settled down to his duties as a member of the Council of the twelve," wrote Joseph Fielding Smith in a letter to Idaho Congressman Ralph R. Harding. "He is going to take a mission to Europe in the near future and by the time he returns I hope he will get all of the political notions out of his system."[4]

---

2. Dorothy O. Rea, "Amelia Smith McConkie," *Church News*, Oct. 31, 1964, 6; Joseph Fielding McConkie, *The Bruce R. McConkie Story: Reflections of a Son* (Salt Lake City: Deseret Book, 2003), 194–95.

3. McConkie, *Reflections*, 195–96; "LDS Assign New Leader of Australian Mission," *Salt Lake Tribune*, Feb. 16, 1961, 22.

4. D. Michael Quinn, "Ezra Taft Benson and Mormon Political Conflicts," *Dialogue: A Journal of Mormon Thought* 26, no. 2 (Summer 1994): 23–25.

Even McConkie joked about his superiors' motive for sending him to Australia. He had just written a lengthy piece—never approved for publication—rebutting the claims to authority made by a Mormon breakoff group, which he titled humorously *How to Start a Cult; or, Cultism As Practiced by the So-Called Church of the Firstborn of the Fulness of Times Analyzed, Explained, and Interpreted; As also Dissected, Divellicated, Whacked Up, Smithereened, Mangled, and Decimated.* It was also given an alternate, shorter title of *An Essay Showing Where All Good Cultists Go.* "After reading the cultist concepts" taught by this group, McConkie wrote in his somewhat sarcastic work, "and discovering how easy it is to dream up doctrines which can be 'proved' from the scriptures and the sermons of the brethren; and after learning there are always some who will accept any sugar-coated opportunity to indulge their lusts; I think I will start a cult of my own." When someone asked him what led to the call to Australia, he thought about this censored work, and said, "Well, I have been writing again."[5]

By accepting this assignment, McConkie had to set some other ventures aside, or at least curtail his involvement for the time being. In August 1960, six months before receiving his call to Australia, McConkie and several LDS businessmen had organized the Memorial Estates Security Corporation (MESC), a financial company formed to establish religiously oriented private cemeteries that provided continual care. The company went public and began offering stocks and bonds to Utah residents in October. McConkie was elected vice-president; the company's president was Alma E. Gygi, a local hotel owner. They, along with the fifteen members of the board of directors, were all active Latter-day Saints. The prospectus told investors there were 200,000 shares of stock available at $1.00 each and 16,000 in bonds at $50 that would mature ten years from the issue date.[6]

Advertisements for the company sought to build trust in investors by publicizing the church affiliation of the officers. Newspapers

5. McConkie, *Reflections*, 311; Bruce R. McConkie, *An Essay Showing Where All Good Cultists Go*, copy in author's possession.
6. "Business News," *Herald Journal* (Logan, UT), Oct. 26, 1960, 11; "Utah Investor," *Deseret News*, Nov. 1, 1960, A9; Lynn Packer, "The Phantom of Fraud," *Utah Holiday*, Oct. 1990, 32; Anson Shupe, *The Darker Side of Virtue* (Buffalo, NY: Prometheus Books, 1991), 57.

showed a photo of Gygi, noting he was a high councilman in his stake. A caption under McConkie's picture stated he was a member of the First Council of Seventy, and photos of three other officers and their current church callings were also prominently displayed. The prospectus publicized this even more by including the photos and church positions of several others, which at least one stockholder found troubling. "I believe that the 'church' is much too intimately involved in this entire operation," noted Royal K. Hunt in a letter to Joseph C. Rich, president of Redwood Memorial Estates, with which MESC had merged its stock shortly after its founding. "I do not in any way mean it to infer that we should divorce ourselves from the church. However, it seems doubtful that it is sound business policy to be so closely tied. There is definitely, in my opinion, too much chance that the church will suffer because of this close tie." The company began hurting financially before McConkie returned from his mission, and in November 1964 it filed for bankruptcy.[7] This would not prove the end of the story, however, and as discussed later, the fallout would linger to the end of the decade.

Although his Australian mission was approaching, McConkie still continued to fulfill assignments as a member of the Seventy. While away at a stake conference assignment, between sessions he ate dinner at the home of an LDS family named Pratt, whose teenage son Ray had been plagued with a deadly skin disease since birth. Although missionaries had given him healing blessings, the young man never found relief through this means. His doctors even told the family that all they could do was keep him comfortable until the condition eventually took his life. McConkie left to head back to the conference, but shortly returned, telling the boy's mother that he wanted to give him a blessing. He asked that she have him at the church by the time the meeting ended. "I got Ray ready and took him to the church," the mother recalled. "When they laid their hands on Ray's head, Elder McConkie was silent. I panicked, thinking there was no blessing for him. I was shedding tears when Elder McConkie started to speak." The blessing McConkie uttered was clear. "Brother Ray Grant Pratt, the Lord has given you this affliction to prepare

7. "Is Your Money Earning 7%," *Herald Journal*, Nov. 20, 1960, 9; Shupe, *Darker Side of Virtue*, 57–58.

you for the work that lies ahead. I promise you in the name of the Lord Jesus Christ that your health will never stand in the way of your serving the Lord." According to McConkie's son, Pratt shortly thereafter recovered.[8]

On June 11, 1961, President David O. McKay of the First Presidency announced that all members of the First Council of Seventy would be ordained as high priests. Earlier that day four had been so ordained, including McConkie, and the rest would soon follow. His ordination occurred under the hands of President Henry D. Moyle. Now members of the Seventy could ordain local men as high priests while at stake conferences throughout the church, something they could not do before.[9]

Less than six weeks later on Thursday, July 20, the McConkie family left Salt Lake City to begin their Australian adventure. Bruce was intentionally not set apart for this calling because, Moyle explained, as a Seventy, McConkie already oversaw missionary work for the church throughout its sixty-four missions and therefore had full authority to perform his duties as a mission president. However, on the day of their departure, McConkie's father Oscar asked to give Bruce a blessing, which Bruce happily accepted. He was now ready to lead.[10]

The family first flew to San Francisco and spent two days seeing various sites before the ship *Canberra* left for a brief stop in Long Beach, where they attended church and Bruce spoke in a ward sacrament meeting. The next stop was Hawaii, where they arrived on July 28. From there they worked their way to Wellington, New Zealand, and for two days endured a storm off the coast. They next made it to Sydney, Australia. The Southern Australia Mission office was located near Melbourne and McConkie disembarked and flew there ahead of his family, who arrived exhausted on the *Canberra* on August 12.[11]

The mission home sat in the Melbourne suburb of Toorak, and as the McConkies immediately discovered, the house was too small to hold the family of eight. But they managed to make it work for the time being. "We moved in with beds, a piano and a 10 year supply of

---

8. McConkie, *Reflections*, 358–59.
9. McConkie, *Reflections*, 177.
10. McConkie, *Reflections*, 196, 230.
11. McConkie, *Reflections*, 197–98; Rea, "Amelia Smith McConkie," 6.

sacrament cups," recalled Amelia, a number shipped due to an error made when someone placed an order intended to number 100,000 but which was accidentally made for a million. The kids had to share bedrooms, but a little over halfway into McConkie's tenure they secured a larger home.[12]

There were then two missions in Australia: the Australia Mission and the Southern Australia Mission. The mission McConkie presided over covered half of the continent, which included Victoria, South Australia, all of Western Australia, and the island of Tasmania. This meant, for example, that members up in Derby lived over 3,000 miles away from mission headquarters. Some even lived farther than that. Perth is 2,100 miles from Melbourne by car, or 1,600 miles by plane.

Having been a member of the First Council of Seventy for fifteen years when he began this assignment, McConkie's reputation would have preceded him. "It was with keen anticipation, a feeling of excitement, a feeling of pride that members of the Church heralded the news of a General Authority as the new Mission President," wrote Donald Cummings of the Perth district about the feeling among members and missionaries.[13]

McConkie spent much of his time teaching and training all his missionaries in monthly sessions that lasted up to ten hours each. On at least one occasion he spent seven hours expounding on a single verse of scripture. He also included a monthly message to them in the mission publication, *The Harvester*. Church members also got to experience his teaching style when he began holding "Share the Gospel Nights." Here the Australian saints brought non-LDS friends or family members to meetings to hear talks, musical numbers, and then to listen to McConkie teach for nearly an hour. He earned many admirers as he spoke to his audience in a manner they had never experienced. The mission's slogan during McConkie's tenure was "Seek the Spirit."[14]

---

12. Rea, "Amelia Smith McConkie," 6; McConkie, *Reflections*, 199.

13. Donald Cummings, "They Came! They Saw! They Conquered!" in "Southern Australian Mission: Notes on Western Australia, 1961–1964," LR 10873 21, Church History Library, Salt Lake City.

14. Robert McDougall, "Bruce R. McConkie Touched Many Lives," *Daily Herald* (Provo, UT), Apr. 20, 1985, 3; "Elder Bruce R. McConkie: 'Preacher of Righteousness,'"

Around a month after settling into his new calling, McConkie had a moment in which he became briefly known to much of the country when he was asked to be one of four clergymen to appear on the Australian television program, *At Random*. The topic was, "Can the Christian Churches unite as one." The three others on the panel were a Catholic, a Methodist, and a Jehovah's Witness. Although the discussion could have focused on ways the various denominations could work together for the good of humanity, they chose to emphasize their differences in a combative way. McConkie played his part in that; in fact, he may have been the instigator. For him, uniting meant that everyone must accept Mormon views on continuing revelation through modern prophets, modern miracles, priesthood authority, ordinances of salvation, and the nature of God, and he was not shy in emphasizing that. When challenged, he even highlighted the concept of the Book of Mormon as a companion volume to the Bible. That he would explain and even sell LDS beliefs during this appearance itself is not surprising. However, he told the Catholic Priest he was a member of the "fallen apostolic faith" and the Methodist that he was part of a sect "who rebelled against them [the Catholics] but lacked priesthood authority." Afterward, in the dressing room, his parting words to his co-panelists before abruptly leaving were "Well, brethren, until we meet in the unity of the faith, cheerio."[15] This lack of diplomacy notwithstanding, McConkie may have reinforced in the minds of church members who tuned in, that powerful, direct preaching, no matter who is offended in the process, is found over and over again in the scriptures.

Those who got to know McConkie in Australia found he was much the same man as a mission president as he was when performing his duties as a member of the Seventy. When he spoke or was involved in the work of the mission—as his appearance on *At Random* demonstrated—he was serious, focused, and never deviated from the task at hand. The missionaries had more interaction with McConkie than most church members, who rarely spoke with a

Ensign, June 1985, 19; McConkie, *Reflections*, 203, 214–15; Dennis B. Horne, *Bruce R. McConkie: Highlights from His Life and Teachings*, second edition with epilogue (Salt Lake City: Eborn Books, 2010), 78.

15. McConkie, *Reflections*, 203–5.

general authority in casual settings. Thus they experienced his lighter side to some degree—as his family always had. His one-on-one time with the elders and sisters was different from what they saw when he was the stern doctrinaire at the pulpit. "I will remember his great sense of humor, his warm, sensitive nature that sometimes seemed to border on shyness," one of those missionaries, Robert McDougall, said later. One example of McConkie's fun side came shortly after the family arrived, when daughter Vivian was due to give birth to her first child. A telegram came to the mission office announcing that Vivian had delivered a boy, and one of the elders gave it to McConkie. The new grandfather kept the news from Amelia at first, perhaps waiting for a special moment to tell her. But during lunch that day with some of the missionaries, the one who gave Bruce the telegram asked about it in front of her, rousing her curiosity.

"What telegram? You got a telegram from home?" Amelia asked anxiously.

"I might have," Bruce responded.

"Did Vivian send the telegram?"

"No," came Bruce's reply.

"Was it her husband, Carlos?" Amelia wanted to know.

"It might have been," Bruce said.

"Did she have her baby?"

"Something like that."

"Is she okay? Is it a boy or a girl?"

Bruce finally revealed that Vivian had born a son. "The missionaries were getting the biggest wallop out of him, that rascal," remembered Amelia.[16]

Personal attention to missionaries could sometimes be neither stern nor humorous but simply compassionate. McDougall reminisced about his initial experience with McConkie. "I have to admit to a great deal of apprehension the day I climbed aboard the plane to answer the call.... I will never forget the feeling of comfort I got when he met me at the airport and took me in his arms and then spent the weekend taking me everywhere he went, talking to me, teaching me, and getting me ready to serve." Another elder, Jay R.

16. McDougall, "Bruce R. McConkie," 3; Dew, "Family Portrait," 51.

Eastley, said that despite McConkie's height and deep voice that people could easily find intimidating, the mission president "soon proved to be love personified.... We began to see that President McConkie was as approachable as he was brilliant, that he genuinely cared about each missionary."[17]

McConkie devoted as much time to his family as he could as he carried out his mission duties. He was usually up between 5:00 and 5:30 a.m. to enjoy a little time outdoors bird watching with Amelia before starting his workday. Amelia kept busy tending to their six children, but she also had her role as mission mother. About six months into their mission, she asked Bruce to give her a blessing, which she treated as the equivalent to being "set apart" for her unofficial position. But this moment also served as setting her apart for her official calling as the new Relief Society president in their Australian ward. Son Mark, who was around thirteen when the family arrived in Australia, remembered taking walks with his father, who used those occasions to teach his son the gospel. One time Bruce stopped as they walked and asked, "Do you have any questions?"

"No," Mark answered.

"Well, junior," replied Bruce, "you should always have questions."[18]

Only nine months into his assignment, on what was Mother's Day in the United States, McConkie and the entire mission experienced a tragedy when two missionaries, Elders Bryan Johnson of Salt Lake City and Steven Denney of Blackfoot, Idaho, were killed when their car was hit by a train about one hundred miles west of Melbourne in the town of Beaufort. McConkie learned about the news as he was about to speak at a training meeting in Perth and was understandably shocked. Amelia found out during that same meeting and let her tears flow. "Elders Johnson and Denney were two of our finest elders," Amelia said. Bruce and Amelia tried to make it through the meeting without addressing the incident so as not to create a distraction during what should have been a happy occasion where fourteen people were baptized. But finally, with the two

17. McDougall, "Bruce R. McConkie," 3; "Preacher of Righteousness," 19; McConkie, *Reflections*, 201–2.

18. Rea, "Amelia Smith McConkie," 6; McConkie, *Reflections*, 212; Joseph Fielding McConkie, "Bruce R. McConkie: A Special Witness," *Mormon Historical Studies* 14, no. 2 (Fall 2013), 196.

missionaries on his mind, Bruce spoke about how tenuous mortality was and that no one knows when their life might end.[19]

People present that day were touched by these remarks, and for a variety of reasons, many found hope in the Mormon message as preached by the missionaries. But not all so touched acted upon it. LDS Sunday services in Australia found many people in attendance who had been investigating the church for months or years but who had never been baptized. McConkie found this unacceptable and developed a plan for getting them to commit, which in some cases required only some simple preaching and a gentle nudge. For others, however, the method turned to force. In one particular meeting McConkie used both methods, which resulted in nine unexpected baptisms after a district conference held in Perth. Two of those baptized, a man named Bancroft and his daughter, had been attending church for some time. The daughter agreed to be baptized when McConkie approached her, but the father refused, saying he was not yet ready to take that step.

"I say you are and that you are going to be baptized," McConkie insisted. "Now you come with me peaceably or I'll get one of these elders to help me carry you out." After Bancroft refused once again, McConkie lifted him by the arm out of the chapel and to the dressing room. When the man refused to give McConkie his pant and shirt sizes, McConkie estimated them, handed him some clothes, and made him dress. When McConkie had to leave to assist with other potential baptismal candidates, he placed a guard outside of the door so that Bancroft could not leave. He was baptized that day. "What we did may seem strange," wrote McConkie in defending his actions, "but it was the right thing under the circumstances, and the Spirit was with us." Bancroft must have believed it was right also, at least eventually. He later named a son Bruce, after the man who insisted he be baptized at what was then, against his will.[20]

Although McConkie was a sitting general authority, the expense and distance involved in flying to the United States allowed him to return for general conference only twice during his mission, the

---

19. McConkie, *Reflections*, 227–28; "Two Missionaries Die in Australia Mishap," *Deseret News*, May 14, 1962, B1, B9.
20. McConkie, *Reflections*, 205–10.

first being October 1962. His talk on this occasion focused on the questions plaguing Joseph Smith that led Smith to the grove of trees whereupon he experienced his First Vision. Although McConkie spoke nothing about his Australian experience, he noted that, "We have in the world now some 12,000 missionaries in the various nations, preaching what we call the message of the restoration." He talked of the responsibilities of those looking into the church. "Every investigator, in due course, stands exactly where Joseph Smith stood. He hears the cry, 'Lo, here is Christ,' and 'Lo, there.' He must decide for himself which of all the churches is right and which he should join. At his peril, he must find where the truth lies." This comes about after learning, listening to relevant testimony, and seeking individual wisdom from God.[21]

Traveling within the mission, although not the distance of the 9,700-mile flight to Salt Lake City, was still long and time-consuming, and during his three years in Australia, McConkie flew or drove a tremendous number of miles. Bruce and Amelia together made thirty-three trips from Melbourne to Perth throughout the thirty-six months Bruce was mission president, each being a 3,200-mile roundtrip by plane. Visitors to the mission who accompanied them on some of these excursions were Apostles Ezra Taft Benson, Gordon B. Hinckley, Howard W. Hunter, Joseph Fielding Smith, and Delbert L. Stapley; Elder Sterling W. Sill of the Seventy; general Relief Society President Belle S. Spafford and one of her counselors, Eileen Dunyon; and McConkie's close friend Glen Rudd, who was then on the church's missionary committee. During Smith's visit in 1963, he ordained his grandson Stephen McConkie a deacon and set Mary apart as a missionary. During the Benson visit, the apostle and McConkie attended the opening ceremony of the Commonwealth Games on November 22, 1962, at Perry Lakes stadium in Floreat Park. They sat in the VIP box with Australian Prime Minister Robert Menzies and the United Kingdom's Prince Philip, Duke of Edenborough. Benson likely secured the seating for the pair, not because of his role as an LDS apostle, but because of his former

21. *One Hundred Thirty-Second Semi-Annual Conference of the Church of Jesus Christ of Latter-day Saints, Oct. 5, 6, and 7, 1962* (Salt Lake City: Church of Jesus Christ of Latter-day Saints, 1962), 8–10.

position as secretary of agriculture from 1953 to 1961 during the Eisenhower administration.[22]

Such activities outside of mission business were rare for Mc-Conkie, but at the mission home he continued to exhibit his sense of fun. For example, Amelia tried constantly to get Bruce to throw away the worn and dirty ties he was adamant about wearing to the office. One morning he asked her if she thought he should throw away the tie he had just put on. "Yes!" she said and took it off him herself and threw it away. The next day, he asked the same question about another tie. Once again, she grabbed it and threw it away. After four days of this Amelia discovered that Bruce had been wearing the same tie each day. "He'd kept pulling it out of the trash. That was a typical Bruce McConkie stunt."

But McConkie cared little for fashion, anyway. Throughout their marriage he preferred to let Amelia cut his hair and often lounged around in worn out socks with holes. "Bruce always said he didn't throw anything away until he'd had the last full measure of devotion," Amelia once said. "He'd wear a shirt until it fell off him."

On another occasion in Australia, after enduring what to him were annoying distractions by Amelia, who had a habit of asking him before spending even the smallest amount of money, Bruce decided to type a note and leave it behind where she would see it.

> Dear Amelia. If the question can be answered by "Yea," or "Nay," the answer is "Yea."
> If it is a matter of "Do" or "Don't," then "Do."
> If it is a question of "Shall I" or "Shall I not," you "Shall."
> If it is one of "Buy" or "Not Buy," you "Buy."
> Anything you do, I approve. Your acts are my acts. Please use your own judgment. And do not trouble me anymore on these matters. Your loving husband, Bruce R. McConkie.
> P.S. It's only money, and we only live once.[23]

When McConkie returned to Salt Lake City for the church's April 1964 general conference, he reported that he had racked up 250,000 air miles over the past three years traveling around the

---

22. "Notes on Western Australia, 1961–1964"; Rea, "Amelia Smith McConkie," 6; McConkie, *Reflections*, 216–225.

23. Dew, "Family Portrait," 50–51, 57; McConkie, "Special Witness," 203.

mission, where some members lived as far as 4,500 miles from head-quarters in Melbourne.[24]

Only four months after this brief visit to Utah, McConkie finished his three-year assignment and the family returned home on Tuesday, August 18, 1964. Australia had seen some tremendous growth for the LDS Church over the past decade, and especially during his time overseeing the mission. During the previous calendar year, the Southern Australia Mission witnessed 1,568 convert baptisms, and McConkie expected the total for 1964 to be around 1,800. While he oversaw the mission, 4,200 people joined the church. "We've been getting good, substantial people in the Church who have leadership qualifications," he told the *Church News* upon his return home. "The growth is stable and secure. The Church in Australia is on a good footing." Missionaries were selling around 1,000 copies of the Book of Mormon weekly, and the book proved to be an effective convert-ing tool. Eleven church buildings had been finished over the past two years and there were then another thirteen under construction. This growth occurred at a time when the church endured opposition through an anti-Mormon ministry that broadcast its criticisms over the airwaves. McConkie addressed these in various talks over his three years in the country.[25]

In summing up the experience, Amelia said, "The daily happen-ings in the mission brought us close together and gave each of the children a desire to fulfill a mission." In fact, Stanford and Mary each received their mission calls during this time, and each was assigned to the Southern Australia Mission where they served under their father. Stanford completed his mission and returned to the United States before his parents did, but Mary still had some time to go and stayed behind.[26] Thus Bruce and Amelia started their assignment with six children in the household and returned home with four.

Donald Cummings wrote an emotional goodbye to the family in a mission publication. "Now after 3 years it is with a feeling of

24. "Pres. McConkie Tells of Growth in Australia," *Church News*, Apr. 4, 1964, 5.

25. "Elder McConkie Notes Upsurge in Converts," *Church News*, Aug. 22, 1964, 15; McConkie, *Reflections*, 213.

26. Rea, "Amelia Smith McConkie," 6; Dew, "Family Portrait," 58; Obituary for Mary Ethel McConkie Donoho, Utah Valley Mortuary, utahvalleyfuneral.com, accessed Apr. 10, 2024.

sadness and great personal loss that we realize this wonderful family have completed the great work they were sent her[e] to perform, and that they are now homeward bound." Cummings believed he spoke for all of the missionaries and members when he said, "President, you shall be remembered for your wise counsel, for your god given gift to expound the Doctrines of the Church. Sister McConkie, you shall be remembered for your love[,] sincerity, for your devotion and example as a mother of Zion and your loyalty and support to your husband in his great calling."[27]

McConkie's influence within the mission boundaries was felt for decades and still is among those old enough to remember him, but for some, his style proved divisive. "Perth was a district back then and the leadership was young and highly influenced by Elder McConkie," explains John Bowie, whose family moved to Perth from Scotland in 1966 when he was a small child. A district is an area with too few members to organize a stake. For many of those in charge, McConkie's book *Mormon Doctrine* became the last word on any number of subjects. Bowie recalls that "strict adherence to position and authority became the mandate for all priesthood leaders in Perth." This was much easier to accomplish then, given the time and place. "We were literally on the other side of the world from church headquarters. No internet or influence from Salt Lake City that could compete with *Mormon Doctrine* or McConkie. His influence was so deeply rooted that it took a generation to soften and move from a highly disciplinary style to an empathetic form of leadership."[28]

Whatever the members felt or still feel about McConkie all these years later, the Australian experience had a profound effect upon McConkie personally. "There's nothing to compare with the service that one renders as a mission president," McConkie said later when reflecting on his time there. "It's just a glorious opportunity. I never enjoyed anything more than being with the missionaries." He had overseen 660 of them while in charge in Southern Australia, many of whom went on to serve as ward and stake leaders wherever they

27. Cummings, "They Came! They Saw! They Conquered!"
28. John Bowie, emails to Devery S. Anderson, Jan. 8 and 11, 2024. Bowie served in the England London East Mission with me in the early 1980s.

lived.[29] Certainly it was a rewarding time, and in terms of numbers, a very successful one. Once back home, McConkie resumed his full-time role in the First Council of Seventy and could now set aside more time for writing. That passion put him on course to become a greater doctrinal influence upon the general church membership than perhaps any other general authority in his day.

29. Dell Van Orden, "Elder Bruce. R. McConkie: 'A Challenging Future,'" *Church News*, Oct. 21, 1972, 10.

CHAPTER SEVEN

RETURN TO THE SEVENTY

1964-1972

Upon their return to the United States and to Salt Lake City, the McConkies purchased a new house, this one located at 260 Dorchester Drive, and Bruce settled once again into his full-time role as a member of the First Council of Seventy. His son Stanford had already arranged the sale of the old house before his family came back.[1]

Three months later McConkie learned that a teacher at the LDS Institute at the University of Utah had criticized his teachings about Catholics during a classroom discussion. Reed Durham, who taught a course made up of student wives, had centered a lesson on Doctrine and Covenants 18:20, which says, "Contend against no church, save it be the church of the devil." When he asked his students what "church" that referred to, they responded that it meant "all the forces of evil." One student who knew of McConkie's teachings in *Mormon Doctrine* pointed out that according to McConkie, this was a reference to the Catholic Church. After another student raised her hand and reaffirmed that McConkie meant it to mean any force of evil in the world, Durham pushed back and reiterated that the general authority had, in fact, taught that these church of the devil references in scripture were primarily aimed at the Catholic Church. After class someone pointed out to Durham that the student who raised her hand was Vivian Adams, McConkie's daughter. Perhaps fearing a backlash or worries that he had offended her, Durham later called Adams at home and told her that he had not meant to attack

---

1. Sheri L. Dew, "Elder Bruce R. McConkie: A Family Portrait," *This People*, Dec. 1985/Jan. 1986, 58; Dorothy O. Rea, "Amelia Smith McConkie," *Church News*, Oct. 31, 1964, 6.

her father. Adams mentioned that she told her father what Durham had said but that McConkie simply laughed it off by stating there were many people who did not agree with him.

However, Durham's lesson must have struck a nerve, because McConkie wrote him a letter almost immediately and reprimanded him. He claimed he had not only heard about Durham's criticisms from his daughter, but also from someone else. "I have received from two sources informal reports of statements you have made to your students about my teachings, writings, and conduct," he wrote on November 20, 1964. "If these reports are true your course has been unwise and injudicious. If you have been misunderstood and mis-interpreted, still the effect on some of your students has been such as to weaken their faith and lessen their respect for church officers." Apparently, Durham had known about the blowup at church head-quarters over *Mormon Doctrine* and told the students about it. "If you are perturbed or upset or lacking in understanding about any matter that involves me, I suggest you come in and discuss the matter with me rather than parade the problem before your students."[2]

Durham responded in a letter to McConkie and explained his intent when he brought the subject up to his class and assured Mc-Conkie of his faith and that he was a devout member of the church. McConkie found his words encouraging and told Durham in a let-ter dated December 2 that he never intended "to exhibit any concern as to whether you agreed or disagreed, either with me or any of the Brethren, as to any point of doctrine." However, "I did intend to express some concern as to what was reported to me as your attitude and manner of presentation—the main report on this coming not from my daughter, but from an independent source. Obviously I am aware that such reports are often due to misunderstanding and are seldom wholly reliable."

McConkie learned also that Durham told his class that general authorities do not always agree with each other on items of doctrine or policy, and so he chose to give Durham some counsel. "Empha-size agreement; minimize and explain away seeming divergence of

2. Notes on exchange between Reed C. Durham and students during his institute class, recorded Nov. 23, 1964; Bruce R. McConkie to Reed C. Durham, Nov. 20, 1964, copies of both courtesy of Smith–Pettit Foundation, Salt Lake City.

views," he said. This applied to scripture also. "Learn to interpret and explain every passage of scripture as being in harmony with every other passage." As to the general authorities specifically, "Seek to make it appear that all the Brethren believe and teach the same things—as they do on all the fundamentals; and such divergences of views as may be unearthed are either insignificant, or pertain to matters not essential to salvation; or stand as statements which we improperly interpret." He pointed out one example—Brigham Young's statements that Adam was God, which McConkie insisted were misunderstood. Joseph Fielding Smith had cleared up this matter, McConkie believed, "and interprets them in such a way as to show they are in harmony with the revelations, thus presenting an excellent illustration of how to handle this sort of thing." McConkie would eventually learn, if he hadn't already, that Young had in fact taught the Adam-God doctrine precisely as critics said he did, and that any attempt to harmonize the statements were naïve at best or disingenuous at worst. And, as shown later, he eventually came to chastise those who sought to square such conflicting views, despite having just encouraged Durham to do so here.

"The marvel is not that through misunderstanding, errors in reporting of sermons, and what the title page of the Book of Mormon calls 'the mistakes of men,' there are occasional differences of view," McConkie said in concluding his letter and the entire exchange. "The marvel is that a whole nation of leaders and teachers, called from all walks and with varying backgrounds, should in the end show forth such a striking unanimity of doctrinal understanding and presentation."[3]

McConkie not only wrote letters such as these, but he also received them throughout his years in the hierarchy by countless people asking doctrinal questions, criticizing his views, or seeking the final word on just about every subject, all of which enhanced his reputation as the church's authority on doctrine. That would only get stronger over the next few decades—as would the controversy.

In October 1965, the First Presidency called McConkie as supervisor of the British Isles to serve under Apostle Mark E. Petersen. In fact, his first assignment was to temporarily preside over one of

---

3. Bruce R. McConkie to Reed C. Durham, Dec. 2, 1964, copy courtesy of Smith–Pettit Foundation.

the missions there while its president, O. Preston Robinson, and his wife, Christine, returned to Salt Lake City for two weeks while Christine underwent surgery. From there, McConkie visited the other missions in Britain and attended stake conferences in Glasgow, Leeds, Manchester, and Sunderland. He flew home midway through December.[4]

Just as he returned, the *Deseret News* began advertising his new 886-page book, one that he likely started while still serving in Australia and that he wrapped up over the last year. This was volume one of what would be a three-volume work titled *Doctrinal New Testament Commentary*, and this first volume covered the four Gospels. The preface, dated December 1, 1965, explained that "this work uses latter-day revelation and the teachings of modern prophets as a means of interpreting and understanding the Gospels." He was quick to add that "it is not, however, a Church publication; I alone am responsible for the interpretations and views set forth." It sold for $7.50.[5]

A book like this is what McConkie had longed to see. Years earlier when he so vocally criticized an LDS Sunday School manual that relied on and advocated the views of non-Mormon scholars, he believed that church members needed the very book he now offered. His views on Biblical scholarship had clearly not moderated. In fact, his disdain toward what he considered a worldly approach had only deepened over the years. In his entry titled "Higher Criticism" in *Mormon Doctrine*, after thoroughly denouncing the views of the "uninspired Biblical scholars of the world," he seemed to hurl a criticism at that manual and perhaps other publications like it. "Occasionally some of these views are even found in the true Church and creep into lessons and class discussions." He later aired his views further, admitting that he read these studies and explained why. "If I'm working on something like the 'Doctrinal New Testament Commentary,' obviously I read what the commentators of the world have said about these various things, but I certainly don't read them to learn. I read them primarily because they make me angry at the modernistic and unstable views that are presented." This allowed him to "write

---

4. "Elder McConkie Assigned," *Church News*, Oct. 23, 1965, 2.
5. Advertisement, *Deseret News*, Dec. 14, 1965, 8C.

from our perspective with a good deal more vigor than I would have done if I hadn't seen the absurd, sectarian delusions that fill them."[6]

He spent several pages at the beginning of the book harmonizing the Gospels by subject matter and then created a scriptural index for each of the four books. After a twelve-page introduction, the text of the King James Version of the Gospels and his own commentary make up the rest of the book. McConkie cites additional scripture throughout, but of the 287 citations he included outside of the standard works, 37 percent of those were from *Mormon Doctrine*, then out of print. Of the rest, 26 percent came from Joseph Smith, 16 percent from Apostle James E. Talmage, 8 percent from non-Mormon scholar J. R. Dummelow (one of the few outside the church he trusted), with the rest attributed to a dozen other sources.[7]

That McConkie would cite *Mormon Doctrine* so extensively meant that he still believed in the importance of his banned book, despite the controversy it created and the feeling among the First Presidency and at least a few of the apostles that it was riddled with errors. By referencing it repeatedly in his *Commentary*, McConkie was either trying to open the door for it to be republished, or its inclusion inspired him to think it should be.

Either way, McConkie came to see President David O. McKay by prearrangement on July 5, 1966, and asked the ninety-two-year-old president about the possibility of republishing *Mormon Doctrine*. McKay's diary notes that "I asked him a number of questions about the original publication, about the need for the book, and asked him to give me the facts about what has been done since we stopped the publishing of the book." In response, McConkie said that one of the brethren had read it thoroughly but that "no one has gone over the corrections he has made since the reading." McKay said that Apostle Spencer W. Kimball, former chairman of the reading committee, would go over McConkie's changes.[8]

---

6. Bruce R. McConkie, *Mormon Doctrine* (Salt Lake City: Bookcraft, 1958), 324–25; David Croft, "Spare Time's Rare to Apostle," *Church News*, Jan. 24, 1976, 4.

7. David John Buerger, "Speaking with Authority: The Theological Influence of Bruce R. McConkie," *Sunstone*, Mar. 1985, 10.

8. David O. McKay, diary, July 5, 1966, in Harvard S. Heath, ed., *Confidence amid Change: The Presidential Diaries of David O. McKay, 1951–1970* (Salt Lake City: Signature Books, 2019), 663.

Three days later, at the request of McKay's secretary, Claire Middlemiss, McConkie followed up about the matter in a memo to her. Middlemiss, who kept McKay's diary at this time, used this memo to form the basis for the journal entry documenting the meeting between her boss and McConkie. There is one significant difference between McConkie's memo and McKay's diary entry, however. The diary says, "I told Brother McConkie that should the book be re-published at this time, he would be responsible for what is in it, and that it will not be a Church publication." McConkie's memo states that "President McKay indicated that the book should be re-published at this time, said that I would be responsible for what was in it, that it would not be a Church publication." McConkie, in other words, claims that McKay gave him a mandate to republish the book, while McKay's diary suggests that the church president was hesitant and would only allow it provided certain conditions were met. Middlemiss may have sought clarification from McKay and thus worded the diary to reflect what she concluded was his take on the meeting.[9]

Why did McKay grant that even a corrected version of *Mormon Doctrine* be published, considering that he, his counselors, and the Twelve were adamantly opposed to the idea just six years earlier? By 1966, First Presidency counselors J. Reuben Clark and Stephen L Richards were dead. McKay, at ninety-two and in failing health, may have been more easily manipulated and may not have accurately recalled those earlier discussions and all the associated controversy over the book. Middlemiss told BYU president Ernest L. Wilkinson a year earlier that McKay was "slowly deteriorating" and that he "does not remember anything after conferences had with him unless he has a written memorandum on it."[10] What's more, Joseph Fielding

---

9. Bruce R. McConkie to Clare Middlemiss, July 8, 1966, in David O. McKay diary under that same date. Much of the text of the memo is produced in Heath, *Confidence amid Change*, 663n29. In *The Bruce R. McConkie Story: Reflections of a Son* (Salt Lake City: Deseret Book, 2003), 183–84, Joseph Fielding McConkie says McKay initiated the meeting by inviting his father to the office and that McKay "directed him" to reprint the book. He makes no reference at all to McKay's diary, which portrays the meeting differently. Joseph McConkie says that he learned this directly from his father and that "I am in possession of handwritten papers by my father affirming that direction." This is likely the memo to Middlemiss, or, if handwritten, a draft of that memo.

10. Ernest L. Wilkinson, diary, July 7, 1965, as quoted in D. Michael Quinn, *The Mormon Hierarchy: Extensions of Power* (Salt Lake City: Signature Books, 1997), 54;

Smith became a member of the First Presidency in 1965 and his influence with McKay had grown. It is possible that McConkie asked his father-in-law to try to warm McKay to the idea and that the July 5 meeting came about because of that. In fact, Smith may have been the man among "the brethren" who McConkie told McKay "had read it thoroughly."[11] But McKay would not have "directed" the publication of a book not officially under church auspices and then warn the author that he would be responsible for its contents.

McConkie noted to Middlemiss that he had already talked with Kimball about reviewing the changes and that "Brother Kimball graciously agreed to do this as his time and circumstances permitted." Any review of the book he undertook or supervision he gave McConkie was not significant enough for Kimball to even mention in his journal. But whatever attention he gave the matter was done quickly. Four months after McConkie and McKay met, on November 11 newspapers began advertising the second edition of *Mormon Doctrine*, which was by then available for sale.[12]

Two weeks before the book came out, McConkie spoke to the LDS Student Association at the Salt Lake Institute of Religion at the University of Utah. In this talk, titled, "Are the General Authorities Human," he used some rare doses of humor over the pulpit as he discussed church leaders, their limitations, and how they all have their own biases and opinions that can be uninspired or wrong. This was a new approach for him in dealing with these kinds of issues, considering how he had advised Reed C. Durham to handle them two years earlier. He even joked about the controversy surrounding his book when he told the students, "I would like to read you a couple of quotations. I know these are good quotations because I wrote them myself. The first one is under the heading 'General Authorities' in a book entitled, *Mormon Doctrine*, which is reputed to have said more than it ought to have said on some subjects and this may be one of them." He quoted liberally from the book throughout his talk, and

Stirling Adams, "The End of Bruce R. McConkie's *Mormon Doctrine*," *John Whitmer Historical Association Journal* 32, no. 2 (Fall/Winter 2012): 66–67.

11. Stirling Adams, "Oh, Say, What Was Mormon Doctrine?" 20, unpublished essay, copy in my possession courtesy of the author.

12. McConkie to Middlemiss; Advertisement, *Deseret News*, Nov. 11, 1966, 4A.

although he did so from the first edition in every case, those quotations remained unchanged in the revised edition then at press.[13]

McConkie's son Joseph says that Kimball provided a report to the First Presidency after completing his task and that he went over fifty-six changes McConkie made to *Mormon Doctrine* and approved them all. It is puzzling that McKay asked Kimball to do this after Apostles Marion G. Romney and Mark E. Petersen had spent nearly a year examining the book and knew it better than anyone. Although Romney had spelled out several problems with the first edition in his January 28, 1959, letter to McKay following his own reading, the expanded committee in 1960 found that *Mormon Doctrine* contained 1,067 errors. Those were never made public and may not have even been shown to McConkie, since at the time the First Presidency opted to have the book go out of print rather than allow McConkie to publish a revised version.[14]

Whatever those errors were, the second edition clearly failed to address more than a handful of them, but there were far more changes made than the fifty-six Joseph McConkie admits to. That number affected only the changes made to the blatant anti-Catholic references, which softened the rhetoric. Total changes numbered around 480, but 80 percent of those only affected the tone, thus the original meaning remained intact. McConkie added eight new entries and deleted twenty-five others. There were ninety-three words or phrases removed while 250 other changes affected an entry's wording. The book went on to sell several hundred thousand copies over the next several decades and has been used and cited by members more than almost any LDS title outside of the scriptures.[15]

In time, the entries on race proved to be problematic, but it was

13. Elder Bruce R. McConkie, "Are the General Authorities Human," talk delivered at the LDS Institute of Religion, Oct. 28, 1966, copy courtesy of Smith–Pettit Foundation.

14. McConkie, *Reflections*, 187, 191; Marion G. Romney to David O. McKay, Jan. 28, 1959, inserted in McKay diary, Jan. 7, 1960.

15. David John Buerger, unpublished review of *Mormon Doctrine*, copy courtesy of Smith–Pettit Foundation; Adams, "End of Bruce R. McConkie's *Mormon Doctrine*," 65–66. For further comparisons between the two editions, see Dennis C. Davis, "McConkie's *Mormon Doctrine* Changes in Parallel Columns," (1971) and David Dye, comp. and ed., *Changes in Mormon Doctrine: Comparison of the 1958 and 1966 Editions by Bruce R. McConkie* (Mona, UT: FIG Project, 2007).

well over a decade before McConkie gave that any thought. Most church leaders assumed that Joseph Smith had initiated the ban that kept Black members from holding the priesthood or attending the temple, but later research showed it started with Brigham Young in 1852. McConkie and others in the hierarchy believed the ban was directed by God, and they maintained a theology to explain and justify it. McConkie laid it out in *Mormon Doctrine* but he was only echoing those who came before him. For example, an entry in his book titled "Negroes" maintained that the ban's root cause had to do with the pre-existence—the period before birth where, in LDS theology, those born into mortality lived with God before coming to earth. Two-thirds of those spirits, according to LDS beliefs, followed Christ's plan involving the freedom to choose good or evil and the risks associated with that. One third chose to follow Satan, who proposed forcing everyone to do good and thus, all humankind would be saved. Those who followed Satan were never born into this world and were denied mortal bodies. "Of the two-thirds who followed Christ, however, some were more valiant than others.... Those who were less valiant in pre-existence and who thereby had certain spiritual restrictions imposed upon them during mortality are known to us as the *negroes*. Such spirits are sent to earth through the lineage of Cain, the mark put upon him for his rebellion against God and his murder of Abel being a black skin." He explained that Blacks are denied the priesthood and that "under no circumstances can they hold this delegation of authority from the Almighty." He then declared that, "The negroes are not equal with other races where the receipt of certain spiritual blessings are concerned, particularly the priesthood and the temple blessings that flow therefrom, but this inequality is not of man's origin. It is the Lord's doing." This entry, as originally worded in the first edition of *Mormon Doctrine*, is preserved intact in the second edition of 1966.[16]

McConkie made no changes to his racial teachings between the first and second editions because his view of Blacks mirrored those found in LDS teachings at the time and nothing he said on the subject was controversial to his colleagues or to most church members.

---

16. McConkie, *Mormon Doctrine*, first edition, 476–77, and second edition, 526–27.

McConkie could well have reached many of his conclusions early in his youth by studying any number of LDS authorities at the time, but no point of view on the subject was better known or more accessible to him than that of Joseph Fielding Smith. In 1931, when McConkie was only sixteen years old, Smith published *The Way to Perfection*, which spent two chapters explaining the church's theology on Blacks. Smith was hardly ambiguous. "Not only was Cain called upon to suffer, but because of his wickedness he became the father of an inferior race. A curse was placed upon him and that curse has been continued through his lineage and must do so while time endures." The result is that "Millions of souls have come into this world cursed with a black skin and have been denied the privilege of Priesthood and the fulness of the blessings of the Gospel. These are the descendants of Cain. Moreover, they have been made to feel their inferiority and have been separated from the rest of mankind from the beginning." Smith then spent a chapter backing up his views by quoting nineteenth-century church leaders. This book was a popular title among Latter-day Saints, went through eighteen printings, and until *Mormon Doctrine* at least, was the primary source for explaining the church's stand on the racial issue.[17]

McConkie briefly addressed his views on the inferiority of Blacks shortly before the second edition of *Mormon Doctrine* appeared when he spoke to departing missionaries at the Salt Lake Mission Home. One who remembered this moment was future Massachusetts governor, Republican presidential nominee, and US Senator from Utah Mitt Romney, then nineteen years old and about to embark on a mission to France. After McConkie instructed the group not to proselyte "negroes," Romney asked during the question-and-answer session, "We believe that all people are equal, right?"

"Do you think you're equal to Jesus Christ?" McConkie asked him, staring down at the young missionary as he did so. "Do you think you're equal to Joseph Smith?"

Romney sat silently but said later that he wished he'd have

17. Joseph Fielding Smith, *The Way to Perfection: Short Discourses on Gospel Themes* (Salt Lake City: Genealogical Society of Utah, 1931), 101, 103–11; Adams, "End of Bruce R. McConkie's *Mormon Doctrine*, 61; Matthew L. Harris, "Joseph Fielding Smith's Evolving Views on Race: The Odyssey of a Mormon Apostle-President," *Dialogue: A Journal of Mormon Thought* 53, no. 3 (Fall 2022): 4–5.

responded by saying "Yes, yes, we *are* all equal. We can all achieve the highest level of glory."[18]

The civil rights movement that began in the mid-1950s had culminated in the Voting Rights Act of 1965, which President Lyndon B. Johnson signed into law on August 6 of that year. America's attitude about race was changing, but racist views and actions still occurred everywhere, and some parts of the South were still fighting the laws that gave Blacks equal rights. In 1970 a fact-finding committee of four white and four Black students and faculty members from the University of Arizona spent three days at Brigham Young University in Provo to investigate charges of racism at the Mormon school. Their report concluded that the campus was "no more or less (racist) than any other university," even though the report called the school "sterile" in that only fifteen Blacks were then enrolled there. However, the United Front Organization criticized that report and provided evidence that BYU did support racism. It cited an entry in *Mormon Doctrine* called "Races of Men," where McConkie taught that, "Racial degeneration resulting in differences in appearances and spiritual aptitude has arisen since the fall [of Adam]. We know the circumstances under which the posterity of Cain were cursed with what we call Negroid racial characteristics. The Book of Mormon explains why the Lamanites received dark skin and a degenerate status." Bruce Eggers, president of the Associated Students of the University of Arizona, tried to counter this teaching by citing instances in LDS scriptures that speak of the equality of humankind.[19] For many, however, there was a clear contradiction between the teachings Egger's cited and actual practice.

McConkie's resurrection of *Mormon Doctrine* occurred during a time of family bereavements mixed with celebrations. Earlier that spring, McConkie's seventy-eight-year-old father, Oscar, died after a lengthy illness. In July Joseph Fielding Smith turned ninety and Bruce spoke at his birthday celebration. In January 1967, son Stanford, then enrolled at Brigham Young University, married nursing

---

18. McKay Coppins, *Romney: A Reckoning* (New York: Scribner, 2023), 294.

19. Dick Fowler, "'Fact-Finders' Criticized for BYU Report," *Arizona Daily Star* (Tucson), Oct. 5, 1970, B1.

student Kathleen Sorensen in the Salt Lake Temple. Bruce performed the marriage ceremony.[20]

Around this time the troubles over the Memorial Estates Security Corporation, of which McConkie was the founding vice president, reached a peak after its 1964 bankruptcy filing. In 1966 fifteen of its officials, including McConkie, were sued by James and Caroline Cottam, a senior couple from Veyo, Utah, who represented the 270 stock and bondholders in the business venture. These investors believed they had been misled by the 1960 company prospectus into thinking, among other things, that MESC was a church-approved business. Half of the 210 investors who completed a questionnaire about their reasons for investing noted that the Mormon leaders involved, specifically McConkie, were their reasons for trusting MESC in the first place. "We relied upon the integrity of corporate officers shown in the Prospectus," noted the Cottams. "We relied heavily on the name of Bruce McConkie because we were sure that anything he was connected with would be completely reliable and honest." Investors, the Cottams insisted, were kept in the dark regarding the company's financial problems. One investor wrote to McConkie directly. "We should like the $800, plus interest, we paid for the bonds returned immediately," they demanded, and then asked, "Could you please help me?" McConkie never responded. In 1969 the parties settled the lawsuit just three days before it was set to go to trial and stockholders received back only a fraction of their original investment.[21]

How involved was McConkie in the MESC fiasco? He may have done little more than lend his name to the enterprise, since he spent most of its solvent years in Australia and was likely out of the loop. But even so, his official involvement in a leading role within the company made him partially accountable for its mismanagement. He appears to have said nothing about it publicly and probably saw it as an unfortunate business failing. It is not uncommon for people in such positions to separate business ventures from their religious

20. "Rites Tuesday for Ex-Judge," *Deseret News*, Apr. 11, 1966, B1; Henry A. Smith, "Pres. Smith to Note 90th Anniversary," *Church News*, July 16, 1966, 3; "Sorensen-McConkie Wedding," *Deseret News*, Jan. 26, 1967, 2C.

21. Lynn Packer, "The Phantom of Fraud," *Utah Holiday*, Oct. 1990, 32; Anson Shupe, *The Darker Side of Virtue: Corruption, Scandal and the Mormon Empire* (Buffalo, NY: Prometheus Books, 1991), 58–61.

lives and personal morality, even when there are painful consequences that hurt and financially damage others as that business crumbles.

McConkie explained later that he wrote *Mormon Doctrine* and his *Doctrinal New Testament Commentary* primarily on holidays and days off, but a colleague in the Seventy, Paul H. Dunn, said McConkie and others at church headquarters also used office time and staff on their personal projects. General authorities take the entire month of July as vacation time, but the summer of 1967 proved different from McConkie's typical experience. This year he was recruited to teach two religion courses at Brigham Young University during its second summer session. The first course, Religion 510, The Gospels, may have come about because of the reputation that followed the publication of his *Commentary*. The other, Religion 530, LDS Theology, was also a subject well within his wheelhouse.[22]

In other memorable moments that summer, he, along with Apostles Mark E. Petersen and Thomas S. Monson represented the church to over 200 guests at the opening of the Mormon Visitor's Center in the Ogden Tabernacle. In August he dedicated a plaque in New Orleans commemorating the immigration of 18,000 Latter-day Saint converts who came from England to the United States between 1840 and 1855. Eighty-one voyages across the Atlantic during that fifteen-year period brought them to New Orleans before they went on to either Nauvoo, Illinois, or Salt Lake City. The plaque, gifted by the Daughters of Utah Pioneers, was mounted in the building of the New Orleans and Jefferson wards.[23]

In November, McConkie sat with religious leaders of the Catholic, Lutheran, and Unitarian churches at the Hansen Planetarium in Salt Lake City on a panel discussion called "Life Beyond the Earth," meaning the possibility of life on other planets, moderated by Dr. Robert Kadesch, physics professor at the University of Utah. Rev. John Fallon of Judge Memorial Catholic School told the gathering

22. Croft, "Spare Time's Rare to Apostle," 4; "Church Official to Teach in Second Session," *Daily Herald* (Provo, UT), Apr. 21, 1967, 4A; Leonard J. Arrington, *Confessions of a Mormon Historian: The Diaries of Leonard J. Arrington, 1971–1997*, ed. Gary James Bergera, 3 vols. (Salt Lake City: Signature Books, 2018) 1:293.

23. "LDS Church Open's Visitor's Center in Ogden Tabernacle," *Ogden Standard Examiner*, July 15, 1967, 11; "New Orleans: Plaque to Note Historic Period," *Deseret News*, Aug. 12, 1967, 4.

that, "Theology at the present time cannot dispute or formulate principles regarding life beyond earth because we just don't know. If science shows there is life like ours beyond earth, it seems the principle of redemption through Christ would be applicable there." Universalist minister Hugh Gillilan countered that "Redemption and the moral code are products of mankind, not necessarily applicable to life beyond Earth which may be subject to entirely different problems and circumstances." Much as he had in Australia when speaking on national television, McConkie set himself apart here from the other religious leaders on the stage and spoke with the certainty that had come to define his approach as a leader in the LDS Church. In this case Latter-day Saint scripture addressed this topic with clarity, which allowed him to affirm that there were "worlds without number" inhabited by beings related to those on earth because they come from the same creator.[24]

A few years earlier, the missions of the church were divided into twelve areas, each directed by a member of the Twelve Apostles, with supervisors called from either the Assistants to the Twelve or First Council of Seventy. In May 1968 McConkie was assigned to serve with Elder Ezra Taft Benson in overseeing what was called the Oriental Missions, which included the Korean, Northern Far East, Southern Far East, and Philippines missions. During the three years McConkie served in this capacity he and Amelia went to Asia four times and held seminars with mission leaders. In Saigon the McConkies once got to spend time with their son Joseph, who served as a chaplain there. The following year Benson and McConkie traveled to Djakarta, Indonesia, to visit the one small LDS branch located there. Before they left, Benson, with McConkie by his side, dedicated the country for missionary work. McConkie also gave a short talk. Before going home, they spent a few days in Jerusalem. In 1970 while on assignment in Osaka, Japan, he and Amelia found time for relaxation and attended the world's fair.[25]

In addition to his work overseas, McConkie had many opportunities to speak at home to college-aged Latter-day Saints, whether

---

24. "Don't Rule Out 'Other' Life, Minister Says," *Deseret News*, Nov. 4, 1967, 10A.

25. "General Authorities Assigned New Areas," *Church News*, May 25, 1968, 9; McConkie, *Reflections*, 334–45.

at devotional services at BYU or talks at LDS institutes of religion. From September 25 through December 6, 1968, he taught two Monday night classes at the Salt Lake Institute. One was called "Messages from the Book of Mormon," and the other was "LDS Doctrine and Philosophy." He was one of twenty-seven instructors, including three general authorities, who taught at the institute that fall. A few weeks before his courses started, he taught young and older adults at the opening lecture of a thirty-week Know Your Religion series at BYU.[26]

While McConkie spoke to students at an institute fireside in March 1969, someone asked him about *Dialogue: A Journal of Mormon Thought*, an independent publication founded three years earlier to help satisfy the needs of intellectuals and independent thinkers in the church. "The church no longer feels threatened by anyone. The church is established and nothing can destroy it except our own wickedness," he answered. Although *Dialogue* was not meant to harm the church but to help thinkers within it find reasons to stay, McConkie felt that any well-meaning intent on its part to aid such members or even to help the church in that way was wrongheaded because he did not believe *Dialogue*, with its intellectual slant, could contribute to the spiritual life of Mormons. One of the journal's founding editors, Eugene England, learned of McConkie's comments when he spoke at a similar fireside the following month and had a few words of his own. "When a general authority expresses his view on Dialogue, it is just like when he votes—it is not doctrine. It is his point of view."[27] McConkie and England would have occasion to disagree on other matters in a little over a decade, but that conflict, through some unfortunate leaks, would become public in a way neither intended.

Less than three weeks into the 1970s, ninety-six-year-old David O. McKay died of congestive heart failure. He had served as church president since 1951 and had been in failing health for several months. McKay was beloved by Latter-day Saints worldwide and

---

26. Ad for the fall schedule for the Salt Lake Institute of Religion, *Daily Utah Chronicle*, Sep. 24, 1968, 20; "News Notes at Home and Abroad: New Religion Series Set," *Deseret News*, Aug. 24, 1968, 2.

27. Mardell C. Parrish, "England Stresses 'Dialogue's' Purpose," *Student Life*, Apr. 9, 1969, 2; Parrish, "Dialogue Editor Calls for Larger Perspective," *Herald-Journal* (Logan, UT), Apr. 9, 1969, 9.

was the only prophet many could even remember, and understandably his death had a tremendous impact upon the membership. But for the McConkies, it meant something beyond that, as Amelia's father was next in line as the church's new president. Joseph Fielding Smith, then ninety-three, had been ordained an apostle in 1910 and since 1951 had been president of the Quorum of the Twelve. Upon the deaths of the eight previous church presidents, the senior apostle assumed the office (although not always immediately), but in this case, Smith's age and mental decline were both factors for possibly reconsidering that. If ordained, he would be the oldest person ever to take on the top leadership position. Earlier, Hugh B. Brown, while still serving as McKay's first counselor, told Alvin R. Dyer, another counselor in the presidency, that Smith was "too old" for the role and that the tradition of selecting the most senior apostle for the job was simply that, tradition. He believed that the most senior after Smith, seventy-year-old Harold B. Lee, should be selected instead. Dyer disagreed, telling Brown that, "If the Lord does not want President Smith to be the President, He would make it known to him or would remove him."[28]

Brown was not the only one in the hierarchy who wanted to bypass Smith. Apostle Spencer W. Kimball, who sat just behind Lee in seniority, told Brit McConkie after McKay's death that, "We'll have a *younger* Prophet now, instead of an older Prophet." Bruce also learned about these rumors and was unbending in his view that tradition be maintained and that his father-in-law be ordained the next prophet. He even held an evening with the family where he taught succession by seniority to be doctrine.[29]

On the day before McKay's funeral, Smith and his wife, Jessie, paid a visit to Lee at his office in the Church Administration Building. The Smiths were deeply troubled by the idea that the presiding brethren might, for the first time, appoint a church president other than the senior member of the Twelve. They told Lee that should

---

28. Alvin R. Dyer, diary, Oct. 8, 1969, as quoted in Gregory L. Prince and Robert Wright, *David O. McKay and the Rise of Modern Mormonism* (Salt Lake City: University of Utah Press, 2005), 402; Francis M. Gibbons, *Joseph Fielding Smith: Gospel Scholar, Prophet of God* (Salt Lake City: Deseret Book, 1992), 453.

29. D. Michael Quinn, *Chosen Path: A Memoir* (Salt Lake City: Signature Books, 2023), 267–68.

Smith be appointed, Smith wanted Lee "by his side," which to Lee was an assurance that he would be asked to serve as a counselor in the First Presidency.[30]

At a meeting in the Salt Lake Temple on January 23, 1970, the apostles all spoke their feelings on the matter, beginning with the most junior member. Lee spoke last and proposed that Smith be ordained tenth president of the Church of Jesus Christ of Latter-day Saints. Smith chose Lee and N. Eldon Tanner as first and second counselors respectively. Spencer W. Kimball obviously had come around because he seconded the motion. Lee then, with the Twelve now united behind him, ordained Smith as prophet, seer, revelator, and president of the church.[31]

In addition to these events that directly affected the McConkie family, it was also a busy time for Bruce outside of his work in the Seventy. Before the end of the year, he finished the second volume of his *Doctrinal New Testament Commentary*, a 544-page book that covered Acts through Philippians. As with the first volume, he quoted and referenced *Mormon Doctrine* heavily, but this time did it all from the second edition. Utah newspapers began advertising volume two for sale in early April 1971.[32]

McConkie's church work never let up. In May he received a new assignment after three years supervising missions in Asia. Now he would be doing so in the South American region with Elder Milton R. Hunter, who served in the Seventy with him. They were to work under Elder Howard W. Hunter of the Council of the Twelve, who would direct the region. This area covered missions in Bolivia, Chile, Columbia, Venezuela, Ecuador, Peru, two in Argentina, three in Brazil, and one throughout Uruguay and Paraguay.[33]

As busy as he was with his church assignments, writing in his spare time remained a passion for McConkie. But it was not his only one. "I go on the theory that someone who is working with his mind

---

30. L. Brent Goates, *Harold B. Lee: Prophet and Seer* (Salt Lake City: Bookcraft, 1985), 403.

31. Goates, *Harold B. Lee*, 404–5; Gibbons, *Joseph Fielding Smith*, 455–56.

32. See Bruce R. McConkie, *Doctrinal New Testament Commentary, Volume Two: Acts Through Philippians* (Salt Lake City: Deseret Book, 1970); see ad in *Deseret News*, Apr. 1, 1971, A15.

33. "General Authority Mission Assignments," *Church News*, May 29, 1971, 7.

all the time needs to do something with his hands," he explained. After once helping daughter Sara on an assignment for her geology class, he became interested in "rock hounding," and with Amelia began going to the desert and mountains during the summer months hunting for agates, jasper, and petrified wood. Then he would spend the rest of the year, when he could, in his garage using a diamond saw to shape them into various items, such as jewelry, paper weights, and bookends. These items then became gifts for friends and family. "I get a real genuine satisfaction; it's a creative thing," he said of this interest. "There's a sense of accomplishment and there's always a sense of expectancy and wonder at what you're going to get when you cut something."[34]

Amelia described her husband's hobby as excessive. "Before I knew it I was trotting all over with him looking for rocks.... We had a yard full of rocks we'd found. And when he polished them he'd rub his hands against those abrasive wheels until his fingers bled, but he'd just keep at it. A little pain didn't stop him. He'd say the blood of Israel was in those stones."[35]

The gathering process led him to a close call with death, much as he had experienced as a child when falling off his horse and catching his leg in the stirrup. On one occasion he was out rock hunting with Finn Paulsen, a regional representative of the Twelve. They were in Salina Canyon digging under an overhanging cliff, and the pocket they were working on was a yard deep. They started on opposite ends, and for several hours worked on this with a sledgehammer, chisel, and crowbar, all done in a lying position. They slowly worked their way toward each other and got close enough where they had to reposition so that McConkie could continue to use his crowbar. After he got up, moved, and laid down again, the cliff caved in, and tons of rock came crashing down. "One rock about 18 inches or two feet in diameter came down where my head and shoulders had just been five seconds before. It came so close to my head that I felt it go through the top of my hair." Paulsen started rolling away and barely escaped a fatal accident himself. "Neither one of us had a scratch

34. Croft, "Spare Time's Rare to Apostle," 4; Dell Van Orden, "Elder Bruce R. McConkie: A 'Challenging Future,'" *Church News*, Oct. 21, 1972, 3.

35. Dew, "Family Portrait," 54.

on us. All we lost was his chisel which was under two tons of rock."
From there they calmly put their rocks in a sack and climbed down
to their car unnerved.[36]

McConkie also found satisfaction in physical exercise. He had
always been an avid walker and after the move to Dorchester Drive,
which sits at the bottom of Ensign Peak, he began walking the near
two-mile journey to the Administration Building every morning.[37]

Bruce and Amelia probably watched with some concern as President Smith delivered conference sermons and traveled outside of
Utah. Smith had been in his new role for about a year and a half
when his wife, Jessie, became ill on July 9, 1971, and was hospitalized with a heart condition. She returned home on July 30 but died
four days later on August 3 at age sixty-eight, leaving her husband,
twenty-six years her senior, a widower for the third time. She was
buried two days later. Jessie had been a part of Amelia McConkie's
life since 1938, a total of thirty-three years, a period longer than her
own biological mother.[38]

President Smith was scheduled to travel to Manchester, England,
for an area conference, but Jessie's death drained him of any desire
to go. Church members in Britain, however, had been anticipating
his appearance there and, in the end, after some prodding by his
counselors, he decided not to let them down. He arrived on August
26 and returned home to Salt Lake City a few days later. While he
was overseas, without his knowledge Bruce and Amelia arranged to
move his essential belongings from the church-owned Eagle Gate
apartments where he had been living to the McConkie home, where
he would now be living. He was surprised and upset; the move took
place without his consent and he lamented the loss of freedom he
had been used to all his life. But those in his inner circle knew he
could no longer live on his own or care for himself.[39]

Bruce and Amelia still had children living at home, fourteen-
year-old Sara being the youngest, when Smith moved into a spare
bedroom at their house. The grief he felt over Jessie's death and a new

36. Van Orden, "Elder Bruce R. McConkie," 3; Croft, "Time's Rare to Apostle," 4.
37. Croft, "Spare Time's Rare to Apostle," 4.
38. "Jessie Evans Smith Dies of Heart Illness," *Deseret News*, Aug. 4, 1971, 1; Gibbons, *Joseph Fielding Smith*, 480.
39. Gibbons, *Joseph Fielding Smith*, 481–85.

living situation he did not choose affected his health greatly. During a First Presidency meeting in September, he fainted but recovered almost immediately and insisted on attending the temple meeting afterward. A month later he began suffering abdominal pains during another meeting of the presidency and needed help leaving the room. In December he injured his shoulder, some ribs, and a hip due to a series of falls, which forced him to use a wheelchair when out and about, and a pushcart while at home or at his office. This obviously added stress to Bruce and Amelia, and with Bruce away so often on church business, the brunt of the care given to Smith would come from his daughter. Church security was not present at the house, neither did nurses make any kind of regular visits.[40]

Smith's physical decline was only part of the problem. He also suffered from advanced dementia, but this was not easily discerned when people observed him in public reading talks at conferences, which he could still do with apparent ease. Nephew James McConkie learned directly from Wilford W. Kirton Jr., the church's top lawyer and who attended meetings of the First Presidency, that Smith's counselors made all administrative decisions, only asking Smith afterward if their decision was correct, which he usually replied by answering, "Yes, it is." There were times he even forgot he was the church's president. When he began setting apart Myrthus W. Evans as the new Los Angeles Temple president on March 8, 1970, two months after becoming church president, Smith stated he was doing so under the authority given to him by President David O. McKay. This forced Harold B. Lee to intervene and correct him. Another time, Smith's grandson Stanford McConkie asked Smith what it was like to be president of the church, to which Smith replied, "Yes, President McKay is a good man."[41]

Yet some days were better than others. Amelia said later that "It was a thrill to have Dad living with us," and she paid particular attention to the prayers he uttered. During that time Bruce wrote Smith's conference talks and the dedicatory prayers that Smith read

40. Gibbons, *Joseph Fielding Smith*, 485–88; James W. McConkie, interview with the author, July 20, 2023.

41. Quinn, *Chosen Path*, 269; "New President of Los Angeles Temple Named," *Church News*, Feb. 21, 1970, 3.

at the dedication of the Ogden, Utah, temple in January 1972 and at Provo, Utah, the following month, although he consulted with Smith when doing so. McConkie sent these prayers to Harold B. Lee in October 1971 and told him Smith had approved them.[42]

Whatever fond memories built, or challenges faced during the time Smith lived with his daughter and son-in-law, it all ended after only ten months. On Sunday, July 2, 1972, Amelia took him to his home ward for sacrament meeting, and then his son Reynolds drove him to visit a daughter, Josephine, in Bountiful. After he returned to the McConkie home he ate dinner and then sat in a chair in the living room and talked with Amelia as she wrote a letter. She left the room for a few moments to get the recipient's address and when she returned, she saw her father slumped over in the chair. Bruce, who was at home, came to the room and brought oxygen and tried to administer it, but within moments had to concede it was too late. Smith was officially declared dead at 9:25 p.m., just seventeen days before his ninety-sixth birthday. He died in the same chair that Jessie had passed away in eleven months earlier. Bruce was holding his hand when the church president's pulse stopped.[43]

McConkie spoke at Smith's funeral on Thursday, July 6, after which the prophet was laid to rest. "I have been overshadowed by a great feeling of calmness and peace since the passing of President Joseph Fielding Smith—a calmness and peace that carries with it the absolute assurance that the will of the Lord has been done," he told mourners in the tabernacle on Temple Square. "Truly when the Lord took his prophet, there was no sting. President Smith did not taste of death but went to meet his earthly and his heavenly Father with a name and a character worthy of their approbation."[44]

Soon the First Presidency was reorganized with Harold B. Lee ordained as the eleventh president of the church. He called N. Eldon

---

42. Gerry Avant, "Mrs. McConkie Honored," *Church News*, Apr. 28, 1973, 4; McConkie, interview with the author.

43. Gibbons, *Joseph Fielding Smith*, 493–94; "Church Leader Dies at 95," *Deseret News*, July 3, 1972, 1; "Church Tribute to Pres. Smith: 'Spiritual Giant, Devoted, Gentle,'" *Deseret News*, July 6, 1972, 1; "Elder McConkie Speaks for Kin," *Church News*, July 8, 1972, 13; Bruce R. McConkie, "Joseph Fielding Smith: Apostle, Prophet, Father in Israel," *Ensign*, Aug. 1972, 27.

44. "Elder McConkie Speaks for Kin," 13–14; McConkie, "Joseph Fielding Smith," 27–28.

Tanner and Marion G. Romney as First and Second Counselors respectively. Smith's death and Romney's move created a vacancy in the Quorum of the Twelve, which would be filled in October at the church's semi-annual general conference. Twenty-six years earlier McConkie had been called to the Seventy, and now, as he soon began to suspect, another call was about to take place.[45]

---

45. Gibbons, *Joseph Fielding Smith*, 496–97.

CHAPTER EIGHT

JUNIOR APOSTLE, INFLUENTIAL VOICE
1972-1978

McConkie's talk during the July 6, 1972, funeral of his father-in-law had a lasting impact on many individuals. Some wrote about it and others talked about it among themselves. "Bruce McConkie's tribute was masterful," recorded Leonard Arrington in his journal. "It will be a primary source on Joseph Fielding Smith as a person and as a prophet before the historians of the future." Arrington, called earlier that year as the LDS Church Historian, also noted the remarks of Harold B. Lee, who would be ordained church president that next day. Lee spoke of having received a personal revelation about "what must be done," which Arrington interpreted to mean Lee's role as the new church president, who his counselors in the First Presidency should be, and "possibly also the name of the person who will be named to the vacancy in the Quorum of the Twelve."[1]

Spencer J. Condie, a friend of McConkie who taught at BYU, also watched Smith's funeral service, and after McConkie gave his tribute, Condie turned to his wife. "There is the next apostle of the Lord," he predicted. The vacancy would not be filled for another three months until the church's general conference in October, but in late August McConkie himself believed he received a spiritual confirmation that he would indeed be called. He and Amelia were at a large area conference in Mexico where the names of the general authorities were read for the members to sustain with an uplifted

---

1. Leonard J. Arrington, *Confessions of a Mormon Historian: The Diaries of Leonard J. Arrington, 1971–1997*, ed. Gary James Bergera, 3 vols. (Salt Lake City: Signature Books, 2018), 1:183.

hand. When the names of the eleven apostles were presented, "I, however, heard the twelfth name. It was mine."[2]

If McConkie's funeral sermon was getting people to talk, many likely still had his April 1972 general conference talk on their mind, having been touched by his personal testimony of Jesus, during which he read all eight verses of a poem he had written entitled "I Believe in Christ." Years later it was set to music and became a popular LDS hymn.[3]

On Sunday, October 1, with general conference approaching, President Lee sought inspiration on some pressing matters. "Today while fasting, I went to the most sacred room in the temple," he wrote in his journal. "There for an hour I prayerfully considered the appointment of a new Apostle. All seemed clear that Bruce R. McConkie should be the man." He discussed this with his counselors to find that they, too, had already settled on McConkie. Three days later when Lee met with McConkie to issue the call, he put his arms around him and said, "The Lord and the Brethren have just called you to fill the vacancy in the Council of the Twelve."

"I know. This is no surprise to me. I have known it for some time," McConkie responded. He then told Lee about his experience in Mexico and that he had spent time in the temple himself struggling with the knowledge he had been given.[4]

The general conference opened on Friday, October 6. McConkie brought his wife and four of their children to the tabernacle that day but had not told them about his new calling. He took his seat with the First Council of Seventy as he always had. This conference was different than most because it included the Solemn Assembly where a new church president is sustained for the first time. Five new general authorities were also called and sustained that day, but

---

2. Joseph Fielding McConkie, *The Bruce R. McConkie Story: Reflections of a Son* (Salt Lake City: Deseret Book, 2003), 324–25.

3. *One Hundred Forty-Second Annual Conference of the Church of Jesus Christ of Latter-day Saints, held in the Tabernacle, Salt Lake City, Utah, April 6, 8, 9* (Salt Lake City: Church of Jesus Christ of Latter-day Saints, 1972), 133–34. The music for "I Believe in Christ" was written by John Longhurst and included as hymn #134 in *Hymns of the Church of Jesus Christ of Latter-day Saints* (Salt Lake City: Church of Jesus Christ of Latter-day Saints, 1985).

4. L. Brent Goates, *Harold B. Lee: Prophet and Seer* (Salt Lake City: Bookcraft, 1985), 494–95; McConkie, *Reflections*, 327.

only one name caught the attention of the family. When N. Eldon Tanner read the names of the Twelve, the name Bruce R. McConkie was included at the end. Then all twelve stood to be sustained by the members present. After all the business of the Solemn Assembly concluded, President Lee spoke and invited McConkie to sit with the rest of the apostles. "This is sort of a foot of the ladder, Brother McConkie. We welcome you." Each of the new general authorities took their seats as well.[5]

After Lee finished speaking, he invited McConkie to come to the podium. "I am grateful beyond any measure of expression, beyond any utterance in my power, for the blessings the Lord has so abundantly showered upon me, upon my family, and upon the faithful Saints in all the world," the junior apostle began. After noting the importance of the "gifts of the spirit," he declared that "I have a perfect knowledge that Jesus Christ is the Son of the living God and that he was crucified for the sins of the world." He bore testimony of the role of Joseph Smith in the Restoration, and that prophecy and revelation were with the church and its people in abundance. "I know there is revelation in the Church because I have received revelation. I know God speaks in this day because he has spoken to me."[6]

Not all of the McConkie children learned about their father's new calling immediately because some could not tune in to the conference and watch it live. One son called home later that day to talk about nothing in particular and learned about it then. That evening Bruce and Amelia called three other children who now had families of their own and lived away from Utah. All were happy with the news.[7]

At the time of McConkie's call to the apostleship he was fifty-seven years old and Amelia was fifty-six. Their five married children had made them grandparents thirteen times over. Three of the McConkie offspring had master's degrees and one had earned a PhD. Two others were then working on their doctorates, one of whom was only a few months away from receiving it. Two attended Brigham Young University. In April 1973, six months after Bruce's call, the

5. *One Hundred Forty-Second Semi-Annual Conference of the Church of Jesus Christ of Latter-day Saints, October 6, 7, 8, 1972* (Salt Lake City: Church of Jesus Christ of Latter-day Saints, 1972), 4–17.

6. *One Hundred Forty-Second Semi-Annual Conference*, 21–22.

7. "Families Respond with Joy to New Appointments," *Deseret News*, Oct. 7, 1972, A3.

LDS sorority Lambda Delta Sigma honored Amelia as its "Woman of the Year" at a special institute program at Idaho State University.[8]

Five months after McConkie's call to the apostleship, he published the final volume of his *Doctrinal New Testament Commentary*. All three volumes were published over a span of eight years. When completed it was a massive, three-volume work of over two thousand pages and was the first such commentary ever written by an apostle or general authority at any level.[9]

Two of McConkie's earliest assignments as an apostle helped carry on the work of the church, but in different ways. On September 21, 1973, nearly a year after becoming a member of the Twelve, McConkie was assigned to the Bible Aids Committee, joining Thomas S. Monson and Boyd K. Packer, and replacing Marvin J. Ashton. The name was later changed to the Scriptures Publication Committee. Before McConkie came along the committee had approached Spencer W. Kimball, acting president of the Council of the Twelve, and presented him with the idea of producing an LDS edition of the King James Bible. Kimball received approval from the First Presidency and on October 27, 1972, he reached out to two BYU professors proficient in Greek and Hebrew and asked them to take part in the creation of the new Bible, one with cross references to the church's other scriptures and which would include a new atlas, concordance, dictionary, photographs, and other reading aids. The committee began meeting in January 1973. It was clear that when McConkie was asked to come on board eight months later it was because he possessed an unusual familiarity with the LDS canon. He also supervised the creation of the footnotes and the inclusion of excerpts from the Joseph Smith translation of the Bible. A major task for him was creating the brief headings for each chapter of the Old and New Testaments, which he did alone. It would take nearly seven years to complete the Bible project.[10]

---

8. "Lambda Delta Sigma Units to Honor 'Woman of Year,'" *Idaho State Journal*, Apr. 11, 1973, B3; Gerry Avant, "Mrs. McConkie Honored," *Church News*, Apr. 28, 1973, 4.

9. Ad in *Odgen Standard-Examiner*, Mar. 30, 1973, 18B.

10. Lavina Fielding Anderson, "Church Publishes First LDS Edition of the Bible," *Ensign*, Oct. 1979, 11–12; Robert J. Matthews, "The New Publications of the Standard Works—1979, 1981," *BYU Studies* 22, no. 2 (Fall 1982): 387–89; Fred E. Woods, "The Latter-day Saint Edition of the King James Bible," in *The King James Bible and the Restoration*,

Earlier, on December 13, 1972, McConkie began serving as an advisor to the Church History Department. One of Arrington's staff members, D. Michael Quinn, was not happy with this news. "Bruce R. McConkie has been appointed to serve with Howard W. Hunter as the two Apostles to oversee HDC [Historical Department of the Church] and be our representatives in the Quorum," Quinn noted in his diary. "This was a double disappointment, since I have long felt these two men have Dark Age attitudes about church history." Quinn felt this way because a nephew of McConkie had told him more than once that his uncle believed "it would be better if MSS [manuscripts] having negative information about the Church were destroyed." Quinn tried to remain optimistic, however. "Although having these two men in charge of our Archives is a frightening prospect to me, I want to acknowledge my determination to sustain God's will."[11]

McConkie's response to historical writing where its conclusions were critical or simply differed from the church's traditional viewpoint came out on at least one occasion. By April 1973, an article by Lester Bush called "Mormonism's Negro Doctrine: An Historical Overview," was slated for publication in *Dialogue: A Journal of Mormon Thought*. Through primary sources Bush debunked the popular theological rationale that McConkie, Joseph Fielding Smith, and others had long used to explain the priesthood and temple bans. Bush even showed conclusively that the restrictions did not originate with Joseph Smith. Apostle Boyd K. Packer learned about the forthcoming article and not only read a copy of the manuscript that Bush had sent him, but he also examined Bush's separate, 400-page compilation of primary source material and statements on Blacks given over the course of the church's history. Joseph Anderson, managing director of the History Division, also read the article. Both understood the sensitive nature of the issue and gently tried to persuade Bush during two meetings in May and June to delay publication

---

ed. Kent P. Jackson (Salt Lake City and Provo: Deseret Book and Religious Studies Center, 2011), 260–63; Dennis B. Horne, *Bruce R. McConkie: Highlights from His Life and Teachings*, second edition with epilogue (Salt Lake City: Eborn Books, 2010), 189, 193.

11. Arrington, *Confessions*, 1:377–78; D. Michael Quinn, journal, Dec. 14, 1972, D. Michael Quinn Papers, WA MSS S-2692, box 28, Beineke Library, Yale University, New Haven, CT, copy in my possession.

or to publish it somewhere other than *Dialogue*, a publication that many of the brethren found suspect.[12]

Apparently McConkie did not read Bush's piece prior to publication, but he soon read it with keen interest after its publication the following August. As expected, he was not pleased. Ed Ashment, who then worked for the Church Translation Division, came to see McConkie at his office about unrelated business, and as he entered, he noticed McConkie reading the article. In a sudden burst, however, McConkie turned his chair around, slammed down his issue of *Dialogue*, and called it "CRAP!" McConkie may well have accepted some of the messiness in the history of the priesthood ban, but he was not about to discard the theology he had long advocated, and which lent it God-given legitimacy. A year later when he addressed the October general conference, his message to Bush and anyone else troubled by the matter was clear. "Am I valiant if my approach to the Church and its doctrines is intellectual only, if I am more concerned with having a religious dialogue on this or that point than I am on gaining a personal spiritual experience? Am I valiant if I am deeply concerned about the Church's stand on who can or who cannot receive the priesthood and think it is time for a new revelation on this doctrine?"[13]

Despite his attitude about Bush's scholarly treatment of a controversial issue, in the two years he served as an advisor to the Historical Department, McConkie proved to be the least of Arrington's worries and, overall, Arrington felt he had Hunter and McConkie's support. The Arrington team and their advisors held a meeting in late November 1974 in response to criticisms voiced in a letter by Apostle Packer to the First Presidency about a proposed project sponsored by the History Division. McConkie assured Arrington that, "We have to write history. We cannot avoid the responsibility. And as long as we have to do it, we have to get competent professional people. We

12. Lester Bush, "Writing 'Mormonism's Negro Doctrine: An Historical Overview' (1973): Context and Reflections, 1998," *Journal of Mormon History* 25, no. 1 (Spring 1999): 247–55.

13. Bush, "Writing 'Mormonism's Negro Doctrine,'" 264–67; *One Hundred Forty-Fourth Semi-Annual Conference of the Church of Jesus Christ of Latter-day Saints, October 4, 5, 6, 1974* (Salt Lake City: Corporation of the President of the Church of Jesus Christ of Latter-day Saints, 1975), 46.

cannot expect it to be done by an 8th grade Sunday School teacher or someone not trained." Moments like this were gratifying to Arrington. "In essence," he recorded, "we have a vote of confidence from Elders Hunter, McConkie, and Anderson, and they see the letter as posing no threat to us or our program."[14]

Two months later when Arrington sought McConkie and Hunter's opinion on a planned book examining the practice of plural marriage among the Mormons, Arrington noted that "both said they supported the idea and said they would take it to the Quorum of the Twelve and try to obtain their support for the task." When they asked Arrington to make an oral response to new criticisms by Packer, they accepted Arrington's defense and assured him they were on his side. After suggesting Arrington speak with Packer directly, they gave Arrington a warning: "They said he will try to indoctrinate me, but I should attempt to explain in as clear and logical and persuasive a manner as possible the point of view of historians on this and related matters. I was grateful for their expressions of support."[15]

McConkie himself benefited from his role with the Arrington team. On October 30, 1973, the Historical Department and First Presidency met to discuss the possibility of exchanging some documents with the historians of the Reorganized Church of Jesus Christ of Latter Day Saints. The First Presidency was willing to give them copies of revelations of Joseph Smith that were never included in the LDS version of the Doctrine and Covenants. Church archivist Earl Olson said he would provide McConkie a photocopy of the handwritten Kirtland Revelation Book and other non-canonical writings, which McConkie would look at after he returned from an assignment in the South Pacific a few weeks later. After the meeting McConkie, who still served on the Scriptures Publication Committee, told Arrington's team that, "This opens the door I have looked forward to; namely, the opportunity of considering additional revelations in a new edition of the Doctrine and Covenants." McConkie said he would even make a recommendation to the First Presidency

---

14. Arrington, *Confessions*, 1:753–56.
15. Arrington, *Confessions*, 1:794–95.

about these possible additions. In time the apostle would be both gratified and disappointed in the outcome of his efforts.[16]

McConkie's near-weekly assignments to preside over stake conferences continued after he became a member of the Council of the Twelve. He had other speaking opportunities also. In June 1973 he addressed the 185 graduates of LDS Business College at their commencement exercises and told them, "Principles of eternal truth make for a balanced personality. Don't spend your whole time seeking wealth. Be the balanced person you need to be to grow spiritually." He gave them three principles that he said would help them obtain "influence, eminence and sufficient of this world's needs to get along in this life." Those were faith in God, following the prophets, and rising above the world.[17]

In addition to his other duties, McConkie was assigned to the Melchizedek Priesthood Committee, serving with Thomas S. Monson, Boyd K. Packer, and Marvin J. Ashton. As part of the church's new correlation program implemented by President Harold B. Lee, in October 1972 the Mutual Improvement Association (MIA) began functioning under the priesthood. The MIA program for youth became the Aaronic Priesthood MIA and the program for adult singles was designated the Melchizedek Priesthood MIA, with the latter correlated under the apostles responsible for the Melchizedek Priesthood Committee. Managing directors would be James E. Faust, Marion D. Hanks, and L. Tom Perry of the First Council of Seventy. This new program was announced at a conference in June 1973. A year and a half later the committee oversaw the publication of a new thirty-four-page *Melchizedek Priesthood Handbook*, which updated and condensed information that was previously spread across six different manuals totaling over two-hundred pages. In an interview for the *Church News*, Monson summed up the handbook as "an effort to 'teach correct principles' of priesthood government, using the scriptures as basic reference material."[18]

---

16. Arrington, *Confessions*, 1:607. The Kirtland Revelation Book has since been published in Robin Scott Jensen, Robert J. Woodford, and Steven C. Harper, eds., *The Joseph Smith Papers, Revelations and Translations, Volume 1: Manuscript Revelation Books* (Salt Lake City: Church Historian's Press, 2011), 308–481.

17. Robert Copier, "LDS Graduates Counseled," *Deseret News*, June 9, 1973, A4.

18. "President Lee on Correlation: New Methods, Same Purpose," *Deseret News*,

The day after Christmas 1973, President Harold B. Lee died suddenly. Lee had woke feeling tired and later entered the hospital.[19] His death, which came less than a year and a half after he took office, stunned church members and made Spencer W. Kimball the new president. The vacancy created in the Council of the Twelve was filled by L. Tom Perry at the church's general conference the following April. With Perry in the quorum, McConkie was no longer the most junior member.

The new First Presidency was set apart in the Salt Lake Temple on December 30. McConkie spoke at a BYU devotional two months later on February 27, 1974, and used his talk to discuss succession in the presidency. The upcoming April conference would see another Solemn Assembly, as Kimball would receive the sustaining vote of the entire church for the first time. McConkie, perhaps using the same arguments that he did at a family gathering in 1970 to explain why Joseph Fielding Smith had a right to the office, told the BYU student body that the manner of succession was determined because it was doctrine. "It was not required, nor was it requisite or needed, that the Lord give any revelation, that any special direction be given. The law was already ordained and established. God does not look down each morning and say, 'The sun shall rise.' He has already established the law." Thus, the transfer of leadership from Lee to Kimball was a natural occurrence. After recounting the three-and-a-half-hour leadership meeting from December when Kimball was set apart, McConkie emphasized again that succession in the church presidency is "orderly and systematized." Each member of the Twelve holds the keys, but they lay dormant until the most senior among them becomes the president, at which time those keys can be used by him alone. Here McConkie echoes Joseph Fielding Smith, whose teachings on this subject McConkie had compiled in *Doctrines of Salvation* nearly two decades earlier.[20]

Jun 22, 1973, A1, A9; "New Handbook to Help the Priesthood Printed," *Church News*, Feb. 8, 1975, 3; Francis M. Gibbons, *Harold B. Lee: Man of Wisdom, Prophet of God* (Salt Lake City: Deseret Book, 1993), 474–75. See *Melchizedek Priesthood Handbook* (Salt Lake City: The Church of Jesus Christ of Latter-day Saints, 1975).

19. Goates, *Harold B. Lee*, 575–80; Gibbons, *Harold B. Lee*, 497–99.

20. "Apostle McConkie to Speak," *Daily Herald* (Provo, UT), Feb. 26, 1973, 3; "Succession in Presidency," *Church News*, Mar. 23, 1974, 7–8; Bruce R. McConkie, comp., *Doctrines of Salvation: Sermons and Writings of Joseph Fielding Smith*, 3 vols. (Salt Lake City: Bookcraft, 1956), 3:155–56.

As an apostle, McConkie's visits to stake conferences included organizing stakes and calling new stake presidents, something members of the First Council of Seventy could not do at the time. On January 12, 1975, he presided over a conference that formed the Merthyr Tydfil Wales Stake, the first stake in that country. His committee assignments also grew when the board of trustees at BYU was reorganized in April to be led by the First Presidency, five apostles (including McConkie), two members of the First Council of Seventy, the presiding bishop, and the general Relief Society president.[21]

In early 1976 the *Church News* ran two stories in its January 24 issue that spotlighted Bruce and Amelia. The writeup on Bruce highlighted just how busy he was by its title, "Spare Time's Rare to Apostle." McConkie talked about his various writing projects and stressed that "the very large percent of any study I do is on the scriptures themselves.... I think that people who study the scriptures get a dimension of their life that nobody else gets and that can't be gained in any way except by studying the scriptures." He said that church members "eternally" wrote to him seeking answers to questions that they could easily find on their own. "I mean, I don't have any more obligation than they do to know what the answers to these things are and they have the same sources to look to that I do." He would tell his family the same thing when they asked him questions that he believed they should have sought answers to themselves.[22]

He talked about his rock hounding hobby, his sense of humor, and his commitment to exercising. His travels around the world, especially the regions he supervised in Asia and South America, allowed him to see little else than the airports at his various destinations and the church members who lived there. But "it's the people that count, and everywhere you go you find the best and finest people in the world—that is one of the beauties of this."[23]

Amelia talked about her childhood and upbringing, meeting her husband, and her hobbies, such as sewing, knitting, crocheting, and

---

21. McConkie, *Reflections*, 360–61; "First Stake of Zion in Wales Organized," *Church News*, Feb. 8, 1975, 13; "Genesis of the BYU Board of Trustees," *Daily Herald*, Aug. 28, 1975, 36.

22. David Croft, "Spare Time's Rare to Apostle," *Church News*, Jan. 24, 1976, 4; "Bruce R. McConkie: A Special Witness," *Mormon Historical Studies* 14, no. 2 (Fall 2013): 53.

23. Croft, "Spare Time's Rare to Apostle," 4.

making clothes for her then twenty-one grandchildren. She used time on airplanes accompanying Bruce to assignments to create some of her handcrafted projects. She said she also enjoyed painting and embroidery and, like her husband, made jewelry out of the rocks they collected.[24]

McConkie's life was about to get even busier for the next several weeks when, on February 12, he accompanied Presidents Spencer W. Kimball and N. Eldon Tanner of the First Presidency, Apostle David B. Haight, and six other general authorities on a three-week tour holding conferences in Pago Pago, American Samoa; Apia, Samoa; Hamilton, New Zealand; Suva, Fiji; Nuku'alofa, Tonga; Melbourne, Brisbane, and Sydney, Australia; and Papeete, Tahiti. Over 100,000 church members were invited to participate in these events. Kimball saw this trip as "a great new adventure in taking the whole program of the church out to the people of the whole world."[25]

McConkie told the saints in Pago Pago that "all men are the spirit children of the Eternal Father; all are members of His family; all dwelt with Him in the premortal life." Those who are in the church and live the gospel develop "a special kinship," one, however, "which is not found elsewhere." They are those who "are adopted into the family of Jesus Christ and become His sons and His daughters." He continued to emphasize Christ and his role when speaking at conferences in New Zealand, Tonga, and Fiji during ten different sessions the following week.[26]

A month after McConkie and the others returned from their South Pacific assignment, the church's one hundred forty-sixth annual general conference was held in the tabernacle on Temple Square. It must have been highly satisfying to McConkie. On Saturday, April 3, 1976, after N. Eldon Tanner read the names of church leaders for the routine sustaining vote, he explained that at a meeting held a little over a week earlier, the First Presidency and Twelve gave approval to add two revelations to the Pearl of Great Price. One had been given to Joseph Smith in the Kirtland Temple

---

24. Gerry Avant, "Amelia Smith McConkie: Measuring Up to Great Shadows," *Church News*, Jan. 24, 1976, 5.

25. "Officials of LDS Visiting Pacific," *Salt Lake Tribune*, Feb. 13, 1976, C3.

26. "Samoans Urged: Develop Spiritual Strength," *Church News*, Feb. 21, 1976, 3. "Conferences Continue in South Seas," *Church News*, Feb. 28, 1976, 4.

on January 21, 1836, and was a vision of the celestial kingdom and taught about the status of those who die with no understanding of the gospel. The other was President Joseph F. Smith's October 1918 vision on the redemption of the dead. McConkie had recommended and pushed for these two older revelations to be canonized a year earlier on February 28, 1975. He had been on the Scriptures Publication Committee for three and a half years and was in a position of influence to help elevate these revelations to the status of scripture.[27]

The Scriptures Publication Committee had been busy creating the new LDS version of the King James Bible and updating and cross referencing all the standard works, but seeing the fruits of those labors was still a few years away. In June 1976 McConkie became part of yet another committee when the First Presidency and the Quorum of the Twelve created four new executive committees, each led by three apostles: The Melchizedek Priesthood Executive Committee, the Temple and Genealogy Executive Committee, the Missionary Executive Committee, and the Correlation Executive Committee. Apostles Thomas S. Monson, Bruce R. McConkie, and David B. Haight would lead the Missionary Executive Committee, which oversaw all the global functions of the missionary department. At the time there were 23,000 missionaries serving throughout the church, more than the combined number that had served worldwide between 1830 and 1910.[28]

That summer McConkie may have felt nostalgic when he attended the Hill Cumorah Pageant in Palmyra, New York. He had been a missionary there forty years earlier when the Eastern States Mission held the first performances of the annual pageant in 1936. The event, which ran July 23–31, was significant this year because the nation was celebrating its bicentennial. To pay tribute to the founding of the United States, over one hundred pageant members carried a large forty-eight by eighty-foot flag up the hill, and people

---

27. "New Scripture Voted; 4 Authorities Called," *Church News*, Apr. 3, 1976, 3; President N. Eldon Tanner, "The Sustaining of Church Officers," *Ensign*, May 1976, 18–19; Horne, *Bruce R. McConkie*, 193; McConkie, *Reflections*, 383. As discussed later, in 1981, five and a half years after their brief inclusion in the Pearl of Great Price, the two revelations were moved to the Doctrine and Covenants.

28. "4 New Committees Formed," *Church News*, June 5, 1976, 3; "Missionaries Go Directly to LTM," *Church News*, Jan. 3, 1976, 3.

portraying several of the Founding Fathers performed a ten-minute tribute. McConkie spoke at a mission conference to the six hundred cast members of the pageant, then later addressed a fireside.[29]

That fall McConkie released a twenty-four-page illustrated booklet called *Let Every Man Learn His Duty*, which he wrote as a member of the Melchizedek Priesthood Committee. It was divided into two sections called "The Ten Commandments of Priesthood Correlation," and "The Home Teaching Constitution" and sold for $1.95. It laid out the various duties of priesthood holders and his "ten commandments" were all written in an authoritative style. Each injunction began with "Thou Shalt," such as "Thou shalt teach correct principles and let the people govern themselves," and "Thou shalt perfect the Saints through home teaching." The language was quintessential McConkie.[30]

McConkie was a supervisor in the South American region and had traveled to the stakes there numerous times since 1971. On November 21, 1976, he presided over a conference in Lima, Peru, and created a third and fourth stake out of the two already in existence there. A week later he formed a new stake in Vina del Mar, Chile. His actions in South America highlighted the dramatic growth of the church there.[31]

In mid-April 1977 his assignment changed, and he began a two-and-a-half-week tour of the churches in Hawaii, Tonga, and Samoa. While there he had some spare time to work on the scripture project and managed to write 250 chapter headings for the forthcoming edition of the Bible.[32]

Meanwhile, McConkie had been working diligently on yet another writing project, a new multi-volume series that would result in a massive study of the life and mission of Jesus Christ. The first volume, a 626-page tome that dealt with all the scriptural prophecies and teachings foretelling the savior's mission, would be released in March 1978 and titled *The Promised Messiah: The First Coming of Christ*. In preparation for writing the book he reread all the standard

29. "Pageant Adds Patriotism," *Church News*, July 31, 1976, 5.
30. Bruce R. McConkie, *Let Every Man Learn His Duty* (Salt Lake City: Deseret Book, 1976), 1, 10; see ad in *Deseret News*, Sep. 30, 1976, A13.
31. "5 Stakes Reflect Church Growth," *Church News*, Dec. 18, 1976, 12.
32. McConkie, *Reflections*, 345, 347.

works of the church and took fresh notes on anything to do with the prophecies of a messiah. Advertisements for the book billed it as the first of three volumes, the second dealing with Christ's mortal life, and a third focusing on his prophesied second coming.[33] In the end it become a six-volume series, with four volumes alone devoted to a study of Christ's mortal mission. While McConkie toiled away on this project, behind the scenes at LDS Church headquarters a long-festering issue had moved to the forefront.

Like his predecessor David O. McKay and a few other church leaders, Spencer W. Kimball felt anxious about the restrictions that the church had long imposed upon its members of African descent. External pressure had grown as outside groups pushed to end the ban; some college sports teams refused to play against BYU because of the church's racist policies. Internal changes also made the race-based restrictions less sustainable, especially after Kimball announced in May 1975 plans to build a temple in São Paulo, Brazil. Interracial marriages there had been so prevalent for so long that it was nearly impossible to determine who among the members had African blood. Kimball began sending several church leaders to Brazil to determine the leadership potential of Black members there. One of those sent was McConkie, who knew many of the members and leaders well, having earlier been assigned to the South American region.[34]

By June 1977 the issue weighed heavily on Kimball's mind, and it would continue to occupy his thoughts and actions for the next year. That month he asked three apostles—Boyd K. Packer, Thomas S. Monson, and McConkie—to submit memos laying out their thoughts on the matter. A document by McConkie titled "Doctrinal Basis for Conferring the Melchizedek Priesthood Upon the Negroes" appears to be the memo he wrote on this occasion, and it explained his current thinking. Despite what had long been his vocal, unwavering, and unapologetic views on the subject, made most evident in *Mormon Doctrine*, McConkie now believed the time for

---

33. Sheri L. Dew, "Bruce R. McConkie: A Family Portrait," *This People*, Dec. 1985/ Jan. 1986, 53; See ad in the *Salt Lake Tribune*, Mar. 31, 1978, B4.

34. Edward L. Kimball, *Lengthen Your Stride: The Presidency of Spencer W. Kimball, Working Draft* (Salt Lake City: Benchmark Books, 2009), 339; Matthew L. Harris, *Second-Class Saints: Black Mormons and the Struggle for Racial Equality* (New York: Oxford University Press, 2024), 205.

Blacks to achieve full and equal status may have finally arrived. He made five arguments about why they should receive the priesthood and backed up each of them with scripture:

[1] The Gospel and all its blessings are for all mankind
[2] The gospel is given successively to those of different races, nations, and lineages on a priority basis
[3] The gospel and all its blessings are to go to all races, nations, and lineages before the Second Coming
[4] All those who receive the gospel become members of the family of Abraham and are entitled to all of the blessings of the gospel
[5] Gentile blood—including Negro blood—is purged out of a human soul by baptism, the receipt of the Holy Ghost, and personal righteousness.

Under this fifth point, he stressed that "There is only one blood, human blood." McConkie's arguments, of course, begin with the premise that the racial restrictions had all originated from God as part of a divine plan. But from this moment he became a witness to history in the making and an advocate for change. Within a year, long-awaited events came to pass and resulted in the most significant changes seen in the church in the twentieth century.[35]

Since at least February 1978 Kimball spent an excessive amount of time alone in the Salt Lake Temple praying about this issue. On March 9 he met with his counselors N. Eldon Tanner and Marion G. Romney and the Quorum of the Twelve, and each of the apostles spoke. They felt if there was to be a change it would need to come about by revelation and that Kimball would need to announce it. Kimball encouraged each one of them to learn the Lord's will on the matter through fasting and prayer. Kimball himself had looked at all the reasons why the ban should stay in place and one by one those justifications began to fade away. On March 23 he told Tanner and Romney that he had spent much of the previous night awake and felt impressed to end the restrictions. They told him they would support him in that decision should he decide to do so. Rather than rush the matter, however, they decided to talk further with the Quorum of the Twelve. A month later, on April 20, Kimball asked that

---

35. Harris, *Second-Class Saints*, 212–13; Bruce R. McConkie, "Doctrinal Basis for Conferring the Melchizedek Priesthood Upon the Negro," copy in author's possession.

the First Presidency and Twelve together pray that God would show them the way forward on this issue. Kimball also met individually with the apostles to talk about it.[36]

Then, on May 4, an unusual thing occurred during a meeting of the First Presidency and the Twelve where they had discussed the church's racial policies. Apostle LeGrand Richards addressed the group and said "Brethren, I have something to tell you. A little while ago, I saw a man seated above the organ there and he looked just like that." He then pointed at a portrait of Wilford Woodruff, fourth president of the church. "I saw him just as clearly as I see any of you Brethren." Richards assured them that "I am not a visionary man.... This was not imagination," and explained that, "It might be that I was privileged to see him because I am the only one here who had seen President Woodruff in person."[37]

A few weeks later, on May 30, Kimball read to Tanner and Romney a statement he had written where he removed the racial restrictions on the priesthood and said he had a "good, warm feeling" about it. This indicated that the decision was all but finalized, but he still needed the Twelve's approval. On this occasion the First Presidency reviewed all past statements made by church presidents about when and how the ban could be removed and asked G. Homer Durham, who then supervised the Historical Department, to research this in greater depth. Kimball canceled a luncheon scheduled for two days later that was to follow the combined monthly meeting of all general authorities. He asked the apostles to instead plan to continue with their fast.[38]

On Thursday, June 1, all the general authorities met together beginning at 9:00 a.m. Their meeting lasted three and a half hours. After it ended, Kimball asked the Twelve to remain. That this was not planned is evident by the fact that two of them had already left to change out of their temple clothing and had to be called back into the room. Apostle Mark E. Petersen was on assignment in South America and Delbert L. Stapley was in the hospital. Kimball then

36. Kimball, *Lengthen Your Stride*, 346–47.
37. Lucille Tate, *LeGrand Richards: Beloved Apostle* (Salt Lake City: Bookcraft, 1982), 291–92; Kimball, *Lengthen Your Stride*, 348.
38. Kimball, *Lengthen Your Stride*, 349; Gibbons, *Spencer W. Kimball: Resolute Disciple, Prophet of God* (Salt Lake City: Deseret Book, 1995), 294–95.

told the ten apostles present that because he had canceled lunch, he would like them to remain in the temple.

"I have been going to the temple almost daily for many weeks now, sometimes for hours, entreating the Lord for a clear answer" regarding the racial restrictions, he told them. "I have not been determined in advance what the answer should be. And I will be satisfied with a simple Yes or No, but I want to know. Whatever the Lord's decision is, I will defend it to the limits of my strength, even to death." He talked about how the objections to a change in this policy had been fading away and that he was becoming more convinced that lifting the restrictions was the right thing to do. When he asked the Twelve to speak, McConkie did so immediately and explained that he could see no scriptural obstacle that would forbid a change. Seven others spoke voluntarily and then Kimball called on the two who had thus far opted to remain silent to say something. All spoke in favor.

After they discussed the issue for another two hours, Kimball asked the assembled brethren, "Do you mind if I lead you in prayer?" Dressed in their temple robes, they formed a circle around the altar as Kimball knelt and prayed for around ten minutes. "The Lord took over and President Kimball was inspired in his prayer, asking the right questions, and he asked for a manifestation," McConkie wrote a few weeks later.

As Kimball prayed, everyone experienced something they described as a spiritual outpouring. L. Tom Perry said two weeks later that, "While he was praying we had a marvelous experience. We had just a unity of feeling. The nearest I can describe it is that it was much like what has been recounted as happening at the dedication of the Kirtland Temple. I felt something like the rushing of wind. There was a feeling that came over the whole group. When President Kimball got up he was visibly relieved and overjoyed." He had received an answer and the others had too. Kimball himself said several months later that "this revelation and assurance came to me so clearly that there was no question about it." After the prayer, before everyone departed, someone reminded Kimball of LeGrand Richards's vision of Wilford Woodruff the month before, to which Kimball responded, "President Woodruff would have been very much interested, because he went through something of the same sort of experience" when he issued the Manifesto in 1890 that announced the end to the church's practice of plural marriage.[39]

Any talk about the revelation outside of the thirteen present that day would have to wait. On June 7 Kimball told his counselors that he wanted to make a public announcement and asked Gordon B. Hinckley, Boyd K. Packer, and McConkie to write up drafts of a statement, which they did. Afterward, First Presidency secretary Francis M. Gibbons wrote up a composite announcement taken from the three submitted drafts. The First Presidency then made some revisions. The next day, a week after the revelation was received, the First Presidency and Twelve met and the apostles were given the presidency's version. They suggested additional revisions and discussed just when to make the announcement. Some wanted to wait until the next general conference in October; others favored doing it at a mission president's seminar scheduled for the following week. But McConkie chimed in, saying they should do it right away. The news will get out, he assured them, and "we have to beat Satan. He'll do something between now and then to make it appear that we're being forced into it." Packer suggested turning the announcement into a letter to general and local church leaders throughout the world but that it should be released through the media first so that everyone would learn about it immediately.[40]

Apostles Petersen and Stapley still had not been told about the revelation. Kimball called Petersen in Ecuador, where he was staying with a member of the Seventy. "I felt the fact of the revelation's coming was more striking than the decision itself," he later said, but he told Kimball he accepted it "one hundred percent." The First Presidency visited Stapley in the hospital and he too was on board, telling them "I'll stay with the Brethren on this."[41]

That Petersen and Stapley were in agreement with their colleagues

39. Kimball, *Lengthen Your Stride*, 350–52; Gerry Avant, "President Kimball Says Revelation Was Clear," *Church News*, Jan. 6, 1979, 15.

40. Kimball, *Lengthen Your Stride*, 355–56; Arrington, *Confessions*, 2:563; Edward L. Kimball, diary, May 12, 1982, copy in author's possession courtesy of Christian Kimball and Mary Kimball Dollahite. Thanks to Matt Harris for making this source known to me.

41. Kimball, *Lengthen Your Stride*, 356–57; Peggy Petersen Barton, *Mark E. Petersen: A Biography* (Salt Lake City: Deseret Book, 1985), 176.

was stunning. They, along with Ezra Taft Benson, had been the least open to change among the Twelve and had made that known to Kimball in the past.[42] Had Petersen and Stapley been at the meeting on June 1 they may have voiced opposition that would have quashed Kimball's efforts at that time. It was not coincidental that Kimball talked to them after the revelation had been given for their take on the matter and not immediately before.

McConkie kept the revelation quiet, but it may not have been easy. During the week between the revelation and the announcement, his brother Brit, working in the Philippines and serving as a patriarch, gave a patriarchal blessing to a woman with African ancestry and told her that she would receive her temple ordinances; to a black man, he promised both the priesthood and temple blessings in his lifetime. When Brit shortly returned to Utah and told his brother about this, Bruce said only that, "I am glad to know you have given those blessings." At some point that week McConkie hinted to Amelia that something big was going to be announced and assured her, "You'll be surprised."[43]

On June 9 at 7:00 a.m., all the general authorities met together in the temple, dressed in their temple clothing. None of the seventy or presiding bishopric knew anything yet about the revelation. After a hymn and everyone knelt for a prayer offered by Ezra Taft Benson, Kimball told them how he had long thought about the priesthood and temple restrictions and had always asked those above him about it. "Then one day the mantle fell on me." He told them of the many nights he came to the temple alone and "poured out my heart" to God. "Now the Lord has answered me and the time has come for all worthy men to receive the priesthood." Francis Gibbons read the statement lifting the ban and Kimball wanted to know their thoughts. They all approved it unanimously. Several, including McConkie, spoke to the assembled group. Kimball then told N. Eldon Tanner, "Eldon, go tell the world." Tanner left the room and gave the

---

42. Harris, *Second-Class Saints*, 216, 219, 222.

43. "Events Surrounding the 1978 Revelation"; "Revelation of Extension of Priesthood to Negro"; "The 1978 Negro Revelation"; all in David John Buerger, comp., "The 1978 Negro Revelation: A Unique Compilation of Events," in David John Buerger, Papers, MS 0622, box 32, fd, 12, Special Collections, Marriott Library, University of Utah, Salt Lake City; McConkie, *Reflections*, 379; Kimball, *Lengthen Your Stride*, 364n39.

statement to Heber Wolsey, the church's managing director of public relations, who was waiting outside. Wolsey knew an announcement was coming but did not know what it was about. He immediately released it to the press and before the brethren finished their meeting and returned to their offices, the phones were ringing off the hook.[44]

The announcement was on the front page of the *Deseret News* that afternoon, and news outlets around the country held up their presses to make room for the story. In the Church Office Building, seventeen telephone operators took calls from all over the world. For a two-hour period between 11:00 a.m. and 1:00 p.m., those phones never stopped ringing. President Jimmy Carter sent Kimball a telegram saying, "I welcomed today your announcement as president and prophet of The Church of Jesus Christ of Latter-day Saints that henceforth all worthy men in your church without regard for race or color may have conferred upon them the priesthood in your church." As could only be expected, Black Latter-day Saints were brought to tears of joy at the news, and the press reached out to several for comments. Monroe Fleming, a convert of twenty-seven years, spoke for many when he said, "It's like not feeling you're a guest in your father's house anymore."[45]

As this event-filled morning and afternoon came to an end, after the announcement had gone out and the world was talking, Amelia came to pick Bruce up from his office at the Church Administration Building, as she often did. After Bruce got in the car, she turned to him and joked, "Well, what are you boys going to do for an encore?"

"It may have to be the Second Coming," Bruce quipped.[46]

Before the end of the month McConkie spoke about the revelation on a few different occasions. The first occurred on Friday, June 16, at a family home evening at his home. These meetings were held monthly and were always taught by Bruce, who usually dressed casually in his short sleeved Hawaiian shirts. They were attended by immediate and many extended family members. On this occasion

44. Kimball, *Lengthen Your Stride*, 358–60.
45. "LDS Church Extends Priesthood to All Worthy Male Members," and "Priesthood News Spurs Calls, Stops the Presses," *Deseret News*, June 9, 1978, A1, A3; "Carter Praises LDS Action," and "Tears Tell Feelings of Black Members," *Deseret News*, June 10, 1978, A1, A3.
46. Kimball diary, May 12, 1982.

Bruce's brother Oscar Jr. was there, as was a sister, Margaret Pope (also known as May), and her husband, Bill. Among the others was James McConkie, a nephew.

James McConkie called this evening "unforgettable." He also provided context for the setting. Bruce was well known for his sense of humor and ability to tease, but what is perhaps lesser known is that family members could easily tease him in return. On this occasion they playfully asked, "Hey, what about *Mormon Doctrine?* Look at all the things you said about Blacks there!" But the apostle suddenly turned serious and told them, "I just want the family to know that everything I ever said about Blacks not holding the priesthood—everything I've ever written about it, everything I've ever thought about it—is wrong. And I repent of it."[47]

He then spoke about the June 1 experience in the temple. Margaret was so enthralled by her brother's presentation that she took copious notes and stayed up until 2:00 a.m. typing them up. Her husband, Bill, a stake president at BYU, provided details on Saturday night at a stake conference on campus. "When we were all seated in the living room, Bruce began to tell us some of the events and the details about this revelation," he told the congregation in attendance. McConkie gave his family permission to share what he had told them but stressed that they were "not to embellish it." Pope said McConkie "often wondered what Paul had meant in the Book of Acts by cloven tongues of fire," but after witnessing the revelation, "he now understands what Paul meant, because he experienced it." Pope explained that when someone at the family gathering asked McConkie, "Was it like the day of Pentecost in the Restored Church" at the dedication of the Kirtland Temple in 1836, when "some saw angels, some saw others and so forth?" McConkie responded, "It was like that." When people tried to get McConkie to reveal who may have visited from the spirit world "he was very careful to say it was like that day and would not go into detail."[48]

On June 26 Oscar McConkie told a similar account to Jay Todd, editor of the church's *Ensign* magazine, as did McConkie's son Joseph, who talked to Todd the next day. The younger McConkie was

47. James W. McConkie, interview with the author, July 20, 2023.
48. Bill Pope, "Address (ca. 1978)," MS 6886, Church History Library.

not present at the family gathering, but he got the story directly from his father. Todd then shared the details with Leonard Arrington, who wrote them in his journal. "At the end of the prayer, a Pentecostal experience occurred. All thirteen experienced and saw 'just the way it was at Kirtland.'" Arrington learned that McConkie used that same phrase several times as he answered questions posed by the family. "The rushing of a great wind? 'Just like Kirtland.' Angelic choirs? 'Just like Kirtland.' Cloven tongues of fire? 'Just like Kirtland.'" Arrington echoed Bill Pope in saying that here, McConkie said he came to understand what Paul meant by this occurrence as reported in the Book of Acts. "Visitors from across the veil?" Again, McConkie responded, "Just like Kirtland." After he avoided a question about the past presidents of the church appearing, his sister, who had been writing down their names, started crossing them off. McConkie noticed and said to her, "I didn't say they didn't come, May. I just said I wasn't telling."[49]

That naturally left people with a clear impression that dead prophets appeared that day in the temple, and the Popes and perhaps others hearing this weren't about to keep quiet. On June 18, the day after Bill Pope spoke at BYU, he gave a talk in his ward that evening. He told the congregation that in addition to the experience of the First Presidency and Twelve being "as it was in the days of Pentecost and the Kirtland temple era," that "many members of the early church appeared, including Pres. [Joseph] Smith, [John] Taylor, and [Brigham] Young. Tongues of cloven fire fell upon all the thirteen men instantaneously, confirming a positive answer to President Kimball's prayer." McConkie, he said, "was not able to describe the scene in words. He said it was the greatest spiritual experience of his life."[50]

Joseph McConkie told a priesthood quorum on June 25 that during the revelation all previous presidents of the church appeared. He also reiterated the similarities of the Kirtland Temple experience. He told Jay Todd a few days later that "Joseph Smith had come to instruct

49. Arrington, *Confessions*, 2:560–62.
50. Annie B. Whitton, "An Account of the Revelation Which Extends the Priesthood to All Worthy Members," June 18, 1978, quoted in Harris, *Second-Class Saints*, 235. Whitton was present for Pope's talk and took notes.

them in the doctrine."[51] Had Joseph McConkie been told these stories by his father or was Joseph, too, reading more into what happened?

Apostle McConkie spoke again later that month at a gathering in Nauvoo, Illinois, at the home of J. LeRoy Kimball, president of Nauvoo Restoration Inc. President Spencer W. Kimball knew by now the stories circulating by McConkie family members about the alleged details of the revelation; or perhaps he heard about what McConkie himself said at the June 16 family meeting. Regardless, he was troubled by it. He asked McConkie to provide him with an account of what he said in Nauvoo. "Pursuant to your request I have prepared the attached document," McConkie wrote in a cover later to his paper. "It summarizes what I said in the home of Dr. LeRoy Kimball in Nauvoo on Wednesday, June 28, 1978." The result was a lengthy piece McConkie titled "The Receipt of the Revelation Offering the Priesthood to Men of All Races and Colors." Kimball looked it over and made several revisions to it, perhaps providing an authorized script for McConkie to use for future talks. For example, in six different places Kimball added the words "temple blessings" to "priesthood," to clarify all ordinances and rites now available to Black members.[52]

There was nothing objectionable or exaggerated in the document, suggesting McConkie either toned it down before giving it to Kimball, or else he had learned by the time of the Nauvoo meeting to be more circumspect in what he said. In the document he detailed what the typical Thursday meetings in the temple consist of and what transpired on June 1. In recounting Kimball's prayer as witnessed by his counselors and ten of the Twelve, McConkie said that "a great pentecostal outpouring of the Spirit such as none of those present had ever before experienced" occurred. He said it was something that words could not describe and that, "It was something that could only be felt in the hearts of the recipients and which can only be

51. Arrington, *Confessions*, 2:562; Harris, *Second-Class Saints*, 235; "Revelation of Extension of Priesthood to Negro," notes made by Duane Jeffery, June 26, 1978, after conversation with Clayton White, who attended the meeting, located in Buerger, "The 1978 Negro Revelation."

52. Harris, *Second-Class Saints*, 236; Bruce R. McConkie, cover letter to "The Receipt of the Revelation Offering the Priesthood to Men of All Races and Colors," June 30, 1978, quoted in *Kimball, Lengthening Your Stride*, 343n1.

understood by the power of the Spirit." All of this wording apparently had Kimball's blessing.

In describing the Pentecostal part of the experience, he said that in the Book of Acts, "it is recorded that cloven tongues of fire rested upon the people. It is thought that this is an attempt to find language which would describe the overwhelming power and impact of the Holy Ghost upon the hearts of people." Without giving the impression that other-worldly visitors came or that the brethren heard audible voices, McConkie simply reiterated that "On this occasion in the upper room of the temple something akin to the day of Pentecost occurred."[53]

This version contained little if anything that others could easily embellish without knowingly doing so. However, McConkie had to deal with the fallout from the stories he had already told that others had echoed and exaggerated publicly. To do so, he had someone call family members, and, as James McConkie remembers it, that person was very direct. Apostle McConkie had received a call from church headquarters about the stories afloat and had a message for everyone. "You've got to stop talking about this—period—because it's causing problems." Thus, as James explains, "we were all sworn to secrecy."[54]

By then a young researcher, David John Buerger, had compiled the various accounts from McConkie as told by Bill Pope and Joseph Fielding McConkie. Buerger also received notes from Gary James Bergera taken during an address by Max Pinegar, the president of the Missionary Language Training Center. Pinegar spoke to missionaries on the day the revelation was announced. Pinegar got the story earlier that day from his twin brother, Rex, a member of the First Quorum of Seventy. Buerger wrote up a summary of everything he had heard second hand and sent it to Apostle McConkie for verification. "Due to the numerous sources of the same basic account, I tend to place credence in it," Buerger wrote in a cover letter on July 5. "If the enclosed copy of my synopsis is not accurate however, would you please indicate where its details are at fault, and, if possible, provide a correct rendition of your experience."[55]

---

53. McConkie, "Receipt of the Revelation."

54. McConkie, author interview.

55. Harris, *Second-Class Saints*, 236–37; David John Buerger to Bruce R. McConkie, July 5, 1978, in Buerger, "The 1978 Negro Revelation."

McConkie responded the next day, assuring Buerger that Spencer W. Kimball had received a revelation "by the power of the Holy Ghost" on June 1, 1978, that extended the priesthood to all worthy males. "Aside from this, and for all practical purposes, everything else in the document you enclosed is false. Such reports that have come to me on what President Pope said are in the same category." McConkie asked Buerger to help educate others on the falsity of these stories and concluded his letter by saying, "The rumors going around in my judgment are not in the best interests of the Church."[56]

A woman in Pope's ward who heard Pope speak there on June 18 about past prophets appearing in the temple also wrote up those details and gave her report to several members of her own family, which McConkie soon learned about. He wrote and asked her to stop spreading "unfounded rumors." When she told him she was only reporting what Pope had said, plus some additional details that Pope's wife Margaret had given her, McConkie wrote back and said that Margaret was prone to embellish stories. When Buerger interviewed Joseph McConkie shortly after this, asking about the accuracy of the things the Popes were saying, some of which was similar to what he too had shared, Joseph Fielding McConkie also blamed his aunt and told Buerger that "Margaret doesn't tell an accurate story. She's never told an accurate story in her life." When Buerger explained that the account actually came from her husband, Joseph said, "Well, I would have appreciably more confidence in an account given by Bill than I would by Margaret," and then, laughing said, that "he may have lived with Margaret too long."[57]

James McConkie acknowledged decades later that Margaret did in fact embellish when telling stories and that this was known within the family.[58] Yet that does not explain how Bruce's brother Oscar listened to Bruce at the family gathering on June 16 and stated to

---

56. Harris, *Second-Class Saints*, 237; Bruce R. McConkie to David John Buerger, July 6, 1978, in Buerger Papers, box 32, fd. 12.

57. Bruce R. McConkie to Annie B. Whitton, July 31, 1978; Annie B. Whitton to Bruce R. McConkie, Aug. 6, 1978, and McConkie to Whitton, Aug. 21, 1978, all in Harris, *Second-Class Saints*, 237–38; David John Buerger, "An Interesting Conversation," recorded and transcribed interview between Buerger and Joseph Fielding McConkie, July 10, 1978, Buerger Papers, box 32, fd. 12.

58. McConkie, author interview.

Arrington that Bruce refused to confirm or deny the appearance of past prophets, thus leaving the door open for rumors to spread. If others were telling falsehoods, Bruce had clearly set the stage.

Joseph, deviating from his father's assessment, told Buerger that Buerger's synopsis was two-thirds correct, that the only inaccuracy was the story about the appearance of heavenly visitors. But he also said his father had reasons for declaring everything in Buerger's synopsis as false. "He's been deluged by the kind of letters that you wrote, I would assume. He doesn't have the time or strength or the interest, I think, to try to go through and say this is true and this isn't." Although Joseph never directly acknowledged that he or his father had spread any falsehoods relating to the revelation, he told Buerger that, "He's embarrassed, I'm embarrassed; I don't know if Bill Pope's embarrassed but if he's got good sense he's embarrassed."[59]

This raises questions about what exactly happened during the revelation, what was said at the family gathering, and why those present were instructed to stop talking about it. McConkie's refusal to clearly state whether heavenly beings appeared or not allowed for others to fill in the blanks with their own assumptions as to what he was trying to say. James McConkie, who was present at the June 1978 family meeting, insists that his uncle never intended to embellish in his account of the event, and explains that doing such a thing was not in his nature. Family members had long tried to encourage the apostle to make his conference talks more interesting by including stories, but he refused, believing that when people tell stories, they can't help but exaggerate. He also believed that those who told stories would eventually be forgotten, while those who preached doctrines would always be remembered and quoted. When McConkie said the revelation experience was "just like Kirtland," James believes, he understood that people did not all experience or see the same thing at the 1836 temple dedication, and neither did those who gathered around the temple altar one hundred and forty-two years later. In Kirtland, James pointed out, "some saw Jesus, and some didn't; some spoke in tongues, some people didn't." Therefore "you can all be in the same room, but some people might have a day vision, and some might see an angel."[60]

59. Buerger, "An Interesting Conversation."
60. McConkie, author interview; McConkie, "Special Witness," 205.

Thus, James continued, "When Bruce said to the family that 'it was like Kirtland,' that's what he meant," meaning McConkie may have been one of the few, or perhaps the only one in the temple that day, to sense the presence of heavenly visitors, or even see them. He had claimed to the family in the past to have had visions and seen into the spirit world. When he performed the wedding for James and Judy McConkie, for example, he told them that James's father, Bruce's deceased brother James, was there. He also said that during the funeral of Joseph Fielding Smith, that Smith's father, President Joseph F. Smith, was present.[61] Along these lines, none of LeGrand Richards's colleagues believed he was fabricating or hallucinating in May when he announced that he had just seen Wilford Woodruff in the temple, even though they did not experience it themselves.

L. Tom Perry and Gordon B. Hinckley each described the June 1, 1978, revelation experience differently. Perry said shortly after that he "felt something like the rushing of wind" when describing the experience. But Hinckley said specifically ten years later that, "There was not the sound 'as of a rushing mighty wind,' there were not 'cloven tongues like as of fire' (Acts 2:2–3)," contradicting both Perry and McConkie, although neither of them said specifically that they heard it, and McConkie, like Perry, may have only claimed to have felt it. As Hinckley also described it, "No voice audible to our physical ears was heard. But the voice of the Spirit whispered with certainty into our minds and our very souls."[62]

Joseph McConkie, however, when asked by Buerger if "at that family gathering, if he [Bruce] got a little carried away," admitted, "Well ... He might have, I don't know." But when Buerger asked the same thing to Bill Pope in a telephone interview the next day, Pope was emphatic. "He never gets carried away ... He knew exactly what he was saying." Still, Apostle David B. Haight was convinced while speaking at a meeting in Washington state fifteen years later that McConkie "overstated the experience" concerning the revelation.[63]

To put an end to the rumors they had helped to spread, Bill and

61. McConkie, author interview; Horne, *Bruce R. McConkie*, 118.

62. Kimball, *Lengthen Your Stride*, 351; Gordon B. Hinckley, "Priesthood Restoration," *Ensign*, Oct. 1988, 70.

63. Buerger, "An Interesting Conversation," and "Bill Pope Interview," July 11, 1978, both in Buerger Papers; Harris, *Second-Class Saints*, 236.

Margaret Pope wrote a letter to the *Daily Universe* at BYU stating that, "There have been many false rumors and stories attributed to us concerning the new revelation received in the Church of Jesus Christ of Latter-day Saints that all worthy males may now hold the priesthood. This revelation came by the Holy Ghost. There were no messengers involved. All other such stories are false." But the Popes' letter, according to James McConkie, had a purpose lost on its readers. "They got themselves in a position where they had to pull back, and the only way to pull back was to just say it wasn't true."[64]

Whatever McConkie believed to have happened on June 1, 1978, in his letter to Buerger, he stressed that, "Until the Brethren speak in General Conference or publish matters officially in the Church Magazines there is nothing more that I know which can be said about this matter." However, on August 18, a month and a half before the church's next conference, McConkie gave what has likely become the most read account of the revelation when he spoke at BYU to seminary and institute personnel at the Book of Mormon Symposium. His account, titled, "All Are Alike unto God," was published with the proceedings from the Religious Educators Symposium on the Book of Mormon the following year. After discussing the priesthood restriction and the revelation, he said "people write me letters and say, 'You said such and such, and how is it now that we do such and such?' And all I can say to that is that it is time disbelieving people repented and got in line and believed in a living, modern prophet." Then, in words that have been quoted throughout the church ever since, he said, "Forget everything that I have said, or what President Brigham Young or President George Q. Cannon or whomever has said in days past that is contrary to the present revelation. We spoke with a limited understanding and without the light and knowledge that now has come into the world."[65]

The revelation forced McConkie to make some revisions to the 1966 edition of *Mormon Doctrine*, which he did the following year. Under the heading "Negroes," the old article was gone. A new one

64. Harris, *Second-Class Saints*, 238; Bill J. and Margaret Pope, "Denies Rumor," *Daily Universe*, Aug. 3, 1978, 15; McConkie, author interview.

65. Bruce R. McConkie, "All Are Alike unto God," *The Second Annual Church Education System Religious Educators Symposium, 1978: The Book of Mormon* (Salt Lake City: The Church of Jesus Christ of Latter-day Saints, 1979), 3–4.

said that nations and people receive the gospel at various times, and that Blacks received the priesthood through a revelation. He then provided in full the letter announcing the revelation. Nothing was said in the article about Blacks being unvaliant in the pre-existence or that they were members of an inferior race. However, the article did say to see those entries titled "Cain," "Ham," "Pre-existence," and "Races of Men." Under "Races of Men," McConkie held to his previous views. "Racial degeneration, resulting in differences in appearance and spiritual aptitude, has arisen since the fall. We know the circumstances under which the posterity of Cain (and later of Ham) were born with the characteristics of the black race." He also addressed how Native Americans, or Lamanites as they are called in the Book of Mormon, "received dark skins and a degenerate status." Because we don't know how other races came to be, he continued, "we know only the general principle that all these changes from the physical and spiritual perfections of our common parents have been brought about by departure from the gospel truths."[66] The revelation granting Black members priesthood and temple blessings may have come, but the racist folklore that justified the previous denial of those blessings remained firmly entrenched in the LDS Church.

It took decades, but in 2013 the LDS Church officially repudiated these teachings when it issued a carefully crafted article titled "Race and the Priesthood" as part of its Gospel Topics series intended to address and answer difficult subjects. "Today, the Church disavows the theories advanced in the past that black skin is a sign of divine disfavor or curse, or that it reflects unrighteous actions in a premortal life; that mixed-race marriages are a sin; or that blacks or people of any other race or ethnicity are inferior in any way to anyone else. Church leaders today unequivocally condemn all racism, past and present, in any form."[67] It turns out that McConkie's counsel to "forget everything that I have said," in time, came to apply to far more than anything he intended at the time or would ever imagine.

66. Bruce R. McConkie, *Mormon Doctrine*, 2nd ed. (Salt Lake City: Bookcraft, 1979), 526–28, 616.
67. "Race and the Priesthood," Gospel Topics, Church of Jesus Christ of Latter-day Saints, at churchofjesuschrist.org.

CHAPTER NINE

HERESIES AND REPRIMANDS
1978-1982

Church members certainly anticipated some talk about the June revelation at the October 1978 general conference. First Presidency counselor N. Eldon Tanner read the June 8 letter that had served as the official announcement and asked those present in the tabernacle to sustain the action of the brethren with an uplifted hand. Beyond that, any remaining discussion about it was left to McConkie, which he took care with one long sentence in a talk centered on revelation. "We cannot speak of revelation without bearing testimony of the great and wondrous outpouring of divine knowledge that came to President Spencer W. Kimball setting forth that the priesthood and all of the blessings and obligations of the gospel should now be offered to those of all nations, races, and colors."[1]

McConkie would soon have other things to think about and prepare for. The following month he fulfilled an assignment to travel to Dhahran, Saudi Arabia. The church had a small presence there of around six hundred members who mostly hailed from the United States and Canada, the majority of whom worked in the oil industry and related fields. Through an arrangement with Ernest A. Weeks, who served as the church's district president there, Bruce and Amelia were both allowed to enter the country, which was a rare thing for a non-Muslim man to be able to do at the time, but a feat nearly impossible for a non-Muslim woman. They left the United States early enough to spend a few days in London touring, where Bruce

1. *Official Report of the One Hundred Forty-Eighth Semi-Annual General Conference of the Church of Jesus Christ of Latter-day Saints, Held in the Tabernacle on Temple Square in Salt Lake City, September 30–October 1, 1978* (Salt Lake City: The Church of Jesus Christ of Latter-day Saints, 1978), 22, 91.

saw the collection of Bibles at the Natural History Museum and the Egyptian materials at the British Museum. They also went to Dusseldorf, Germany, where Bruce officiated at a stake conference.[2]

The McConkies had to follow the strict laws and customs of Saudi Arabia and learned before they even arrived that they would have to leave behind any religious items, including their scriptures, or risk losing them or seeing them vandalized. Women could not drive and had to veil their faces when out in public. The church could not proselyte there and anyone who joined a non-Muslim faith could be executed. The Latter-day Saints were allowed to hold an annual district conference, this one attended by around 350 members. The McConkies did some sight-seeing by arrangement of local church members and flew over deserts and oil fields, which they found fascinating. Before they returned to America, they stopped in Athens, Greece, and then went back to Germany so Bruce could preside over another stake conference, this one in Stuttgart.[3]

The Bible collection in London would have been a natural draw for McConkie, but it certainly held greater interest to him due to his work on the Scriptures Publication Committee, which he had then been a part of for nearly six years. The work of the committee in forming the LDS edition of the King James Bible was now complete. Typesetting had started in January 1978 and had wrapped up by May. The church had contracted with Cambridge University Press, which had been producing Bibles for hundreds of years. Designers there used the old method of hot metal monotype to do it. McConkie had written the chapter headings for all 1,189 chapters in the Old and New Testaments. Other features that made this publication unique were new cross references to all the scriptural texts of the church, and over 600 excerpts from Joseph Smith's "Inspired Version" of the Bible, a project the prophet took up during the early 1830s. McConkie was the driving force behind getting these included. There were new language notes, a topical guide featuring 750 categories, a thoroughly revised Bible Dictionary, and twenty-four pages of color maps. All of the Biblical text of the King James

2. Joseph Fielding McConkie, *The Bruce R. McConkie Story: Reflections of a Son* (Salt Lake City: Deseret Book, 2003), 348–49.

3. McConkie, *Reflections*, 349–50.

Version remained unchanged, but the additional study aids brought the work to 2,432 pages. In creating the dictionary, the committee relied heavily on McConkie's *Mormon Doctrine* when considering doctrinal teachings. After the dictionary was finished, McConkie read it over and gave a few suggestions for revisions. The supplements provide a strongly conservative bent in their interpretations of biblical scholarship.[4]

Part of the inspiration for shaping the new Bible probably came from *The Analytical Bible*, published in 1973, and which McConkie had become so enthralled with that he gave copies of it to all eight of his children. His son Joseph noted that "It takes no stretch of the imagination to see how this work may have influenced the creation of what we call the new edition of the scriptures."[5]

The committee supervised the work of numerous volunteers who put in thousands of hours on the project. As typesetting progressed, McConkie served as one of several readers who went over the proofs. The first copies of the bound, finished product were ready on August 7, 1979, and arrived in Salt Lake City by air express that very next day. It became generally available for purchase by late fall.[6] The work of the committee was not yet done, however. A new edition of the Book of Mormon, Doctrine and Covenants, and Pearl of Great Price was still in the works and would not be released for another two years.

As McConkie saw years of labor on the new Bible come to fruition, he also celebrated the release of some of his own independent work done outside of that project. In October 1979 Deseret Book published *The Mortal Messiah Book 1*, which dealt with the

4. Lavina Fielding Anderson, "Church Publishes First LDS Edition of the Bible," *Ensign*, Oct. 1979, 9, 11, 13–15; Fred E. Woods, "The Latter-day Saint Edition of the King James Bible," in *The King James Bible and the Restoration*, ed. Kent P. Jackson (Salt Lake City and Provo: Deseret Book and Religious Studies Center, 2011), 263, 268–69; Philip L. Barlow, *Mormons and the Bible: The Place of the Latter-day Saints in American Religion*, updated edition (New York: Oxford University Press, 2013), 225; Dennis B. Horne, *Bruce R. McConkie: Highlights from His Life and Teachings*, second enlarged edition with epilogue (Salt Lake City: Eborn Books, 2010), 195.

5. Joseph Fielding McConkie, "Bruce R. McConkie: A Special Witness," *Mormon Historical Studies* 14, no. 2 (Fall 2013): 197.

6. Michael De Groote, "And it Came to Print: Creating a New LDS Version of the Bible," *Deseret News*, Aug. 13, 2009, at deseret.com.

beginnings of Christ's earthly ministry, and only five months later in March 1980 *The Mortal Messiah Book 2* came out, which brought the narrative up to events recorded in Matthew 15 and Mark 7. Together, these two volumes totaled nearly 950 pages. McConkie relied primarily on the New Testament accounts of Christ's life, supplemented by conservative non-LDS scholars Alfred Edersheim, F. W Farrar, and Cunningham Geike, all of whom Apostle James E. Talmage cited throughout his 1915 study, *Jesus the Christ*. McConkie also cited himself, Joseph Smith, and a variety of others.[7]

Having been a general authority for thirty-four years now, McConkie had delivered dozens of talks at general conferences and countless other meetings while presiding at stake gatherings. He had also had numerous opportunities to speak to college and university students and even taught some institute classes. But if there was a talk for which he would always be remembered, it was the one he gave at a fireside at BYU on Sunday, June 1, 1980, called "The Seven Deadly Heresies." Although he acknowledged in his opening lines that the talk would focus on things people "would consider to be controversial," he believed that need not be the case. Despite his hopes, this talk proved to be memorable only because it *was* controversial. The heresies on his list, he believed, were ideas that had "crept in among us" but which had to be corrected. Four of the seven generated significant discussion afterward. Introducing the first on the list, he said, "There are those who say that God is progressing in knowledge and is learning new truths," teachings he declared to be "false—utterly, totally, and completely. There is not one sliver of truth in it." The Mormon teaching of eternal progression as it applies to God, meant only that "God progresses in the sense that his kingdoms increase and his dominions multiply—not in the sense that he learns new truths and discovers new laws." To describe those who believed God was still learning, McConkie injected some humor. "I have been sorely tempted to say at this point that any who so suppose have the intellect of an ant and the understanding of a

7. Ad for *The Mortal Messiah Book 1*, *Salt Lake Tribune*, Oct. 7, 1979, 2D; ad for *The Mortal Messiah Book 1* and *2*, *The Myriad* (Mount Pleasant, UT), Mar. 6, 1980, 11; David John Buerger, "Speaking with Authority: The Theological Influence of Elder Bruce R. McConkie," *Sunstone*, Mar. 1985, 11.

clod of miry clay in a primordial swamp, but of course I would never say a thing like that." The audience erupted in laughter. He removed that line in the print version for fear the intended humor would be misunderstood. The second heresy had to do with organic evolution and whether it can be harmonized with "revealed religion." In his mind, the answer was no. That topic had long been a sore spot for McConkie. In *Mormon Doctrine*, the entry denouncing evolution was the lengthiest in the book.

In describing heresy number five, McConkie stated, "There are those who say that there is progression from one kingdom to another in the eternal worlds or if not that, lower kingdoms eventually progress to where higher kingdoms once were." This idea, also, was a falsehood. Throughout his talk McConkie was silent on the fact that the church had no official stand on these three "heresies," but his dogmatic denunciations implied that it did.

Heresy number six declared: "There are those who believe, or say they believe that Adam is our father and our god. That he is the father of our spirits and our bodies, and that he is the one we worship."[8] McConkie did not acknowledge this, but these were actually teachings of President Brigham Young that the church had long rejected. At the time McConkie spoke out against this idea, only fundamentalist Mormons taught and believed it.

Over the years McConkie had no doubt been asked repeatedly about these various ideas so often that he finally decided to formulate his thoughts into a talk. One of the catalysts for refuting the teaching that God still progresses in knowledge may have come after his son Joseph complained to him about an incident at BYU, where Joseph taught religion. Nine months earlier, on September 13, 1979, Professor Eugene England was set to deliver a paper to the school's honor students that he titled "The Lord's University," in which he encouraged the students to continue a life of learning patterned after the church's doctrine of eternal progression as outlined in Joseph Smith's King Follet Discourse. Joseph McConkie had read a copy of the paper and warned England that his apostle father would likely

8. Bruce R. McConkie, "The Seven Deadly Heresies," talk delivered at BYU on June 1, 1978, original version, in *Doctrinal Differences: The Bruce R. McConkie–Eugene England Affair, an Exchange of Ideas* (N.p.: privately published, nd), 37–42.

take issue with it. Joseph too was so bothered by England's teachings that he told him he no longer felt right attending the temple with him. To smooth things over, England invited Joseph McConkie to the event and asked him to state his objections directly to the audience. After England presented his paper, the younger McConkie told those present that both his father and grandfather, Joseph Fielding Smith, taught that God had already obtained all knowledge and did not progress in that way. "Though I accord a man the privilege of worshiping what he may, there is a line—a boundary—a point at which he and his views are no longer welcome," and then stated that "I do not see the salvation of BYU in the abandonment of absolutes, and with the prophets whose blood flows in my veins, I refuse to worship at the shrine of an ignorant God."[9]

That Joseph McConkie would cite any individual in his bloodline as the final word on anything was problematic, and many in church leadership were unhappy with his father after he delivered his "Seven Deadly Heresies" talk. President Spencer W. Kimball's son Edward confirmed that his father spoke to McConkie about the address. On June 25, the church president "asked me [Edward] whether I had heard the talks at BYU by Brother [Ezra Taft] Benson and Brother McConkie." Benson had given a controversial talk at BYU back on February 26 called "Fourteen Fundamentals in Following the Prophet," which, Ed noted to his father, some observers read as Benson "setting up his own position in the event he should succeed Dad." Kimball talked to Benson about it, which the younger Kimball "inferred that he had suggested that Brother Benson should be more careful in what he said." Ed told President Kimball that as to McConkie's "Seven Deadly Heresies," "I thought Elder McConkie's labeling the viewpoints he disapproved [of as] 'heresies' put too strong a label on most of them." Although President Kimball did

9. Rebecca England, "A Professor and Apostle Correspond: Eugene England and Bruce R. McConkie on the Nature of God," in *Doctrinal Differences*, 4; Eugene England, "On Spectral Evidence," *Dialogue: A Journal of Mormon Thought* 26, no. 1 (Spring 1993): 144; Terryl L. Givens, *Stretching the Heavens: The Life of Eugene England and the Crisis of Modern Mormonism* (Chapel Hill: University of North Carolina Press, 2021), 162–63; Kristine Haglund, *Eugene England: A Mormon Liberal* (Chicago: University of Illinois Press, 2021), 17–18. The published version of the talk is in Bruce R. McConkie, "The Seven Deadly Heresies," *BYU Devotional Speeches of the Year, BYU Devotional and Fireside Addresses* (Provo: Brigham Young University Press, 1981), 74–80.

not detail to his son the conversations he had held with these two apostles, Ed concluded from his father's demeanor "that Dad's position was that Brother McConkie could properly believe and teach what he did, but that he ought not brand as [a] heretic anyone who disagreed with him."[10]

Kimball was more upset than he let on to his son. After McConkie delivered his talk, his good friend Marion D. Hanks confronted him about it and then complained to the First Presidency. Kimball assured Hanks that he was taking care of it. "The brethren were just livid," Hanks told Eugene England. Hanks was firm in his view that only the president of the church had the right to declare doctrine and believed that McConkie made claims "which were not in any way official." He also said that they "chastised him and told him he had to change it."[11]

McConkie made the most significant changes to the portion on organic evolution. In the version as spoken to the students, he said "Try as you may you cannot harmonize the theories of men with the inspired word." When published, that read as a question: "Can you harmonize the theories of men with the inspired words..." Again, when he gave the talk, he said, "If death has always prevailed in the world, there was no fall of Adam which brought death to all forms of life." He changed this in the printed version to read, "My reasoning causes me to conclude that if death has always prevailed in the world..." Hanks was still not happy. "So he changed part of it. Mainly just the part about evolution. And then circulated it with the statement saying it had been approved by the first presidency." Hanks, a believer in progression from kingdom to kingdom in the afterlife, preferred that McConkie had eliminated or at least revised his denunciation of that teaching as well.[12]

10. Edward L. Kimball, diary, June 26, 1980. This and all excerpts quoted are from copies in my possession courtesy of Christian Kimball and Mary Kimball Dollahite. Thanks to Matt Harris for making this source known to me; Edward L. Kimball, *Lengthen Your Stride: The Presidency of Spencer W. Kimball, Working Draft* (Salt Lake City: Benchmark Books, 2009), 51.

11. Author telephone interview with Hanks's son, Richard D. Hanks, June 13, 2023; Givens, *Stretching the Heavens*, 164–65.

12. Givens, *Stretching the Heavens*, 165; the original of "Seven Deadly Heresies" as quoted above is found in *Doctrinal Differences*, 40, 50; the revised portion is in *1980 Devotional Speeches*, 76–77.

McConkie was regularly inundated with letters from people with doctrinal questions, and he received even more after delivering this talk. His secretary fielded thirty-five calls for copies in a two-hour period alone. Due to this intense interest, a month later, on July 1, he drafted an eight-page letter to "Honest Truth Seekers," that he began sending to inquirers. This saved him countless hours that otherwise would have gone to personally addressing people's concerns. "I receive a flood of letters asking questions about the doctrines, practices, and history of the Church," he wrote as he began the letter. "Several thousand questions are presented to me each year ... Frequently I have a stack of unanswered letters which is six or eight inches high. There are times when weeks go by without an opportunity to read the letters let alone attempt to answer them." Consequently, he listed twelve "general suggestions to those who seek answers to gospel questions," and added lengthy words of counsel under each one. "Seek light and truth," "Search the Scriptures," "Seek to Harmonize Scriptural and Prophetic Utterances," "Leave the Mysteries Alone and Avoid Gospel Hobbies," "Be not Overly Concerned about Unimportant Matters," and "Ignore, if You Can, the Endless Array of Anti-Mormon Literature and Avoid Cults Like the Plague" were only some of them.[13]

McConkie still made exceptions, however, and responded to certain inquirers in writing, or, on some occasions, met with them personally. One of these was Steve Benson, a grandson of Ezra Taft Benson, the president of the Quorum of the Twelve Apostles since 1973. While a student at BYU Steve Benson conducted research for a paper on the LDS Church's official position on organic evolution. On July 7, 1980, he met with his grandfather for over three and a half hours, and while discussing his project, they talked about McConkie's talk, given just a little over a month earlier. McConkie's denunciation of evolution was unwavering, and Steve asked his grandfather if McConkie's view echoed the official church position on the subject. In response, President Benson "lowered his head,

13. "Steve Benson on Seven Deadly Heresies," notes taken of a meeting between Benson and Bruce R. McConkie, July 7, 1980, copy in my possession courtesy of Smith–Pettit Foundation; Bruce R. McConkie to Honest Truth Seekers, July 1, 1980, copy in my possession courtesy of Matthew Christensen.

smiled slightly and replied in careful and measured tones that he did not want to say too much, for fear that he 'might slip.'"

President Benson told his grandson that prior to delivering the talk, McConkie had submitted it to those above him in the hierarchy and offered to make changes to the text, but none of them suggested any. However, "it was understood that the talk represented the views of Elder McConkie" and not the church. During their conversation, President Benson suggested that Steve meet directly with Mc-Conkie over the issue and arranged a meeting at McConkie's home for later that same evening. The two met from 5:45 until 7:30 p.m. Steve Benson was excited yet nervous about speaking with the apostle, but President Benson assured his twenty-six-year-old grandson that McConkie was "a very gracious man" and had sons Steve's age. He also urged him to be open and direct.

When Steve Benson arrived at McConkie's home, McConkie, who had just returned from the office, came to the door wearing a yellow sport shirt and slippers, and thus immediately put his visitor at ease. Mark Benson, Steve's father, had driven his son to the Mc-Conkie home and sat in on the conversation, but he remained silent the entire time. McConkie encouraged the young student "not to hesitate in asking whatever I wanted."

Benson asked directly if McConkie believed in organic evolution, to which he replied that he did not. He even called the theory "logically and scripturally absurd," insisting that Adam was not just the first man but "the first flesh of all flesh." Dinosaurs, he explained, were likely killed off later during Noah's flood because so many of their bones were found buried in mud. He was clear with his guest about his position: "I don't attempt to harmonize the theory of organic evolution with revealed truth. I'm not going to talk about the truth or falsity of organic evolution. I'll leave that up to biologists. I accept revealed religion. If science and religion don't harmonize, then I reject and discard science."

Benson asked McConkie about his recent talk and whether the heresies he condemned represented the church's official position. McConkie replied that "the Church did not have to submit questions concerning doctrine to its membership in order to make them 'the stand of the Church,'" but he did acknowledge that his talk was "my view on what I interpret to be the stand of the Church." This is something McConkie reiterated several times throughout their conversation.

As to a view allegedly held by the late church president Joseph F. Smith that God had not revealed exactly how Adam and Eve's bodies were created, McConkie told Benson that this, in fact, was not the position that prophet had taken; McConkie said he knew this because Smith's son and McConkie's father-in-law Joseph Fielding Smith "told me so." McConkie emphasized to Benson that "a prophet is not always a prophet," and admitted that "I can be just as wrong as the next guy." To McConkie, this meant that, "Prophets can be wrong on organic evolution, of course. And have been wrong." He even said President David O. McKay was "uninspired" when he told BYU students that evolution was a "beautiful theory." McConkie made other statements about the beliefs of church leaders. He dismissed as "underground letters" statements church presidents had sent out affirming that the church had taken no stand on evolution if indeed those letters differed from a statement made by the First Presidency in 1909, which to McConkie was a definitive rejection of the theory.[14]

Surprisingly, McConkie also criticized Joseph Fielding Smith as being "out of his field" when he used science to try to disprove evolution in his 1954 book, *Man: His Origin and Destiny.* "He should have stayed in the areas in which he was trained: scriptures and theology." McConkie said that even prophets get into "trouble" when they go outside of the standard works because people will then start "quoting authority against authority." For McConkie, "see[k]ing authoritative statements doesn't solve the problem. People are always seeking authoritative statements. Authorities conflict." The scriptures were the ultimate source of the church's stand on doctrine, and McConkie reiterated his view that "organic evolution does not and cannot account for a paradisiacal earth, the millennium, an exalted earth and man, the resurrection of man and animals and the pre-existence." If organic evolution claimed that there was death on the earth before the Fall of Adam, McConkie insisted, it simply could not be true.

14. The First Presidency statement was published in *The Improvement Era,* Nov. 1909, 75–81.

McConkie explained—again, this likely being his own view—that the reason the church had not taken an official stand against organic evolution was to avoid picking fights with "vulnerable" members. "It's a matter of temporizing, of not making a statement to prevent the driving out of the weak Saints. It's a question of wisdom, not of truth." He used the example of when he called the Catholic Church the "Church of the Devil" in his first edition of *Mormon Doctrine*. That designation was true, he said, but people had to be circumspect when teaching it because it would offend Catholics.

Before Benson left, McConkie gave him some "inside information," which President Benson confirmed to Steve later. McConkie had been asked to draft an official statement on evolution after Spencer W. Kimball had earlier and coincidentally received a letter from Steve which included several authoritative quotes on the subject. McConkie's response became a forty-two-page document called "Man: His Origin, Fall and Redemption," which according to President Benson, had been "considered favorably by the First Presidency" when McConkie showed it to them on August 30, 1979. Although in the end it was never presented to the church, much of its content was used by McConkie to produce his "Seven Deadly Heresies" talk.[15]

McConkie's passionate anti-evolution stance was clearly shaped in large part by Joseph Fielding Smith, whose teachings (including those on evolution) McConkie had compiled years earlier into the three-volume *Doctrines of Salvation*. Although McConkie certainly held conservative views about the Genesis account of the creation of the earth and humankind, he had to have known that several high church officials had long accepted science when it came to the age of the earth and death on the planet before Adam and Eve. B. H. Roberts, a member of the First Council of Seventy, was perhaps the most vocal in that regard, especially when he publicly clashed with Smith on the subject. But some of Smith's fellow apostles, such as James E. Talmage, John A. Widtsoe, and Joseph F. Merrill, agreed with Roberts in many respects, especially about the earth's age and life and death before the Fall. But Roberts unapologetically defended

---

15. All details of this conversation come from "Steve Benson on Seven Deadly Heresies."

his controversial belief in pre-Adamites. The Smith-Roberts debate became so intense that in 1931 the First Presidency wrote to the church's general authorities that, "The statement made by Elder Smith that the existence of pre-Adamites is not a doctrine of the Church is true. It is just as true that the statement 'there were not pre-adamites upon the earth' is not a doctrine of the church. Neither side of the controversy has been accepted as a doctrine at all....We can see no advantage to be gained by a continuation of the discussion to which reference is here made."[16]

Roberts had written a book length manuscript defending his views, but it was never published in his lifetime. Smith waited until his science-oriented colleagues were all dead when in 1954, he published the anti-evolutionary tome, *Man: His Origin and Destiny*. He believed so passionately in this volume that he tried to have it adopted as a textbook by the church's seminaries and institutes, a move the First Presidency thwarted. McConkie was one of four members of the church hierarchy who Smith said he was "deeply indebted" to "for the encouragement and help which they have given" Smith in writing the book. McConkie would later declare during a debate on the book that "acceptance of the book's account of history is obligatory on all who regard themselves as real Latter-day Saints."[17]

Clearly, President David O. McKay did not agree. His diary captures his feelings about Smith's work, his words nearly echoing those he said a few years later when dealing with the first edition of *Mormon Doctrine*. In a meeting with four concerned institute teachers about the prospect of having to teach Smith's anti-science views, McKay explained to them that "that book should be treated as merely the

16. Richard Sherlock, "'We Can See No Advantage to a Continuation of the Discussion': The Roberts/Smith/Talmage Affair," *Dialogue: A Journal of Mormon Thought* 13, no. 3 (Fall 1980): 63–70.

17. Sherlock, "We Can See No Advantage," 74–75; Gregory A. Prince and William Robert Wright, *David O. McKay and the Rise of Modern Mormonism* (Salt Lake City: University of Utah Press, 2005), 45, 47; Joseph Fielding Smith, *Man: His Origin and Destiny* (Salt Lake City: Deseret Book, 1954), xi; Gary James Bergera and Ronald Priddis, *Brigham Young University: A House of Faith* (Salt Lake City: Signature Books, 1985), 155. Roberts's manuscript was published in two separate editions decades after his death. See *The Truth, The Way, The Life, An Elementary Treatise on Theology: The Masterwork of B. H. Roberts*, edited by Stan Larson (San Francisco: Smith Research Associates, 1994) and *B. H. Roberts, The Truth, The Way, The Life, An Elementary Treatise on Theology*, edited by John W. Welch (Provo: BYU Studies, 1994).

views of one man; that it does not set forth the views of the Church, and should not be prescribed as a text book, but merely as the views of one man. It is true that [this] one man is President of the Twelve, and [that] makes it more or less authoritative, but it is no more to be take[n] as the word of the Church than any other unauthorized book." McKay added McConkie's book for similar clarification in a letter to a Mormon biologist five years later. "The Church has issued no official statement on the subject of the theory of evolution. Neither 'Man, His Origin and Destiny' by Joseph Fielding Smith, nor 'Mormon Doctrine' by Elder Bruce R. McConkie, is an official publication of the Church."[18] McConkie may well have learned from Smith that pushing one's deeply held views was an acceptable course unless, or until, told otherwise.

Decades since McConkie's "Heresies" talk, the LDS Church reiterated its neutral stand on evolution by publishing an article on its official website. This essay acknowledges the varying opinions among church leaders over the years. "In 1992, the First Presidency and board of trustees at Brigham Young University approved a packet of reading material for use in science classes that presented the official 1909 and 1925 statements and other statements from members of the First Presidency on the faithful application of scientific truth." This packet included a church-approved article in the 1992 multi-volume *Encyclopedia of Mormonism*, which affirmed that "the scriptures tell why man was created, but they do not tell how." It also notes that "in 2016, the Church's youth magazine published articles on the pursuit of scientific truth. These articles reiterated that 'the Church has no official position on the theory of evolution' and characterized it as a 'matter for scientific study.'" Still, online statements like these that receive little attention have not done nearly enough to counter the dogmatic assertions of influential leaders like Smith and McConkie. For example, McConkie's influence shaped the Bible Dictionary bound with the 1979 LDS edition of the King James Bible. The closing paragraph under the entry on "Death" states that

---

18. Prince and Wright, *David O. McKay*, 45–49; David O. McKay, diary, Sep. 13, 1954, in Harvard S. Heath, ed., *Confidence amid Change: The Presidential Diaries of David O. McKay, 1951–1970* (Salt Lake City: Signature Books, 2019), 104; Stirling Adams, "Oh, Say, What Was Mormon Doctrine," unpublished paper courtesy of the author.

"Latter-day revelation teaches that there was no death on this earth before the Fall of Adam. Indeed, death entered the world as a direct result of the Fall."[19]

As McConkie's public teachings kept people talking, he took his physical fitness habits to a new level. For some time, he had regularly walked to work purely for exercise. At some point he also became a devoted hiker and often made family members rise early on Saturday mornings and go with him. But around the time he turned sixty-five in 1980 jogging became his new passion after Amelia had him watch a television show on physical fitness. "He bought books about jogging and read them all. He got the kind of clothes and shoes he needed. And he set goals," she said. This worried her somewhat because Bruce was so determined to run the miles he had set out to every day that he refused to let anything get in the way. "Sometimes he was so worn out by the time he got through that he was no good the rest of the day. But he got his miles in." One of his goals was to run one hundred miles as a proxy for every man ever called to be an apostle since 1835. He even dreamed about running a marathon but never really had time to train for it.[20]

One time while on his run he took his usual short cut through a neighbor's lawn but failed to see a new wire fence they had put in, which caused him to injure his foot, and he had to wear a cast while it healed. His obsession became too much for Amelia, who "told him that if he dared say another word about jogging I'd clobber him. I came third—right behind the Church and jogging." Later, in the January 12, 1980, issue of the *Church News* he was featured in a photograph jogging in sweatpants and sporting a shirt given to him by one of his sons bearing the words, "Lengthening My Stride," a play on President Spencer W. Kimball's slogan for church members in the 1970s and '80s. This photo and a few others highlighting older church members doing their part to stay in shape were part of an article on fitness as the new year opened. The photographer who captured McConkie had him run round and round in a confined

19. "Organic Evolution," Church History Topics, Church of Jesus Christ of Latter-day Saints, churchofjesuschrist.org; Bible Dictionary, 627.

20. David Croft, "Time's Rare to Apostle," *Church News*, Jan. 24, 1976, 4; McConkie, *Reflections*, 234; Sheri L. Dew, "Elder Bruce R. McConkie: A Family Portrait," *This People*, Dec. 1985/Jan. 1986, 58; McConkie, "Special Witness," 203.

area so that he could create the perfect photo. After a little bit of this, McConkie joked to the reporter, "You can go home tonight and write in your journal that you had a member of the Twelve running in circles today."[21]

Eugene England, who had upset Joseph Fielding McConkie a year earlier with his paper about the eternal progression of God, wrote Apostle McConkie on September 1, 1980, and asked for some clarification concerning the bold statements in McConkie's speech that had essentially condemned England's views as heresy number one. England mentioned that Joseph McConkie had taken offense at England's BYU speech the previous fall and responded to it negatively. "I was surprised to learn from that response that he considered me out of harmony with the teachings of Hyrum Smith, Joseph Fielding Smith, and yourself." England stressed that he did not want to teach falsehoods, but he knew that the teachings he advocated had been taught by earlier church leaders. Still, he admitted that "I could certainly be wrong," and that he might be misinterpreting those leaders. England had written a new paper where he considered both points of view and tried to harmonize and explain them to demonstrate that leaders on both sides of the issue on the meaning of eternal progression might be right, rather than contradictory. England included a copy of this paper, "The Perfection and Progression of God: Two Spheres of Existence and Two Modes of Discourse" with his letter. He also sent it to apostles Boyd K. Packer and David B. Haight, and to McConkie's son and England's nemesis, Joseph McConkie.[22]

When McConkie received the letter, he had already become aware of England's paper, most certainly through Joseph, and did not read either but put them in a desk drawer, where they sat for the next several months. In the meantime, in January 1981, England began a six-month appointment in London as associate director of

---

21. Horne, *Bruce R. McConkie*, 110–11; Dew, "Family Portrait," 58; McConkie, *Reflections*, 315. For the photograph and article, see Gerry Avant, "1980 Is Big Year for Fitness," *Church News*, Jan. 12, 1980, 6–8.

22. Eugene England to Bruce R. McConkie, Sep. 1, 1980; Eugene England, "The Perfection and Progression of God: Two Spheres of Existence and Two modes of Discourse," both in *Doctrinal Differences*, 57–78.

BYU's study abroad program there.[23] This was not the end of the story, however, and when McConkie revisited England's letter later in the winter, a volcano began bubbling. By the time Eugene England had returned from London, that volcano had erupted.

As England attended to business overseas, McConkie continued his duties at home and wherever his assignments took him. *The Mortal Messiah Book 3* was going to press and was set for a late November release when he spoke at a temple meeting of the Quorum of the Twelve on September 28. This moment had a profound impact on his colleagues. Despite having recently upset some of the brethren and many church members with his BYU fireside talk and his habit of presenting his personal views as church doctrine, the brethren still looked up to him and admired his vast knowledge of the gospel and the scriptures, which indicates that their differences created little if any lasting animosity. Two decades earlier Mark E. Petersen scoured the first edition of *Mormon Doctrine*, found numerous errors, and wanted church members to avoid the book. Now before BYU's student body he had nothing but praise for the things McConkie taught the apostles earlier that morning. "Brother Bruce R. McConkie spoke at length about the tremendous suffering that the Savior went through. He did it in a very touching way and with great solemnity." McConkie told them that while in Gethsemane, "the Savior was not kneeling in that prayer. The suffering that he endured was so infinite, so much beyond our understanding, that even he fell prostrate upon the ground." These teaching moments were uniting, not divisive, and represented McConkie at his best.[24]

In early October McConkie had the opportunity to travel to Rexburg, Idaho, and dedicate a thirteen-year-old building on the Ricks College campus known all that time simply as the Classroom Office Building, or COB, and dedicated it with a new name, the Joseph Fielding Smith Building—fitting, because it then housed the religion department. While speaking at the ceremony McConkie called Smith "the leading gospel scholar and the greatest doctrinal teacher

23. England, "A Professor and an Apostle Correspond"; Bruce R. McConkie to Eugene England, Feb. 19, 1981, both in *Doctrinal Differences*, 6, 79.

24. Mark E. Petersen, transcript of talk given at BYU Fourteen-Stake Fireside, Sep. 28, 1980, copy courtesy of Smith–Pettit Foundation.

of this generation." When he spoke at the church's general conference a few days later, his talk and other news at the conference were picked up by the Associated Press and thus made national headlines. The presence of fifty picketers against the church's stand on the Equal Rights Amendment (ERA) prompted the article. The ERA was fast approaching its June deadline for ratification, being three states short of becoming part of the Constitution. Three women who attended the conference voted against sustaining Spencer W. Kimball as prophet, seer, and revelator of the church, an extremely rare occurrence during the proceedings. McConkie received attention in some of these articles when he issued a warning that "immorality, abortions and homosexual abominations are fast becoming the norm of life among the wicked and ungodly."[25]

In January 1981 McConkie decided to finally read the paper England sent him on the progression of God. He was not happy with it but remained determined not to respond. But soon he began hearing reports that England was teaching the concepts brought out in the paper and so the apostle drafted a nine-page blistering rebuke to England on February 19.

"This may well be the most important letter you have or will receive," McConkie began. He explained his reasons for ignoring it for the last five months and why he now chose to answer. "Over the months various hearsay reports have come to me indicating that you are presenting and championing the views you sent to me." Thus, McConkie felt compelled to respond. "I shall write in kindness and in plainness and perhaps with sharpness. I want you to know that I am extending to you the hand of fellowship though I hold over you at the same time, the scepter of judgment." McConkie assured England that his door was always open to him should England feel the need to talk further.

McConkie spent over two pages directly quoting from "The Seven Deadly Heresies" denouncing the idea that God still progresses in knowledge, since that was the focus of England's paper. He also

25. "Ricks Building Dedicated," *South Idaho Press* (Burley), Oct. 5, 1980, 3; "ERA Backers Vote Against LDS Leaders," *Salt Lake Tribune*, Oct 5, 1980, 3A; for an example of the national coverage the conference received, see "Equal Rights Amendment: Demonstrators Greet Mormons at Church's Semiannual Meeting," *Central New Jersey Home News* (New Brunswick), Oct. 6, 1980, 4.

quoted heavily from his own October 1980 conference talk, and less so from a BYU devotional speech he gave just two days earlier—all to drive home his point that God is all powerful and does not continue to progress in the way England believed. Then he made some admissions that gave the letter significant interest to critics of the church. After praising Brigham Young for his leadership and prophetic teachings "in general," he said: "Yes, President Young did teach that Adam was the father of our spirits, and all the related things that the cultists ascribe to him. This, however, is not true. He expressed views that are out of harmony with the gospel." He also conceded that Young taught that God still progresses in knowledge. But McConkie insisted that at other times Young taught correctly about Adam and eternal progression. "The issue is, which Brigham Young shall we believe and the answer is: We will take the one whose statements accord with what God has revealed in the Standard Works."

But all of this was prelude to some specific counsel McConkie had for England. "If it is true, as I am advised, that you speak on this subject of the progression of God at firesides and elsewhere, you should cease to do so. If you give other people copies of the material you sent me, with the quotations it contains, you should cease to do so." It was not left to England or anyone but leaders of the church to establish the truth. "It is my province to teach to the Church what the doctrine is. It is your province to echo what I say or to remain silent. You do not have a divine commission to correct me or any of the Brethren.... If I lead the Church astray, that is my responsibility, but the fact still remains that I am the one appointed with all the rest involved so to do." There were eternal consequences for the teachings people promote. "If I err, that is my problem; but in your case if you single out some of these things and make them the center of your philosophy, and end up being wrong, you will lose your soul."

Before closing his letter, McConkie took a jab at England that served no purpose other than to embarrass him. "Perhaps I should tell you what one of the very astute and alert General Authorities said to me when I chanced to mention to him the subject of your letter to me. He said: 'Oh dear, haven't we rescued him enough times already.'"[26]

---

26. McConkie to England, Feb. 19, 1981, in *Doctrinal Differences*, 79–87.

McConkie sent the letter to the same three individuals England had sent his: Packer, Haight, and Joseph Fielding McConkie. The copy sent to England went to his office at BYU in Provo. He would be in London for another five months and would not see the letter until it was finally forwarded to him overseas. It was accidentally sent by boat and took three months to arrive, thus England did not get it until May. But a copy, likely the one sent to Joseph McConkie, began circulating at BYU within days after it was written. A friend of England's phoned him in London to ask if it was authentic, but at this point, England knew nothing about it.[27]

When England finally read the letter, he was devastated. He immediately wrote McConkie on May 25 and explained the cause of his late response. He also defended himself against some of McConkie's accusations, insisting that he did not speak on the subject at firesides or anywhere else. Still, he promised to abide by McConkie's counsel and not share his paper with anyone. "Contrary to the hearsay reports you refer to, the subject is not a 'hobby' of mine, I have never actively 'championed' a special position on it, and I am perfectly willing to follow the directions you have given me." He assured McConkie that he had never felt a need to correct the views of church authorities or had a rebellious spirit. His service and sacrifices for the church, he believed, should have already made that clear. "Why, after all this I should continue to be perceived as antagonistic or rebellious, as one who in the words of your colleague, needs to be 'rescued' I must confess is extremely painful and difficult to understand."[28]

Later that fall, McConkie and England spoke over the phone. England never shared the details of that call, but in a follow-up letter he noted that in that conversation, "I felt your warmth and concern and appreciate them very much." England still wanted to talk in person and told McConkie he would set up an appointment with the apostle's secretary. It is not clear if that meeting took place.

A year later England wrote McConkie again, this time because

---

27. Eugene England to Bruce R. McConkie, May 25, 1981; Eugene England to Bruce R. McConkie, Oct. 29, 1982, both in *Doctrinal Differences*, 89, 93; England, "On Spectral Evidence," 146.

28. England to McConkie, May 25, 1981, 89–90.

he had learned that a full copy of his letter had been reproduced by Jerald and Sandra Tanner through their anti-Mormon ministry and was being sold by them. "I have not released my copy to anyone at any time and have made certain it was secure so that no copies could be made. If I had had any way to know in advance of the Tanners' plans I would have exercised my legal rights to stop them, but of course any efforts now would merely be used by them to stimulate interest and sales." He told McConkie that a copy of the letter had been seen on BYU's campus just a few days after it was written. It's unkown if McConkie talked to his son about any breach of confidence. Copies of the letter that the Tanners had for sale had been stamped with the words, "DO NOT REPRODUCE."[29]

This episode says far more about McConkie than it does England, and the apostle's stance against England's paper is puzzling. England was trying to harmonize what seemed to be conflicting ideas from the presiding brethren, just as McConkie had counseled Reed Durham to do back in 1964 when his students were confronted with differing views among leaders. The only time the church had officially taken a stand on the eternal progression of God was on August 23, 1865, when the First Presidency and Quorum of the Twelve issued a statement that denounced the idea that God did *not* continue to progress in knowledge. They have never issued a superseding statement in the years since. As to the idea of progressing from kingdom to kingdom in the next life, the First Presidency wrote a mission president in 1969 that, "For your information we may say that the Church has never announced a definite doctrine on this point." The presidency acknowledged that some church leaders believed that it was possible, while others did not. "But," they repeated, "the Church has never announced a definite doctrine on this point." Although McConkie believed that official statements only cloud and confuse the issue, the burden is still on the church to explain those contradictory teachings, not discipline members who take them seriously. England understood this well. Four years after McConkie's death, believing it was wrong to follow "a single Brother

---

29. England to McConkie, Oct. 29, 1982, 93. The Tanners' publication was called *LDS Apostle Confesses that Brigham Young Taught Adam-God Doctrine* (Salt Lake City: Modern Microfilm Company, 1982).

rather than the Brethren in so important a matter," England published the paper the apostle had so strongly denounced, and did so in *BYU Studies*.[30] How Joseph Fielding McConkie felt when he saw it in print can only be imagined.

The summer and fall of 1981 had McConkie occupied with many other things besides the England matter and any remaining fallout from his "Seven Deadly Heresies" talk. Mid-June saw the release of *The Mortal Messiah Book 4*, leaving McConkie one final volume on Christ's Second Coming to complete this series. As happy as he must have been to see another book from his hand come forth, he simultaneously mourned the death of his long-time friend S. Dilworth Young on July 9 from congestive heart failure. Young's death was a shock, as he and his wife had just returned five days earlier from a two-year assignment as director of the Los Angeles Temple visitor's center. Young and McConkie had served in the First Quorum of Seventy together for twenty-six years and had been known to play pranks and practical jokes on one another throughout their association. McConkie spoke at Young's funeral on July 11.[31]

That fall, as the church geared up for its semi-annual general conference, the work of the decade-long Scriptures Publication Committee culminated in a new edition of the Book of Mormon, Doctrine and Covenants, and Pearl of Great Price. As he did with the Bible, McConkie wrote the chapter and section headings for these three books and composed the introductory material. There were changes and corrections to several verses throughout all three books of scripture, with cross references to each other and the new edition of the Bible. When published together, the three formed what is called the "triple combination," and its new index was now 416 pages. There were also new maps of early church historic sites. The two revelations that McConkie had touted for canonization that were added to the Pearl of Great Price in 1976 were moved to

30. England, "On Spectral Evidence," 146; David O. McKay, Hugh B. Brown, and N. Eldon Tanner to Wilford W. Kimball, Oct. 2, 1969, copy courtesy of the Smith–Pettit Foundation. For England's published paper on the progression of God, see "Perfection and Progression: Two Complimentary Ways to Talk About God," *BYU Studies* 29, no. 2 (Summer 1989): 31–47.

31. "Memorial Rite Set for S. D. Young," *Salt Lake Tribune*, July 11, 1981, 2D; "Elder S. Dilworth Young Dies," *Ensign*, Sep. 1981, 73–74.

the Doctrine and Covenants as sections 137 and 138. Excerpts from speeches of Wilford Woodruff were also added below the text of his 1890 Manifesto announcing the end of plural marriage in what was now designated "Official Declaration—1." The newly added "Official Declaration—2" contained the First Presidency letter dated June 8, 1978, announcing the revelation on priesthood.[32]

Besides some textual corrections, other changes in the Pearl of Great Price were minor. A new "Introductory Note" gave background to the volume, and the title to the opening book, the "Book of Moses," was changed to "Selections from the Book of Moses." The Joseph Smith material was altered as well with the new titles "Joseph Smith—Matthew," and "Joseph Smith—History."

Had McConkie had his way, the Pearl of Great Price would have been changed significantly. In 1980 he finished the creation of a ninety-one-page version of that book and submitted it to the First Presidency. He even had it typeset to mirror the Bible and the pending editions of the other standard works being done at Cambridge. It included a page giving it a 1980 copyright under the name of Spencer W. Kimball, trustee-in-trust for the church. All of this indicated that McConkie was confident that his Pearl of Great Price would be accepted by his colleagues with enthusiasm. The only thing his version did not include at this point, because it was simply a draft submitted for approval, were the cross-references to the other standard works.

In all, McConkie made thirty-three additions to the book, starting with expanding the "Selections from the Book of Moses" from eight chapters to thirteen. Other new material was called "Selections from the Psalms as Revealed to Joseph Smith," which totaled four chapters, and "Selections from the Gospels as Revealed to Joseph Smith," which contained ten chapters. Both books were made up of portions of the Joseph Smith Translation of the Bible. McConkie added several verses to Joseph Smith's History and even included Smith's "Wentworth Letter" as its own book, dividing it into three chapters with eighty-one verses. Written in 1842 to *Chicago Democrat*

32. "Triple Combination Completes New Standard Works," *Daily Spectrum* (St. George, UT), Church Life section, Oct. 2, 1981, 2; Bruce T. Harper, "The Church Publishes a New Triple Combination," *Ensign*, Oct. 1981, 8–17; Robert J. Matthews, "The New Publications of the Standard Works—1979, 1981," *BYU Studies* 22, no. 4 (Fall 1982): 393–417.

editor John Wentworth, the letter explained some of the history and doctrine of the church. McConkie added two additional articles to what had been the thirteen Articles of Faith, and proposed re-canonizing the Lectures on Faith, which had been removed from the Doctrine and Covenants in 1921. McConkie had long championed and quoted from these lectures. The Fifth Lecture, to him, was "the most comprehensive, intelligent, inspired utterance that now exists in the English language—that exists in one place defining, interpreting, expounding, announcing, and testifying what kind of being God is," he noted elsewhere. "It was written by the power of the Holy Ghost, by the spirit of inspiration. It is, in effect, eternal scripture; it is true."[33]

It is not clear why the First Presidency and Quorum of the Twelve did not accept McConkie's expanded Pearl of Great Price, but some sources say that it was simply too much all at once, and that he was too "forward" in his effort to replace the already canonized version. Had he approached the matter differently, some of his changes may have been adopted. Apostle Thomas S. Monson, who chaired the committee, was said to have joked that, "If we included everything in the scriptures that Elder McConkie wanted we would need a pickup truck to carry our scriptures to Church." Whatever internal discussions came out of McConkie's proposed Pearl of Great Price, they remained, for the most part, private. Many of the additions Mc-Conkie hoped for were included among the extracts from the Joseph Smith Translation included in the new Bible but remained apart from the actual scriptural text.[34]

On October 31, 1981, McConkie spoke at a leadership conference at BYU to bishops and stake presidents, and his talk generated widespread discussion, but not for the usual reasons. In this case, his remarks, titled, "Balancing the Saints," delivered a message of moderation for students and to a degree, the general church membership. Much of it was welcome, while parts of it were confusing. He reportedly spoke in a casual manner without notes and took questions throughout the talk. He urged students to become well-rounded and

33. *The Pearl of Great Price: A Reproduction of Elder Bruce R. McConkie's 1980 Proposed Revision of The Pearl of Great Price* (N.p.: privately published, nd); McConkie, *Reflections*, 392.

34. Kent P. Jackson to Devery S. Anderson, May 31, 2023; "Foreword," *McConkie's 1980 Proposed Revision*, iii; McConkie, "Special Witness," 200–1.

find a balance between their spiritual and intellectual needs, and to keep the pendulum from swinging too far in either direction.

McConkie urged his listeners to steer clear of extremism and to discourage it among students. He warned against "religious fads" and even admonished leaders to understand if a student is too busy to accept a church calling. In that regard he cited his own experience as a law student when his stake president, Marion G. Romney, released him as a stake missionary due to the intensity of his studies. Along those lines, he said students should not be discouraged to do homework on Sunday if they need to. Extremism in sabbath observance, he said, was a sign of apostasy.

He also denounced several practices that he believed were faddish as well as extreme, such as asking for "special blessings" outside of patriarchal blessings, administrations for the sick, or father's blessings. He believed this led people to an unnecessary reliance on others and that such practices caused them to expect divine intervention in small matters. He discouraged young people from praying on dates, which he said leads to a relationship that should exist only between married people. He even encouraged people to rely on their own good judgment when seeking a spouse and not to depend on revelation in making their decision.

The Second Coming, he believed, would not occur in the lifetime of anyone currently living; the Lord measured time differently than we do. "The Second Coming will not be in my lifetime or in the lifetime of my children, and I doubt that it will be in the lifetime of my children's children." He said one fad going around the church was seeking a special, "personal relationship with Christ," which he believed was inappropriate. Worship, he stressed, should be reserved for God the Father.

He also said that bishops should not go on a "witch hunt" when conducting worthiness interviews, and reminded the ecclesiastical leaders present that only certain sins need be confessed to priesthood authority. Even then, he noted, time and church service can wipe out some serious, "ancient sins," that had gone unconfessed.[35]

Much of this was surely welcome news. But what did McConkie

---

35. "McConkie Counsels Moderation," *Sunstone*, Nov./Dec. 1981, 59; McConkie, *Reflections*, 292.

mean when he said that church members should avoid seeking a personal relationship with Christ? Such a relationship seemed to be a basic teaching in Mormonism, and now many listeners were hearing otherwise, perhaps for the first time. It turns out that this passing denunciation at this meeting was just the beginning.

Four months after delivering this October talk, McConkie returned to BYU on March 2, 1982, as its Tuesday devotional speaker. His address was titled "Our Relationship with the Lord." He told his audience that "it is no secret that many false and vain and foolish things are being taught in the sectarian world and even among us about our need to gain a special relationship with the Lord Jesus," he said. "I shall summarize the true doctrine in this field and invite erring teachers and beguiled students to repent and believe the accepted gospel verities as I shall set them forth." After laying out and discussing in seventeen specific points what he declared to be the correct mode of worship and a true understanding of the Godhead, he returned to his teaching from the "Seven Deadly Heresies" and insisted that those who believe God still progresses in knowledge, "unless they repent, will live and die weak in the faith and will fall short of inheriting what might have been theirs in eternity."

Much of what he said emphasized that worship is reserved for God the Father only, and that scriptures that teach about worshiping Christ "are speaking in an entirely different sense—the sense of standing in awe and being reverentially grateful to Him who has redeemed us." No member of the Godhead, he stressed, should be singled out for one's sole attention. From there he fully denounced the idea of seeking a personal relationship with Christ and called it inappropriate, a "gospel hobby," and noted that some take it to an extreme and offer "endless, sometimes day-long prayers" to achieve this goal. He quoted unfavorably from a popular Latter-day Saint source to make a point that prayers go directly to God the Father and not through Jesus. "In this connection a current and unwise book, which advocates gaining a special relationship with Jesus, contains this sentence—quote: 'Because the Savior is our mediator, our prayers go through Christ to the Father, and the Father answers our prayers through his son.' Unquote. This is plain sectarian nonsense."[36]

---

36. Bruce R. McConkie, "Our Relationship with the Lord," *Brigham Young University*

The book in question was *What It Means to Know Christ*, written by George W. Pace, a popular BYU religion professor who had been teaching there since 1967 and in 1978 began serving as president of the BYU tenth stake, a position he held until January 1982, three months before McConkie gave this talk to the student body.[37] The book had been released the previous year and fallout from McConkie's speech began immediately. Was what he said universally accepted by the brethren as he claimed? And why call out Pace publicly instead of offering a private rebuke, as McConkie himself had received on occasion, such as when he tried to publish *Sound Doctrine* in 1955 or after the release of *Mormon Doctrine* a few years later? Was Pace's short tenure as a stake president prompted by his teachings?

The next day, BYU's newspaper *The Daily Universe* ran a story about the talk and reached out to Pace, who confirmed that McConkie's quote was accurate and came from Pace's book. He then tried to present himself as unaffected by the criticism. "I think Elder McConkie gave a great talk," he told the paper. "I sustain the Brethren all the way."[38]

Elder Marion D. Hanks, however, believed McConkie was wrong to preach that Latter-day Saints do not worship Christ and thus took exception to the talk for that reason, not to mention the fact that the apostle publicly embarrassed Pace, which Hanks found upsetting and unnecessary. But any criticisms Hanks had were all said privately. Perhaps the most significant response to the address from a faithful Mormon came from forty-one-year-old T. Allen Lambert of Ithaca, New York, who published a letter in the unofficial BYU newspaper, *Seventh East Press* on May 17 addressing the "considerable confusion and consternation exhibited over" McConkie's speech. Lambert noted frankly that McConkie contradicted statements of other general authorities, not to mention McConkie himself. Lambert notes that in *The Promised Messiah*, McConkie taught that "righteous persons do have a close, personal relationship with their Savior" and that answers to prayers "come

---

1981–82 Fireside and Devotional Speeches (Provo: University Publications Division of University Relations, 1982), 102. The quote McConkie read comes from George W. Pace, *What It Means to Know Christ* (Provo: Council Press, 1981), 29.

37. "Three BYU Stakes Obtain New Leaders," *Daily Herald*, Jan. 17, 1982, 39.

38. "Balance Stressed in Talk," *Daily Universe*, Mar. 3, 1982, 1.

from the son," who "pleads our cause. He is our Mediator and Intercessor." Lambert asks, "Now, when someone pleads my cause, does he not take my message? How can a mediator mediate without carrying messages back and forth?" Lambert notes that other general authorities, such as James E. Faust, said something similar. Faust asked during the church's October 1976 general conference, "Is not the greatest need in all the world for every person to have a personal, ongoing, daily, continuing relationship with the Savior?" Elder H. Burke Peterson taught the same thing, encouraging members in October 1981 to "develop *your* personal relationship with the Savior."[39]

Lambert had already gone so far as to write McConkie a letter asking about the April 11 Relief Society lesson titled "Developing a Relationship with the Savior," which quoted both Brigham Young and Marion G. Romney to back up this idea. McConkie wrote back saying that, "It is obviously unfortunate that the Relief Society lesson has the perspective that it does. This will not happen again."[40]

Pace had long taught and talked about the ideas he promoted in his book and did so at the church's Know Your Religion conferences and elsewhere. Despite what he said publicly to downplay the matter, Pace was embarrassed and upset by McConkie's criticism made before the entire student body and faculty. Still, he kept up the charade. He soon approved a five-paragraph statement in support of McConkie written by his former stake presidency counselor Edward L. Kimball. "I sincerely desire to be in total harmony with the Church's teachings and take this means to correct a statement in the book and to clarify what is said there about our proper relationship with the Savior." After addressing the wording in his book that McConkie had publicly denounced, he expressed regret if his teachings on intense prayer "has led people to excess." He concluded by saying, "I mean to stay in the mainstream of the Church, urging any with whom I have influence to listen to the words of our leaders." Pace also had this statement placed as an insert in the copies of his book still available for purchase.[41]

---

39. Hanks author interview, June 13, 2023; T. Allen Lambert, "Developing a Personal Relationship," letter to the editor, *Seventh East Press*, May 17, 1982, 9, 13.

40. Lambert, "Developing a Personal Relationship," 13.

41. George W. Pace statement, copy courtesy of the Smith-Pettit Foundation; David G. Pace, interview with the author, Apr. 15, 2023.

Lengthy excerpts from McConkie's talk were published in the *Church News* on March 20, which now gave it a church-wide audience. The quote from Pace's book remained intact in this article, causing Pace even further embarrassment.[42] When McConkie gave his "Balancing the Saints" talk back on October 31, Pace, was sitting on the stand along with other presidents of campus stakes, unaware that McConkie was about to launch into a discourse where the concepts that Pace and countless others so deeply believed would be called out as wrong. Even though McConkie did not reference Pace's book in that talk, Pace was still hurt. When son David Pace called home from the mission field on Thanksgiving, his father cried when he told him about what had happened. When David called home again after the second talk, the elder Pace did not cry but, as David put it, his father "spoke soberly, numbly." For the next few years family gatherings routinely devolved into discussions about what they called "the incident," or "the McConkie affair," with unsettled resentment and confusion still felt by all. By the time David Pace returned from the mission field and another sibling was about to enter, David described his parents as "living corpses," his mother battling illness and his father losing weight.[43]

Pace advocated in his book that people should pray at length as Book of Mormon prophet Enos did and to do it out loud. In time David had become embarrassed by his father's zeal, and at least once, in 1979, a parent of one of his students complained about a question Pace placed on a test asking students to check what was more important, developing a personal relationship with Christ or God the Father. That complaint let to a talking to by religion chair Larry C. Porter.[44] But if the presiding brethren viewed Pace as a problem, this

42. Bruce R. McConkie, "What is Our Relationship to Members of the Godhead?" *Church News*, Mar. 20, 1982, 5.

43. David G. Pace, "McConkie and Dad: Memories, Dreams, and a Rejection. A Personal Essay," and Lavina Fielding Anderson, "Context and Analysis: 'You Have Heard True Doctrine Taught': Elder Bruce R. McConkie's 1981–1982 Addresses," both in *Case Reports of the Mormon Alliance* 2 (1996): 74–76, 78, 79, 81.

44. Handwritten notes by Gary James Bergera taken from Administration Council Meeting, Religious Instruction, Minutes, Nov. 1, 1979, University Archives 553, box 2, fd. 9. These notes courtesy of Smith–Pettit Foundation; Gary James Bergera and Ronald Priddis, *Brigham Young University: A House of Faith* (Salt Lake City: Signature Books, 1985), 72.

was news to him. He had never been warned or talked to by any of them about his teachings as far as is known.

This seems clear by the reactions of some within church leadership, in addition to Hanks, to McConkie's rebuke. Around June 1982 an LDS bishop in California had the opportunity to ask a visiting general authority about McConkie's talk, and before the bishop could finish asking his question, the general authority stopped him. "I'm familiar with this incident you mention," he said. "In my opinion, that was a very unfortunate and unchristian thing to do. There was no call to do anything like that. And if what that teacher is saying is wrong, then the whole Book of Mormon is wrong." Pace heard from general authorities directly who told him they were bewildered by McConkie's actions.[45]

Four and a half months after McConkie delivered this devotional address, William O. Nelson of Church Correlation called Pace to comfort him and to let him know that McConkie had been talked to about the matter by his superiors. "I just wanted to call you and let you know, assure you, that the brethren love you, and to tell you that *your chastiser has been chastised*."[46]

As helpful as these words may have been, Pace still had to deal with the fact that his credibility had been damaged and as a result, student enrollment in his classes soon dropped to around 50 percent of what it had been. Rumors spread that he had been disciplined and even excommunicated from the LDS Church because of the doctrines he had taught that led to McConkie's public condemnation.[47]

Shortly after this very public scene played out, McConkie released *The Millennial Messiah: The Second Coming of the Son of Man*, which was advertised in papers beginning in mid-March 1982.[48] This completed the six-volume series, which now totaled over 3,200 pages. The books were published over a four-year period and the project was a monumental achievement. Pace's son David believes that the debacle between his father and McConkie came about in

45. Anderson, "Context and Analysis," 92–93; Pace, "McConkie and Dad," 76.

46. This note, dated July 21, 1982, was written by an unnamed person who learned the details from David Whittaker, then university archivist at BYU's Harold B. Lee Library. This note courtesy of the Smith–Pettit Foundation.

47. Pace, "McConkie and Dad," 75; Pace, author interview.

48. Ad for the *Millennial Messiah: The Second Coming of the Son of Man* (Salt Lake City: Deseret Book, 1982), in *Southern Utah News* (Kanab, UT), Mar. 18, 1982, 9.

part because McConkie feared that others writing on Christ at that moment might steal his thunder.[49]

Little did McConkie realize, but the following month after speaking at BYU and calling out George Pace, McConkie was about to be called out for things he had recently said, although he enjoyed the luxury of privacy and diplomacy in the matter. Once again, it involved how he had represented the facts of the June 1, 1978, priesthood revelation—not in any off the cuff moments like he had done when speaking at home four years earlier, but this time for what he said in print. And a few unlikely individuals were involved in handling it.

In the fall of 1981, around the time the new triple combination was released, Deseret Book had published a collection of essays by general authorities called *Priesthood*. McConkie included a revised version of his 1981 talk "All Are Alike unto God" under the title "The New Revelation on Priesthood."

In this published essay McConkie said that all of the brethren present in the temple that day heard "the voice of God" during Kimball's prayer and that the prophet "heard the voice and we heard the same voice." Kimball had been in declining health since undergoing surgeries to remove fluid from his brain just a few months earlier, and in the spring of 1982, he listened as his wife Camilla read the essay to him. When his son Edward came to their apartment on April 25, he found his father upset that McConkie had characterized the experience that way and said that "Brother McConkie should have cleared what he wrote about the circumstances of the revelation before publishing it." President Kimball asked Ed to speak with McConkie and instruct him to change the wording for the book's next printing so as to correct the impression that the brethren heard an actual voice.[50]

On May 10 Spencer Kimball had the essay read to him again, this time by his nurse. The church president got upset all over again, declaring it "bunk," and insisting, "That didn't happen."[51]

---

49. Pace, author interview.

50. Ad for Priesthood, *Daily Spectrum* (St. George, UT), Oct. 2, 1981, 12; Harris, *Second-Class Saints*, 253–54; Kimball diary, Apr. 25, 1982, copy in author's possession; For Kimball's health issues prior to his reading the McConkie essay, see Kimball, *Lengthen Your Stride*, 581–608. The quoted portion of the essay is in Bruce R. McConkie, "The New Revelation on Priesthood," in *Priesthood* (Salt Lake City: Deseret Book, 1981), 128.

51. Harris, *Second-Class Saints*, 253; Kimball diary, May 10, 1982.

Ed Kimball met with McConkie two days later. The younger Kimball found his assigned task uncomfortable and awkward, but he carried it out, nevertheless. They met at 4:00 p.m. at McConkie's office at the Church Administration Building and were joined by First Presidency secretary Francis L. Gibbons who took notes at the presidency's request. Ed Kimball explained to the apostle the purpose of the meeting and how President Kimball felt about the phrasing that all of the brethren "heard the same voice."

McConkie defended his choice of words and told Ed Kimball that he did not think that any readers "could reasonably interpret what he had written as asserting that the Presidency and the Twelve had heard an audible voice because he made clear that it was the power of the Spirit that impressed the assembled men." Besides, he was direct that no heavenly messenger appeared and thus he was trying to keep from exaggerating what happened. But Ed Kimball pointed out that this still did not address the fact that the First Presidency and apostles had not heard an audible voice as part of the revelation. McConkie agreed to revise his wording in future printings of the book but never did. President Kimball's health continued to decline and soon he was no longer able to monitor McConkie's words or anyone else's.[52]

Ed Kimball, who was writing a book about his father's tenure as church president, had previously sent a draft of the chapter concerning the 1978 priesthood revelation to Gibbons. Unbeknown to Ed, Gibbons had sent it to McConkie, and the apostle had it with him during their interview. Ed was relieved that McConkie never brought up any of the criticisms he had written about McConkie years earlier "exaggerating" what had occurred during the revelation. He did, however, give Ed some unsolicited advice about other parts of the chapter, saying "that much of what I had written was unwise divulgence of details." McConkie advised Kimball to allow the First Presidency to look over the manuscript and receive their approval before he published it. Kimball responded that his father had willingly "provided the information, read my account, and asked me to publish it."

---

52. Harris, *Second-Class Saints*, 254; Kimball diary, May 12, 1982.

McConkie urged him to delete references to the brethren gathering in a "prayer circle," but McConkie, in his own account of the revelation, had mentioned publicly that the presidency and apostles prayed around the altar in the temple, which to Kimball was no less revealing. Besides, articles on prayer circles had earlier been published in LDS literature.

The apostle also took issue with Kimball referencing his father's many prayers in the temple prior to receiving the revelation and did not like that Ed wrote in his manuscript that a temple worker stood "guard" over the room to assure privacy while President Kimball was praying. McConkie had a few other suggestions, but Kimball was relieved that McConkie never pointed out any actual errors in the manuscript.[53]

It had been nearly a decade since McConkie had been called to the Quorum of the Twelve, and it had been a productive time in terms of expanding his influence through writing, speaking, and helping shape the direction of the church, its scriptures, and its policies. He had no reason to believe it would not continue for at least another two decades. But before long he began facing, for the first time, real challenges that would alter those plans significantly.

---

53. Kimball diary, May 12, 1982. Kimball's book was eventually published as Edward L. Kimball, *Lengthen Your Stride: The Presidency of Spencer W. Kimball* (Salt Lake City: Deseret Book, 2005). The *Working Draft* referenced in this book is the full, lengthier manuscript published in a limited edition by Benchmark Books in 2009.

CHAPTER TEN

THE FINAL YEARS
1982-1985

When McConkie spoke at the church's April 1982 general conference, things had seemingly settled down in the month since his
latest controversial BYU talk. His conference address centered on
the "doctrine of the priesthood," which he defined as belief in the
correct attributes of God and understanding "that priesthood is the
very name of the power of God, and that if we are to become like
him, we must receive and exercise his priesthood or power as he exercises it." The priesthood is with those who are authorized to use it,
and through that power humankind can enter into eternal marriage
and live in the family unit, as does God. That doctrine means that
through faith temporal and spiritual matters can be governed and
controlled, miracles can occur, and we can "stand in the presence of
God and be like him because we have gained his faith, his perfections, and his power, or in other words the fulness of his priesthood."[1]

McConkie's penchant for teaching straight doctrine over the
pulpit had never waned in his thirty-six years in the church hierarchy. Among his papers are several undelivered talks he prepared
or partially prepared whenever a subject seemed to come to him.
Several unfinished book manuscripts also exist. McConkie's enthusiasm for his subjects is clear but his mind sometimes seemed to
work faster than his ability to capture his thoughts in writing. He
often jotted down things that came to him on whatever he could
find. He kept pens stashed everywhere around the house for that

---

1. *Official Report of the One Hundred Fifty-Second Annual Conference of the Church of
Jesus Christ of Latter-day Saints, Held in the Tabernacle, Salt Lake City, Utah, April 3 and
4, 1982* (Salt Lake City: The Church of Jesus Christ of Latter-day Saints, 1982), 47–50.

purpose. All of this indicates a consistent desire to write, preach, and educate. The many projects he did finish, however, generally required few revisions.[2]

A few months after general conference, on August 13, McConkie traveled to Sydney, Australia, to preside at and participate in the groundbreaking ceremonies of the church's first temple on that continent. It was an important moment for him to witness eighteen years after he had completed his three-year service as president in the Southern Australia Mission. He oversaw tremendous growth there between 1961 and 1964, and the new 12,500 square-foot building would be a tangible symbol of the continued progress made within the church in the years since.[3]

McConkie, Apostles Thomas S. Monson and Boyd K. Packer, and the others who served on the Scriptures Publication Committee received a surprise in October when the church was honored with an award from the Laymen's National Bible Committee for "outstanding service to the Bible Cause." In recognizing the LDS Church's 1979 edition of the King James Bible, Max Chopnick, a New York attorney and vice president of the committee, called the new Bible an "exemplary product" and predicted it would create greater interest in the scripture and would sell copies numbered in the millions.[4]

Around this time, with no children left at home, Bruce and Amelia moved from their home of eighteen years on Dorchester Drive and into a condominium closer to Bruce's office. Things looked bright for their future as empty nesters and Bruce's continued role at church headquarters. He also had more books in progress or in planning stages. He had no reason to contemplate his own mortality as he spoke in Parowan, Utah, on Sunday, March 13, 1983, but he was thinking about the incapacitation of the current church president,

2. Many of these incomplete sermons and book ideas, along with published and unpublished talks, were placed online in 2017, without the authorization of the LDS Church or the McConkie family, by MormonLeaks, now called Truth and Transparency, and are available at mormonleaks.io; Joseph Fielding McConkie, *The Bruce R. McConkie Story: Reflections of a Son* (Salt Lake City: Deseret Book, 2003), 276.

3. "LDS Announce Groundbreaking Set for Sydney Temple," *Salt Lake Tribune*, Aug. 12, 1982, B4.

4. "Laymen's Committee Honors LDS for Publication of New Bible," *Salt Lake Tribune*, Oct. 16, 1982, 16A.

Spencer W. Kimball. His topic was succession in the presidency—a theme he occasionally revisited over the years.

This seemed timely as many wondered about Kimball's ability to continue in so important a role. Kimball's last talk was delivered nearly a year earlier, and he had not been seen in public since. "We do not know how long President Spencer Kimball will be with us," McConkie told the congregation. "We are not concerned as much with the individual as with the overall destiny of the church." He discussed how the keys of the church presidency are transferred to the most senior apostle when the current president dies, and even cited the story of the "transfiguration" of Brigham Young in 1846 as evidence of that. During a speech in Nauvoo, Young was said to suddenly appear and sound like Joseph Smith, who had been murdered weeks earlier. This scene has been taken as a sign that Young was to be Smith's successor, but the story, based generally on late recollections of eyewitnesses, has caused the episode to be called into question by scholars.[5]

The theme of succession continued the following month at the church's April general conference, not only with McConkie but others, as Kimball was noticeably absent from all sessions of the two-day event. "When President Kimball is called home to report the labors of an oh-so-grand and successful ministry," McConkie preached to the saints on Saturday, April 2, "the keys will pass in an instant suddenly to another apostle of the Lord's own choosing." Newspapers noted that outside the gates on Temple Square critics of the church were passing out copies of McConkie's 1981 letter to Eugene England, their purpose being to emphasize McConkie's admission that Brigham Young had taught the Adam-God Doctrine.[6]

---

5. McConkie, *Reflections*, 399; Bill Athey, "Apostle Details the Divine Plan of Succession," *Daily Spectrum* (St. George, UT), Mar. 18, 1983, 4. For examinations of the transfiguration episode, see Richard S. Van Wagoner, "The Making of a Mormon Myth: The 1844 Transfiguration of Brigham Young," *Dialogue: A Journal of Mormon Thought* 28, no. 4 (Winter 1995): 1–24; Reid L. Harper, "The Mantle of Joseph: Creation of a Mormon Miracle," *Journal of Mormon History* 22, no. 2 (Fall 1996): 35–71. For an article defending the story, see Lynne Watkins Jorgensen and *BYU Studies* Staff, "The Mantle of the Prophet Joseph Passes to Brother Brigham: A Collective Spiritual Witness," *BYU Studies* 36, no. 4 (1996–97): 125–204.

6. "Ailing Kimball Absent at Annual Mormon Meeting," *South Idaho Press* (Burley), Apr. 3, 1983, 8; Mara Callister, "Hinckley Opens LDS Conference," *Daily Herald* (Provo, UT), Apr. 3, 1983, 1.

That August McConkie underwent a complete physical examination where he was assured that he was fine. In September he and Amelia traveled to Santiago, Chile, to participate in the dedication ceremonies of the new temple there, held over a three-day period. President Gordon B. Hinckley presided over the ceremonies, assisted by Boyd K. Packer and McConkie. The services were held three times each day before a full house. Amelia and the other two wives also spoke at the ceremonies, a rare thing for women at the time.[7]

In October Amelia noticed a change in sixty-eight-year-old Bruce's appetite and that he seemed tired. He brushed off any thought that there was anything wrong and told her that "all he needed was simple food." He asked her to just include bread, milk, fruit, and cheese in his meals and that everything would be fine. She did this for a while, but she eventually became frustrated and told him so. "He finally admitted he didn't feel good," Amelia recalled. He had also been experiencing stomach pain. "I tried like the dickens to get him to the doctor, but he insisted he didn't need a doctor, just *simple food*."[8]

Finally in January 1984, she told him she was taking him to the doctor immediately. Although he fought her over it, he agreed to go after she came to his office and demanded he come with her. The doctor examined him and although he determined nothing definite, over the next few weeks he had McConkie undergo tests from specialists, all of which came back negative. They noticed something on his liver, however, and recommended he undergo surgery.[9]

During this time McConkie kept working and even spoke at a Tuesday devotional at BYU on January 10 in which he once again addressed popular "heresies" in the church, focusing this time on what he called the false teachings within Protestantism of a three-in-one God and of salvation coming by grace alone. The talk was controversial enough that three clergymen in Utah Valley spoke out against it. "McConkie shows a lack of real understanding of church

7. Sheri L. Dew, "Bruce R. McConkie: A Family Portrait," *This People*, Dec. 1985/Jan. 1986, 62; McConkie, *Reflections*, 352–53.

8. Dew, "Family Portrait," 62–63; McConkie, *Reflections*, 399.

9. Dew, "Family Portrait," 63; McConkie, *Reflections*, 399.

history," said Rev. Steven Barsuhn of both the Payson Bible Church and Nephi Bible Church. "He also shows a lack of understanding for other groups."[10]

Doctors scheduled McConkie's operation for Friday, January 20, at LDS Hospital, which the press learned about right away. The *Salt Lake Tribune* noted on the following day that he had undergone colon surgery and "was listed in serious condition, the normal post-operative condition." By Monday, LDS Church spokesman Don LeFevre announced that the apostle was in "satisfactory condition" and was "progressing very well." McConkie's surgery occurred just nine days after the death of Apostle Mark E. Petersen, putting the Quorum of the Twelve at just ten functioning members.[11]

Despite LeFevre's public comments, the actual prognosis could not have been worse. Right after the surgery McConkie's family received a devastating update. Amelia and her daughter Sara were waiting at the hospital when the doctor approached them. "I'm sorry. I do not have good news for you, and I am not speaking in terms of months." During the surgery they found cancer; it had spread so extensively that there was nothing they could do. Amelia learned later that his condition was such that death could come in a time frame of as little as two weeks, and possibly up to two months.[12]

McConkie was released from the hospital on January 27, one week after the operation. "He will continue recuperation at home" said church public relations director Jerry P. Cahill. Despite McConkie's attempt to keep his condition quiet, rumors began circulating, which forced some public confirmation of his diagnosis. His brother Oscar broke the news to the press in early February. "I saw him [Sunday] and he was feeling much, much better," he said in a story that ran on Tuesday, February 7. Still, he explained that his brother was "seriously ill" with the disease and noted that during surgery doctors took

---

10. Laura M. Janney, "McConkie Tells 'Y' Students Heresies, *Daily Herald*, Jan. 12, 1984, 21; Laura M. Janney, "Clergymen Criticize McConkie Speech," *Daily Herald*, Jan. 22, 1984, 43.

11. "LDS Church Official Undergoes Surgery," *Salt Lake Tribune*, Jan. 21, 1984, 21; "Mormon Church Aide Improving," *South Idaho Press*, Jan. 23, 1984, 3; "McConkie Mends, Hospital Notes," *Salt Lake Tribune*, Jan. 23, 1984, 24.

12. Dew, "Family Portrait," 63; McConkie, *Reflections*, 399–400.

out a cancerous portion of the bowel. In doing so they found that it had spread much farther than they had expected.[13]

Despite what doctors told him, McConkie refused to believe his condition would prove fatal. "He *never* thought he wasn't going to get better," said Amelia. "He told me time and time again that this was the Lord's test for him, and that he had enough faith in and of himself to be healed." On separate occasions President Gordon B. Hinckley and Apostle Boyd K. Packer came to the house and gave him blessings. By February 10 Cahill was reporting that McConkie was "walking and regaining strength." At around this time he began chemotherapy. "Dad has passed the first phase of the chemotherapy with relative ease," wrote Amelia to the family on February 20, explaining that the treatment gave him "slight nausea and exhaustion, but no violent reactions." The pain caused by the cancer, however, was "beyond description."[14]

When Amelia wrote this letter Bruce was already beating the odds. He had just resumed his duties at the office and soon began presiding at stake conferences, but for the most part, these assignments remained within the United States. He spoke at the church's general conference in April and gave a talk on prayer. Citing his own experience, he said that God "has permitted me to suffer pain, feel anxiety, and taste his healing power. I am profoundly grateful for the faith and prayers of many people, for heartfelt petitions that have ascended to the throne of grace on my behalf." Through prayer, he said, the Lord "reaches out his finger and touches us, so we never again are the same."[15]

As he continued to undergo chemotherapy, McConkie became stronger and, in the process, continued to prove the doctors wrong. In June he spoke to members of BYU's religion department about missionary work. At some point he began exercising again

13. "Hospital Releases Mormon Apostle," *Salt Lake Tribune*, Jan. 28, 1984; "'Widespread' Cancer Strikes Mormon Elder," *Arizona Republic*, Feb. 7, 1984, 10; "LDS Apostle Resting After Surgery," *Salt Lake Tribune*, Feb. 7, 1984, 20.

14. Dew, "Family Portrait," 63; McConkie, *Reflections*, 400–1; "Elder McConkie Recovering After Cancer Surgery," *Daily Spectrum*, Feb. 10, 1984, 24.

15. *Official Report of the One Hundred Fifty-Fourth Annual General Conference of the Church of Jesus Christ of Latter-day Saints, Held in the Tabernacle, Salt Lake City, Utah, April 7 and 8, 1984* (Salt Lake City: The Church of Jesus Christ of Latter-day Saints, 1984), 44.

and by the end of August was back up to jogging five miles at a time. Mid-August marked seven months since his surgery and he addressed students at BYU for its 109th summer commencement program, urging them to "love the Lord, keep the faith, walk in the light," and to "put first in your life the things in God's Kingdom." That same month he also spoke to personnel of the Church Educational System, delivering a talk called "The Bible, a Sealed Book." His progress was encouraging to Amelia, and his attitude was contagious, but still, she worried. "Bruce was so confident he'd be healed that when he was home I'd feel optimistic. But when he was away, it was easy to get very discouraged. All the uncertainty was so hard to deal with, though I believed as he did."[16]

Indeed, Amelia had reason to worry and perhaps that element of doubt eased the pain when Bruce's health began deteriorating again in September. Over time he began jogging less and less and finally had to stop completely, reverting to walking instead. The cancer had returned and was quickly taking its toll. He arrived home from work each night completely exhausted. The chemotherapy treatments were then directly injected into his liver, which helped briefly. He received a priesthood blessing from Apostles Packer, James E. Faust, and Dallin H. Oaks and experienced improved health. He managed to speak at general conference on Sunday, October 7, where he asked his listeners ten test questions that they must answer affirmatively to achieve salvation. At the end of the month when the presidency of the church's International Mission wrote a message to the members under its watch, they happily reported that "Elder Bruce R. McConkie seems to be as well as ever, and appears to have no ill effects from his cancer. He acknowledges that he has been healed by the prayers and faith of the Saints and the administration of the priesthood."[17]

16. Dew, "Family Portrait, 63; McConkie, *Reflections*, 402–03; "Love the Lord, Elder Tells Y. Graduates at 109th Commencement Ceremonies," *Salt Lake Tribune*, Aug. 18, 1984, 17.

17. *Official Report of the One Hundred Fifty-Fourth Semiannual General Conference of the Church of Jesus Christ of Latter-day Saints, Held in the Tabernacle, Salt Lake City, Utah, October 6 and 7, 1984* (Salt Lake City: The Church of Jesus Christ of Latter-day Saints, 1984), 101–05; Dew, "Family Portrait," 63; McConkie, *Reflections*, 402; M. Russell Ballard, Jack H. Goaslind, and John K. Carmack to Members of the International Mission, Oct. 30, 1984, Church History Library, Salt Lake City.

Indeed, McConkie had once again rebounded and remained hopeful for his future. On November 3 he spoke on "The Doctrinal Restoration," a talk sponsored by BYU's Religious Studies Center. In early December he addressed all the general authorities as they met together on the first Thursday of the month in the Salt Lake Temple. There, with the Christmas season upon them, he spoke on the birth of Christ, leaving a lasting impression on the three members of the First Quorum of Seventy who made up the International Mission Presidency. "There was no room left in those places of lodgment for strangers, called *caravanserai*, where strangers could get out of the weather and bed down for the night in a bare, open building of rough stones, surrounding an open court in which animals are tied up for the night," McConkie explained to his gathered brethren. "So, Mary and Joseph stayed in a stable with the animals, and smells and in the lowliest circumstances we can imagine for the birth of the great Messiah, the Christ."[18]

On Christmas Day, Bruce and Amelia drove to Provo, where they had dinner with their son Joseph, and Bruce spoke to the missionaries at the MTC. He intended to speak for two hours that day, and although he had been doing better, he wasn't feeling up to talking that long without a break. After speaking for an hour, he took his seat while the missionaries performed several musical numbers. Afterward he returned to the podium for another hour. His usual custom was to stand and shake hands with the missionaries before departing, but on this occasion, he simply lacked the endurance.[19]

For McConkie, 1985 opened with his brief health resurgence about to give way to the cancer he had been determined to beat. On Friday, February 8, he and Amelia traveled to Los Angeles where he, Apostle David B. Haight, and John K. Carmack of the First Quorum of Seventy were to preside that weekend at a regional conference in Santa Barbara. McConkie was so exhausted from undergoing chemotherapy earlier that day that he went straight to the hotel and to bed without having any dinner. At the conference on Saturday and Sunday he managed to speak powerfully before flying back to Salt

18. McConkie, *Reflections*, 403; M. Russell Ballard, Jack H. Goaslind, and John K. Carmack to Members of the International Mission, Dec. 1984, Church History Library.
19. McConkie, *Reflections*, 243–44.

Lake City. Many people at the airport recognized him and spoke to him while he masked the pain that plagued him.[20]

Once home McConkie managed to keep up with his duties, both at home and at church, although not as vigorously. On Friday, February 22, he performed a marriage sealing in the Salt Lake Temple for his grandson David Adams and his fiancé, Lillian Smith. That same month he took part, along with the two other apostles on the Scriptures Publication Committee, in recording a production taped at BYU's Motion Picture Studio on the new scriptures published in 1979 and 1981. McConkie, who had now served on the committee for twelve years, offered to drive to the studio himself but he told Amelia she could come if she wanted to, which she did. They got to the studio at around 11:30 that morning and it was a grueling experience. "They had him standing up, the lights were hot, and I could tell he wasn't feeling well because every time they stopped taping he'd hang onto the pulpit." She had them bring him a chair, which helped him make it through the filming, which did not wrap until 6:00 p.m. When they left, "Bruce didn't say a word to me," but "just got in the passenger side, fell instantly asleep, and I drove home. He'd have never made it alone. He was sick, but he wasn't letting anybody know it." The program, *Using the Scriptures*, was broadcast at stake centers throughout the United States on Sunday, March 10.[21]

It was in February when McConkie's chemotherapy treatments were suspended for a time after it became clear they were no longer working. The family, at Amelia's request, met to begin a fast on his behalf, but did so without his knowledge because they knew that he'd encourage them against it. The male children then went over to the McConkie apartment and gave Bruce a blessing, which he had earlier asked Amelia to arrange. A week later his colleagues in the Quorum of the Twelve, along with Gordon B. Hinckley, gave him another blessing. Soon he went into the hospital for what was supposed to be a two-week stay, where the chemotherapy resumed

20. "LDS Church to Hold Regional Conference on Sunday," *The Signal* (Santa Clarita, CA), Feb. 6, 1985, 9.

21. "Smith, Adams Exchange Vows in Salt Lake Temple Ceremony," *Daily Herald*, Feb. 24, 1985, 33; Dew, "Family Portrait," 63; "LDS Video Focuses on Scriptures," *Salt Lake Tribune*, Mar. 3, 1985, 30; Dennis Horne, *Bruce R. McConkie: Highlights from His Life and Teachings*, second revised edition with epilogue (Salt Lake City: Eborn Books, 2010), 198.

and was again injected into his liver. He experienced fatigue, loss of appetite, and jaundice afterward, but despite this procedure having only a 40 percent chance of success, the treatment worked. Mc-Conkie was released from the hospital five days early.[22]

Doctors continued to visit McConkie at the condo and saw some improvement. One doctor who was a friend came by and offered to give him a blessing, which McConkie accepted. "He rebuked the cells that were rebellious and refusing to act as they should normally do and blessed Daddy that the terrible itching and other problems he's had would cease," wrote Amelia to her children. "He also said that Daddy was well loved in the Church and his work was not finished and he would remain until he had done all he should."[23]

Some of the work McConkie surely hoped to finish was the publication of some book manuscripts he had written. One that he submitted to Deseret Book around this time and was published later that year was called *A New Witness for the Articles of Faith.* In that volume McConkie examined the Articles of Faith penned by Joseph Smith in 1842 as part of the Wentworth Letter and did so from the standpoint of modern revelation and the entire LDS canon. He divided the work into thirteen sections—one for each article—with a total of sixty-nine chapters.[24]

A few years earlier when McConkie hoped to canonize a revised edition of the Pearl of Great Price, he expanded the Articles of Faith from thirteen to fifteen. Although he no longer pushed for the canonization of his two additional articles, he believed them to be important enough to include in *A New Witness,* prefacing them with the sentence, "We might with utmost propriety adopt such declarations."[25]

Another manuscript he submitted for consideration at Deseret Book he titled "These Three: Elohim, Jehovah, Michael." It totaled 299 double-spaced pages and appears to have been written shortly after *New Witness,* because he cites that book with its then working title, "The Living Articles of Faith," leaving blank any cited page numbers because it had not yet been typeset. Why "These Three" was

22. McConkie, *Reflections,* 407–8.
23. McConkie, *Reflections,* 408.
24. See Bruce R. McConkie, *A New Witness for the Articles of Faith* (Salt Lake City: Deseret Book, 1985).
25. McConkie, *New Witness,* 16.

never published is unclear, but one source says it never went through the review process required of general authorities who wished to publish books. Another source, however, says that McConkie had forty copies made that he gave to his colleagues in the Quorum of the Twelve and several others to read and review. As this story goes, they recommended against publication. A former employee at Deseret Book, however, said the book was submitted shortly before McConkie's death but that it was "not approved for publication." It was later sent back to the family.[26]

The manuscript is a study of LDS doctrine surrounding Elohim (God the Father), Jehovah (Jesus Christ), and Michael (Adam), and in ten chapters he expounds upon their roles as co-workers in the pre-existence, as creators of the earth, and through all phases of the plan of salvation through to the exaltation of humankind. "We reach this inescapable conclusion," McConkie states as he introduces his subject. "Elohim, Jehovah, and Michael are the three most important personages in heaven or on earth. They are the ones who have performed the great labors out of which creation, mortality, and redemption come. It is through their acts that salvation is available to all the hosts of men."[27]

McConkie had at least one other bit of unfinished business, and that was delivering a talk at the general conference scheduled for April 1985. On Saturday, March 30, Amelia was in the middle of preparing an apple pie when Bruce came into the room and began reading his talk to her. He became emotional when doing so, which prompted Amelia to stop what she was doing and talk to him. "How are you going to be able to get up and read this?" she asked.

Her husband was determined. "I don't know, but I'm going to do it."[28]

Two days later Bruce's brother Brit came by and gave him a blessing, telling him that he would have the strength to make it through

---

26. Horne, *Bruce R. McConkie*, 447; publisher's "Introduction" to Bruce R. McConkie *These Three: Elohim, Jehovah, Michael* (N.p.: privately published, nd), vi–vii. This edition of McConkie's work was published without the permission of his family and is limited to twenty copies; notes from a Salt Lake City bookseller, shared with me, and written after speaking to the man in question.

27. McConkie, *These Three*, 4.

28. McConkie, *Reflections*, 410.

his conference address. But then on Tuesday, April 2, Amelia received a call from Bruce's doctor, who was direct. "You've got a dying man on your hands," he told her. "He's living on stored energy. You must not let him speak at conference. If he tries, he will collapse on nationwide television. Keep him home, and make him comfortable. That's all you can do for him."[29]

This was the moment when Amelia fully realized that her husband was truly dying. She called her son Joseph to wish him a happy birthday and told him the news. "It crushed her," he recalled. "Up until that time we all still thought he was going to get better." McConkie's bilirubin count was such that the doctors thought he should have already been in a coma. "The doctor wouldn't tell all this to Bruce," she said. "It was hard on me because I believed in Bruce and I had to do what he wanted. The doctor was so worried when he heard Bruce was going to speak, but I couldn't try to stop him." That same day Boyd K. Packer came and blessed McConkie and assured him his work was not yet finished. And McConkie himself was adamant. "I don't think there's anything dad wanted to do more than preach that last sermon at conference," said his son Stanford. After Amelia's call to Joseph, he and Sara got hold of the rest of their siblings to instruct them to begin fasting so that their father would have the strength and ability to deliver that final address. That next day McConkie managed to go to his office and attend meetings but when he came home, he was so worn out he went to sleep. When he got up, he managed to come into the kitchen and eat some of the dinner Amelia had prepared, although at this point his appetite was gone and the aroma of food made him nauseous. Few outside of the family knew how dire his condition was. For example, on April 5 the *Salt Lake Tribune* reported that McConkie had just been elected to the board of directors of Deseret Book, an indication that people at the Church's publishing house thought he was pulling through.[30]

The church's general conference commenced on Saturday, April 6, at 10:00 a.m. That morning McConkie sat on the stand looking noticeably thinner and his skin was yellow. Spencer W. Kimball

---

29. McConkie, *Reflections*, 410; Dew, "Family Portrait," 63.

30. Dew, "Family Portrait," 63; McConkie, *Reflections*, 410–12; "Intermountain Tradewinds," *Salt Lake Tribune*, Apr. 5, 1985, 8B.

was also present, but due to his health problems he did not speak. After remarks by Presidents Gordon B. Hinkley and Ezra Taft Benson, McConkie rose and walked to the pulpit. "I feel, and the Spirit seems to accord, that the most important doctrine I can declare, and the most powerful testimony I can bear, is of the atoning sacrifice of the Lord Jesus Christ." He then spoke for several minutes on Christ's mission, his suffering in the Garden of Gethsemane, his trial, crucifixion, resurrection, and overall mission. These were topics McConkie had spoken about on numerous occasions, but now he distilled them into one talk. It ended with an emotional testimony that has made this address one of the most memorable conference sermons ever:

"I am one of his witnesses, and in a coming day I shall feel the nail marks in his hands and in his feet and shall wet his feet with my tears.

"But I shall not know any better then than I know now that he is God's Almighty Son, that he is our Savior and Redeemer, and that salvation comes in and through his atoning blood and in no other way."[31]

After McConkie sat down his family surely felt a sigh of relief that he had fulfilled the moment he had been living for. He was too ill to attend Sunday's sessions and spent the next week at home, his health deteriorating further.[32]

Then on Sunday, April 14, Elder Packer came to the house and gave him another blessing, telling him that the time had now come for him to accept the Lord's will. McConkie became so emotional that the tears flowed. "It is now all in the hands of the Lord," he said. He then turned to his wife.

"Amelia, do you know what he just did? He sealed me unto death."

Up to this point, as McConkie had tried to remain optimistic that he would live, whenever he napped during the day, he did so on top of the covers in a fully made bed with his clothes on. He also insisted on eating in the kitchen. He even purchased a new suit and some new shoes because he was so sure he would live. Accepting now the realization that death was near, after Packer left, he got

---

31. *Official Report of the One Hundred Fifty-Fifth Annual General Conference of the Church of Jesus Christ of Latter-day Saints, Held in the Tabernacle, Salt Lake City, Utah, April 6 and 7, 1985* (Salt Lake City: The Church of Jesus Christ of Latter-day Saints, 1985), 9–12.

32. Dew, "Family Portrait," 63; McConkie, *Reflections*, 413–14.

out of his clothes and got under the bedding. "This was his way of saying he was submitting," Amelia explained. "He later told me he didn't want anyone fasting or praying for him, that it was all up to the Lord. He desperately didn't want to die. He had been so sure he would live. For him, it was the ultimate test of obedience."[33]

Over the next five days his health continued to fail. The children and other family members and friends came by to tell him goodbye. His ninety-five-year-old mother Vivian was one of them. She spoke of her husband, Oscar, who had died in 1966. "When you see Daddy, you tell him my suitcase is packed and I am waiting at the curb."[34]

Russell M. Nelson, an apostle of one year and a retired heart surgeon, came to the McConkie home on Friday, April 19, to look in on Bruce. After making his observation, he told Amelia that her husband would pass away that day. Nelson was about to leave for Boston with President Ezra Taft Benson to take part in a regional conference in Worchester, Massachusetts. McConkie had been slated to be a part of that. After some phone calls the family gathered and sat in the room that afternoon as Bruce slowly slipped away. They knelt together and Joseph prayed, asking God to "call him home." Bruce Redd McConkie, sixty-nine years old, died immediately after. His mother passed away just three weeks later.[35]

---

33. Dew, "Family Portrait," 63; McConkie, *Reflections*, 411, 414; "Elder Bruce R. McConkie: 'Preacher of Righteousness,'" *Ensign*, June 1985, 15–16.

34. McConkie, *Reflections*, 416.

35. McConkie, *Reflections*, 416–17; "Mormons to Hold Area Conference April 21," *Daily Hampshire* (Northampton, MA), Apr. 12, 1985, 10.

EPILOGUE

Word of McConkie's death spread quickly, and the following day stories began appearing in newspapers across the country after the Associated Press picked up the story.

The funeral service was held in the tabernacle on Temple Square on Tuesday, April 23. Speaking to the assembled mourners, Elder Boyd K. Packer called McConkie "as sensitive a man as ever I have known. I have had my arms around him as he wept openly over what some had said or done. I have delighted in his sparkling sense of humor that few men could equal." Ezra Taft Benson, who had served as president of the Quorum of the Twelve throughout most of McConkie's tenure as an apostle, noted how the First Presidency relied on him to "quote scripture or comment" when a matter of doctrine came before them. Referencing McConkie's general conference address delivered seventeen days earlier, Benson said, "None who heard his last sermon will ever forget his witness."

Apostle James E. Faust spoke of "the size of his heart, the warmth of his soul and the depth of his testimony." Although President Spencer W. Kimball was present, his frail health prevented him from speaking. Gordon B. Hinckley, Kimball's second counselor in the First Presidency, said that during McConkie's illness, "he was indefatigable in his pursuit of the work of the Lord; to open new areas, to strengthen the missionary service, to build the saints, to bear solemn and sincere witness to the reality and the divinity of the Lord Jesus Christ and to the restoration of his work." As a speaker, McConkie's "language was clear, its meaning unmistakable. There was a cadence to it, there was a peculiar strength and beauty in its pattern. He spoke from a cultivated mind, but also from a sincere heart."[1]

For months the McConkie family had planned a trip to Jerusalem, set for May, where son Joseph and his wife had experience leading tours. In preparation for the trip the family began studying about the Holy Land together. Bruce died the month before they were to go, but after his death, when the family prayed together, "we extended the invitation to him to join us at those sacred places of which he had written and preached so much," wrote Joseph. "We have reason to believe that he did so." While listening at the Garden Tomb to a recording of McConkie's recent conference talk, "a dove flew down into the center of our group, where it remained until Father's final amen."[2]

Had the apostle lived to the same age as his ninety-five-year-old mother, he would have contributed much over the next twenty-five years. He may have given another fifty general conference sermons and could have easily authored another half dozen books. He would have spoken at countless firesides and devotionals, and there is little doubt that he would have created more buzz from writing or saying something controversial.

He meant something to everyone, but not everyone viewed him through the same lens. McConkie's family saw a man who lived his faith, loved them, and loved his God. His loyalty to the church sometimes took precedence over everything, sometimes at the expense of others. Once when he faithfully filled an assignment that took him out of town during son Stephen's farewell sacrament meeting and subsequent departure for the mission field, McConkie never complained about that call to sacrifice. On another occasion he was due to speak at a stake conference and miss daughter Vivian's wedding, but his father-in-law intervened and changed McConkie's schedule, something McConkie never would have done on his own. To him there was an urgency in spreading the word and furthering the work of the kingdom, and at least once that manifested itself in

1. "LDS Leaders Salute McConkie's Life," *Salt Lake Tribune*, Apr. 24, 1985, B1, B3.
2. Joseph Fielding McConkie, *The Bruce R. McConkie Story: Reflections of a Son* (Salt Lake City: Deseret Book, 2003), 417–18; Joseph Fielding McConkie, "Bruce R. McConkie: A Special Witness," *Mormon Historical Studies* 14, no. 2 (Fall 2013): 207–8.

the strangest of ways. He and Amelia were in Chile sitting on the stand during a stake conference, waiting to speak. While standing and singing during a congregational hymn, Amelia began to feel dizzy. When the hymn concluded Bruce gently directed her in the direction of the podium. "It's your turn to speak," he told her. But seconds into her talk she fainted. "That's the last thing I remember until I came to, stretched out on the floor behind the pulpit," Amelia said later. It was the only time this ever happened; with no precedent, it would have been natural for the incident to have worried her husband at least as much as it did the frightened members in the congregation, or as it did Elder Robert E. Wells, who looked worriedly at Bruce for a reaction. "She'll be all right," Bruce said as he stepped over his prostrate wife and began preaching.

"This was no ordinary guy," son Joseph said later, chuckling about the episode while defending his father's response. "His wife passes out, he takes his place at the pulpit, and not a syllable is lost. But to him, *the kingdom rolls on!* ... His wife just fell out of the wagon, but *the caravan rolls on.*"[3] Moments like this may have troubled those who witnessed it, and perhaps family members should have thought twice before putting a positive spin on it when speaking about it publicly.

Church members saw McConkie as a man always willing and ready to teach doctrine—forcefully and unapologetically—and that appealed to many. Countless Latter-day Saints loved him because there was no ambiguity in his teachings as he answered the hard questions many were asking. His answers were direct and certain, but this, and the zeal that drove him, also proved to be divisive. In his mind, that was not his problem, but an issue for his rebellious listeners. His teachings were a mix of LDS doctrine, opinion, speculation, and, in hindsight, folklore. Where the church did not take an official stand on a particular doctrine or theory, McConkie often assumed the role of filling the void. Sometimes this happened only to the chagrin of his colleagues or higher-ups in the LDS hierarchy, who now and then corrected him privately. But when BYU professors Eugene England and George Pace unknowingly taught ideas that clashed with McConkie's personal views, he was quick to lash

3. Sheri L. Dew, "Bruce R. McConkie: A Family Portrait," *This People*, Dec. 1985/Jan. 1986, 61.

out and embarrass them, causing unnecessary pain for these men that lasted, at some level, for the rest of their lives.

At his best, he taught in ways that gave his subject its greatest appeal, and in that sense, he was gifted. But his unwillingness to separate his own views from official doctrines was complicated at best. He didn't always know the difference until he was called out, or circumstances changed, such as when the church radically altered its racial policies in 1978. Yet when McConkie announced to his family sixteen days after the revelation that everything he had ever taught about Blacks was wrong, it soon became apparent that he was referring only to the timing for when the priesthood and temple ban would be lifted; he never discarded his conviction that Blacks were cursed, inferior, and less valiant in the premortal existence. He, like most church leaders at the time, believed that the priesthood and temple ban had been the Lord's will while it was in place. "I knew Elder McConkie rather well," wrote Mormon scholar Robert Matthews in 1986. "I know for a fact that in 1980, two years after the 1978 revelation, he did not think or propose that the Church had been wrong in its policy towards the blacks but only that they had misunderstood when the change would come."[4]

Of course, all anyone had to do was look to the 1979 edition of *Mormon Doctrine*, where McConkie retained the racial theories once taught by Joseph Fielding Smith and others before him. While many older works that taught these racist ideas remained in print for decades after 1978, McConkie's 1979 revision holding to those views was the only one written by a general authority *after* the revelation. This made him the most accessible and authoritative source for Latter-day Saints bent on defending those teachings. And many did. As late as 2003 Joseph Fielding McConkie referred to Blacks as "the descendants of Cain" in his published biography of his father.[5]

<hr />

4. Robert J. Matthews, "A Reply to 'Sweet Are the Uses of Fidelity: Why Celestial Marriage is Monogamous,'" a paper delivered by G. Eugene England, on Aug. 30, 1986, at the Sunstone Symposium, Salt Lake City, Utah, Richard Lloyd Anderson Papers, Ms 9073, box 6, fd. 6, L. Tom Perry Special Collections, Harold B. Lee Library, Brigham Young University, Provo, Utah.

5. Stirling Adams, "Racial Folklore in 'Mormon Doctrine,' After 1978," 4, unpublished paper, copy courtesy of the author; McConkie, *Reflections*, 377.

To Joseph, this was established doctrine, and he had his father and grandfather to look to for confirmation of that.

Perhaps Joseph McConkie held to that view because he could hardly tolerate public disagreement with his father, the man he idolized, as Eugene England learned in 1980. The younger McConkie branded those who criticized the teachings of his father, as well as his contemporary firebrands Joseph Fielding Smith and Apostle Boyd K. Packer, as "discontented," "unconverted," and "the avowed enemies of truth."[6] To him it was that simple, that personal.

But Joseph Fielding McConkie, who died in 2013, lived to see the church distance itself from some of his father's teachings. Bruce R. McConkie's most famous and most quoted title, *Mormon Doctrine*, was withdrawn a second time because of a relatively few, but deeply troubling entries. By the time of McConkie's death in 1985, Bookcraft had sold over 376,000 copies of the book.[7] It remained in print another twenty-five years, four years longer than it had been during McConkie's lifetime. After going through forty printings and selling tens of thousands of additional copies, Deseret Book finally let it go out of print permanently in 2010. The stated reason was "slow sales," according to Gail Halladay, the company's managing director of marketing and communications. "The demand is no longer there," she insisted.[8]

There was more of a concerted effort to stifle its influence among church members that Halladay doesn't explain. As of this writing, *A New Witness for the Articles of Faith* is the only book of McConkie's currently available in a print edition.[9] All except *Mormon Doctrine* are available through Deseret Book as ebooks, and it is clearly its racial content keeping it unavailable. It is significant that among Joseph Fielding Smith's books, *The Way to Perfection*, which paved the way for McConkie's views on race, is not available in any format

---

6. McConkie, *Reflections*, 421.
7. Dennis B. Horne, *Bruce R. McConkie: Highlights from His Life and Teachings*, second enlarged edition with epilogue (Salt Lake City: Eborn Books, 2010), 70.
8. Peggy Fletcher Stack, "Landmark 'Mormon Doctrine' Goes Out of Print," *Salt Lake Tribune*, May 21, 2010.
9. Although the three-volume *Doctrines of Salvation* is available in paperback presently in a single volume as well as an ebook, and McConkie's name appears as the editor, the writings are strictly those of Joseph Fielding Smith.

either while most of Smith's other titles are. Ebooks are relatively inexpensive to produce. For the LDS Church to issue its Gospel Topics essay on "Race and the Priesthood" in 2013, it was imperative that it rid its shelves of the very teachings it was trying to reject. Race wasn't the only controversial topic in *Mormon Doctrine* and had McConkie eliminated those entries from the book in his lifetime, it may have survived. His anti-evolution ideas, although controversial to many, were more forgivable in the end. This was obvious when Deseret Book made Smith's science-critical book *Man: His Origin and Destiny* available in its ebook catalog.

LDS Church membership numbered 5,650,000 at McConkie's death.[10] Many among that number have since died, but the church has also tripled in size since then. Few members under the age of fifty remember hearing McConkie speak, and those who become aware of his writings today have generally read selected quotations in lesson manuals, have a passion for LDS doctrine themselves, or have flipped through family copies of *Mormon Doctrine* or any of the other books he published. Yet every active Latter-day Saint is influenced by McConkie more than they realize. When they read their scriptures, they read his words prior to every chapter in all four of the church's standard works. They see his influence in the Bible Dictionary and behind the excerpts included from the Joseph Smith Translation of the Bible.

But however people choose to remember McConkie, it would be unfair to judge him strictly by the controversies surrounding him, as self-imposed and deeply impacting those turned out to be. Only family, friends, and colleagues really got to know him and experience the compassion and sense of humor that was such an integral part of him. This puts everyone else at a disadvantage, but even his harshest critics know that no one is one dimensional. It is therefore worth trusting the various assessments of McConkie by those who knew him intimately. Even without their input, however, all can attest to the dedication to his church that led him to produce the large body of work nearly unmatched by anyone else in Mormonism.

10. *Official Report of the One Hundred Fifty-Fifth Annual General Conference of the Church of Jesus Christ of Latter-day Saints, Held in the Tabernacle, Salt Lake City, Utah, April 6 and 7, 1985* (Salt Lake City: The Church of Jesus Christ of Latter-day Saints, 1985), 25.

Much of it is positive, because central to the tenets of the Latter-day Saint gospel is the role and mission of Christ. No one expounded on that with greater fervor than McConkie. Even his colleagues in the Twelve sat in awe when he spoke to them about that.

At the time *Mormon Doctrine* met its second, final demise, Black Latter-day Saint Darius Gray pondered McConkie's racial teachings and accurately described him as "a good man but a man of his times."[11] As an advisor to President Spencer W. Kimball in the months prior to the priesthood revelation, McConkie proved that he could rise above the prejudices he developed years earlier within a culture where they had been easily nurtured. It is not difficult to assume that he would have come to accept and even champion the church's current teachings on race had he lived long enough to do so. There is every reason to debate his speculations and to reject the most dangerous among them. At the same time, there is sufficient reason to hold a charitable view toward a man who devoted the entirety of his life to a cause he loved so deeply.

11. Stack, "Landmark 'Mormon Doctrine.'"

ACKNOWLEDGMENTS

This biography, part of Signature's Brief Mormon Lives project, would not have been written were it not for Gary James Bergera, then director of the Smith–Pettit Foundation, who originally envisioned this series. I am grateful to him for encouraging me to choose a subject to write on and for occasionally prodding me along the way.

I have long found Bruce R. McConkie to be a fascinating figure within the hierarchy of the Church of Jesus Christ of Latter-day Saints. He is certainly one of the most influential church leaders of the twentieth century. While I served an LDS mission in England my mission president encouraged us to read McConkie's book, *The Promised Messiah*, which I did. I read the five others in that series as soon as they became available. McConkie's no-nonsense style of writing and speaking appealed to me, and his forceful, direct preaching left no doubt where he stood and where he expected the rest of us to stand. I often wondered why he was alone among his colleagues when preaching doctrine and doing so with such passion and certainty.

In time I came to view him differently and became a critic of many of his views, but more particularly, his style, especially when he so mercilessly called out others he disagreed with and caused them tremendous hurt and pain. Yet in researching and writing this book I have gained a renewed appreciation and admiration for him, despite maintaining my firm disagreements with many of the ideas he held until his death.

Although Bergera intended the books in the Mormon Lives series to be brief and to rely mainly on secondary sources, I used some primary sources and created a few of my own through interviews. Some of these sources were supplied by others. Therefore, I must thank Matt Christensen for generously answering questions through email and also when we saw each other at conferences. Christensen plans his own in-depth and far lengthier biography of McConkie. Matthew L. Harris shared drafts of four chapters with me of his groundbreaking and painstakingly researched book, *Second-Class Saints: Black Mormons and the Struggle for Racial Equality*, which were extremely helpful in understanding more fully all that transpired leading up to and in the aftermath of the 1978 revelation on priesthood, and more on McConkie's involvement.

Ardis Parshall shared copies of letters she had transcribed that involved McConkie and his activities. These were very helpful and I am extremely grateful to her. Christian Kimball and Mary Kimball Dollahite provided excerpts from their father Edward L. Kimball's diary that shed light on McConkie from the perspective of their grandfather Spencer W. Kimball. Matt Harris let me know that they were in their possession, and so I am doubly grateful to him. Jonathan Stapley was kind enough to answer questions and lead me to sources as I sought more information on succession in the church presidency, a favorite topic of McConkie.

Stirling Adams went out of his way to give me several items, many written by himself, that helped me immensely. Joe Geisner also shared his research files and sent me hard-to-find manuscripts and other documents. John Bowie of Perth, Australia, gave me insight into McConkie's lasting influence among church members there after the latter's tenure as president of the Southern Australia mission ended.

Two people were kind enough to take the time to sit for interviews. These were David Pace, whose father George had a very public encounter with McConkie in 1982. James W. McConkie, a nephew of Bruce R. McConkie, shared personal reminiscences and helped me come to know his uncle better. I am extremely grateful to both.

I also thank the staffs of the LDS Church History Library, the Utah State Historical Society, and the University of Utah Marriott Library Special Collections for their kind assistance as I researched pertinent collections seeking additional material. The Smith–Pettit

Foundation papers were crucial and contain a thorough McConkie collection. I am thankful that it made them accessible to me.

Bryan Buchanan and Becky Roesler happily read a draft of this manuscript and provided encouragement. The book, as it now appears in your hands, looks and reads the way it does thanks to John Hatch and Jason Francis at Signature Books, who played a significant role in the end. I am thankful to them for their editing, proofing, and designing skills. I'd like to thank them and Beth Brumer-Reeve, as well as their former colleagues Gary James Bergera, Greg Jones, and Keiko Jones for their friendship and many encouraging words of support. Martha Bradley-Evans, current director of the Smith-Pettit Foundation, was always supportive and kind in her comments.

Finally, I want to thank my family for their patience when I was not available for outings and other get togethers when the deadline to turn this manuscript in quickly approached.

INDEX

A

Adam-God Doctrine, 65, 95, 179; BRM denounces, 149, 162

Adams, Vivian McConkie, 55, 78, 192; bears child, 84; birth, 31; on home life, 58; marriage, 68; speaks out in class, 93–94

Anderson, Joseph, 50, 71, 121; and Lester Bush article, 119

Ann Arbor, Michigan, 8; BRM birth at, 7; McConkie family move to, 7, 11

Archuleta, Ramon, murder case against, 8

Arrington, Leonard J., 119, 140; on BRM, 115, 120–21; and priesthood revelation, 136

Ashment, Ed, on BRM, 120

Ashton, Marvin J., 118; Melchizedek Priesthood Committee, 122

Australia. *See* Southern Australia Mission

B

Bennion, Lowell L., on BRM, 38

Bennion, Milton, 37, 38; scolds BRM, 35

Benson, Ezra Taft, 189, 190; controversial talk, 150; on evolution, 152–53, 155; as mission president, 78; and priesthood revelation, 133; serves with BRM, 106; speaks at BRM funeral, 191; visits BRM in Australia, 87–88

Benson, Steve, meets with BRM, 152–55

Bergera, Gary James, and priesthood revelation, 138

Blacks, BRM and, 100–3, 128–29, 130, 135, 142–43, 194; LDS Gospel Topics essay on, 143; LDS racial policy toward, 15, 100–1, 128; revelation about, 130–34; teachings about, 101–2; *see also* racism

Blanding, Utah, 6

Bluff, Utah, 6–7

Book of Mormon, 67, 83, 95, 142; BRM and, 11, 17, 52, 107; and "Church of the Devil," 69; and Hill Cumorah, 19–20; new edition of, 147, 165; pageant depicting, 23; racism in, 103, 143; success of in Australia, 89

Bowie, John, on BRM's Australian legacy, 90

Brigham Young University, 29, 53, 77, 98, 117, 172, 173; Bill Pope speaks at, 136; BRM on board of trustees, 124; BRM speaks at, 123, 142, 148–49, 162, 167–68, 169–70, 180, 182, 183, 184; BRM teaches at, 105, 107; Eugene England speaks at, 149–50, 159; on evolution, 157; Mark E. Petersen's speech at, 160; Oscar McConkie attends, 3; racism at, 103, 128

McConkie, Brit. *See* McConkie, France
Briton "Brit"
McConkie, Bruce Redd, accidents,
14, 22, 110–11; admitted to bar,
30; advise given by, 94–95; adviser
to Church Historical Department,
119–22; affection toward family, 58;
appears on Australian television, 83;
army reserves, 27, 33; Asian mission
service, 106; assessment of sister,
139; assessments of, 58–59, 84–85,
89–90, 191–92, 193–97; attends
University of Utah, 13, 14, 16, 24,
27; attitude on church history,
119–21; author, 60, 62, 63–66,
67–76, 79, 96–97, 109, 118, 127–28,
147–48, 160, 165, 173, 186–87;
baptism, 10; birth, 7–8; birth of
children, 29, 31, 32, 35, 47, 55, 66;
called as apostle, 116; called to Seventy, 50–51; cancer diagnosis, 181;
cancer treatment, 181–82, 183–86;
on Catholicism, 69–70, 83, 93, 155;
childhood, 8; on Christ's mission,
36, 53–54, 117, 125, 127, 160, 169,
189, 197; *Church News* story on, 124;
church travels, 52–53, 54–55, 59–60,
66–67, 68–69, 72–73, 95–96, 105,
106, 115–16, 124, 125, 126–27, 128,
145–46, 178, 180, 184–85, 193; city
attorney, 31, 32–33, 45–46; coerces
baptisms, 86; conflict with Eugene
England, 159–60, 161–65; conflict
with George Pace, 169–70, 171–74;
courts Amelia Smith, 14–16, 24;
criticism of, 170–71, 173, 174,
180–81; criticizes Sunday School
manual, 35–37; death, 190; departs
for mission, 18–19; on *Dialogue*,
107, 120; *Doctrinal New Testament
Commentary*, 96–97, 109, 118;
Doctrines of Salvation, 60–61, 63, 66,
155; early employment, 12, 27; early
gospel training, 9–10, 17; engagement, 24; enters mission home, 18;
on eternal progression, 148–49,
161–62, 169; evolution, 149, 151,

152–55; on exorcism, 36; expanding the canon, 121–22, 125–26,
165–67; extends mission, 24; faith
experiences, 9, 11; family homes,
28, 55, 93, 178; family vacations, 45,
54–55; fraternity life, 13, 24; funeral
of, 192–93; ghostwrites for father-
in-law, 113–14; gospel at home,
57–58; graduates from high school,
13; graduates from university, 27;
high school activities, 13; on higher
criticism, 36–37, 96–97; at Hill Cumorah, 19–23, 126–27; holds Family
Home Evening, 135–36; home life,
9, 57–58, 85; "Honest Truth Seekers"
letter, 152; humor of, 16, 57, 58, 59,
79, 84, 88, 134, 135, 148–49, 159;
illnesses, 18, 29, 34, 180–86, 187–90;
injuries, 8, 10; journalism career,
46–47, 49, 56; law practice, 30, 31;
law school, 28, 30; LDS servicemen's coordinator, 53, 54, 56–57,
67, 73; leadership style, 84–86, 90;
Let Every Man Learn His Duty,
127; literature, 13; matchmaker, 22;
Melchizedek Priesthood Committee, 122; meets Amelia Smith, 14;
meets with Ed Kimball, 175–76;
meets with First Presidency, 64, 71,
75; memo urging change on racial
policies, 128–29; Memorial Estates
Security Corporation, 79–80, 104–5;
mentored by Joseph Fielding Smith,
26–27, 38; military service, 34–35,
45–46; mission experience, 19–24;
mission farewell, 18; on mission
president experience, 90–91; mission
reunion, 29; on moderation, 167–69;
and *Mormon Doctrine*, 67–76, 77,
97–103, 142–43; *The Mortal Messiah*,
147–48, 160, 165; move to Monticello, 8; move to Salt Lake City, 11;
music, 11, 12; *A New Witness for the
Articles of Faith*, 186; offered judgeship, 33; ordinations and callings,
11, 17, 24, 44–45, 51, 78, 81, 96–96,
105, 106, 109, 115–16, 118–22,

"Seven Deadly Heresies," 148–49,
150–51, 161, 165, 169; changes to,
149, 151
Smith, Ethel Reynolds, 14; death, 27
Smith, George Albert, 47, 50; BRM
testifies of, 54; and nepotism, 51
Smith, Jessie Evans, death, 111; mar-
ries, 29; visits Harold B. Lee, 108–9
Smith, Joseph, 2, 14, 54, 64, 68, 149;
Bible translation, 118, 146, 166, 167,
196; First Vision, 21–22, 87; on race,
101, 119; revelations of, 121–22,
125–26; rumor of appearance in
temple, 136–37
Smith, Joseph F., 51, 141, 154; revelation of, 126
Smith, Joseph Fielding, 14, 18, 25,
35, 37, 50, 51, 67, 68, 95, 115, 141,
154, 159, 195; attends conference in
England, 111; birth of grandchildren
noted, 31, 66; BRM reports to, 60,
64; building named for, 160–61; critics of, 195; death, 113; on *Doctrines
of Salvation*, 61; and evolution, 155;
on Ezra Taft Benson, 78; and *Man:
His Origin and Destiny*, 154, 156–57;
mental decline, 108, 112; mentors
BRM, 26–27, 38; and *Mormon Doctrine*, 70, 73, 74–75, 98–99; moves
to McConkie home, 111; performs
wedding, 28; praised by BRM, 61; on
race, 102, 119, 194; remarries, 14, 29;
sickness, 111–12; succession controversy, 108–9, 123; talks with Harold
B. Lee about succession, 108–9;
tends to sick child, 29–30; travels
with BRM, 28; visits Eastern States
Mission, 23–24; visits Southern Australia Mission, 87; *Way to Perfection*,
102, 195; widower, 14, 27, 111
Smith, Lewis, death of, 38
Smith, Louie Emily Shurtliff, 14
Smith, Nicholas G., 18
Smith, Silas, 6
Smith, Silas (doctor), tends McConkie
child, 29–30
Snell, Heber C., 37

Somerville, William, 2
Sound Doctrine, controversy over,
63–66, 68, 76, 170
Southern Australia Mission, 178;
BRM appears on television, 83;
BRM called to, 78; BRM reputation
within, 82; BRM teaches within,
82; BRM travels within, 87, 88–89;
church growth during BRM tenure,
89; missionaries' assessments of
BRM, 84–85, 89–90; missionaries killed, 85–86; possible motive
behind BRM call to, 78–79
Stapley, Delbert L., 87, 130; and
priesthood revelation, 132–33
Swensen, Russel B., 36; McConkie
criticizes manual by, 35–37

T

Talmage, James E., 97, 148; on science,
155–56
Tanner, Jerald and Sandra, distribute
BRM letter, 163–64
Tanner, N. Eldon, 117; announces
priesthood revelation, 133–34; called
to First Presidency, 109, 113–14;
overseas tour, 125; and racial issue,
129, 130; reads priesthood revelation, 145
"These Three," 186–87
Todd, Jay, and priesthood revelation,
135–36

U

United States Constitution, BRM on,
33, 39–44
University of Utah, 32, 34, 38, 69, 93,
105; Amelia attends, 16; BRM and
Amelia graduate, 27; BRM attends,
13, 16, 24; BRM attends law school
at, 28; BRM speaks at, 92; Oscar McConkie attends, 5; Oscar
McConkie teaches at, 12; Vivian
McConkie attends 7

W

Wallin, Marvin, 66n7, 70